An Agenda for India's Growth

An Agenda for India's Growth

Essays in Honour of P. Chidambaram

Editor

SAMEER KOCHHAR

ACADEMIC FOUNDATION

NEW DELHI

First published in 2013
by

ACADEMIC FOUNDATION
4772-73 / 23 Bharat Ram Road, (23 Ansari Road),
Darya Ganj, New Delhi - 110 002 (India).
Phones : 23245001 / 02 / 03 / 04.
Fax : +91-11-23245005.
E-mail : books@academicfoundation.com
www.academicfoundation.com

in association with

S<OCH

Skoch Consultancy Services
www.skoch.in

SKOCH
DEVELOPMENT FOUNDATION

Skoch Development Foundation
www.skoch.org

INCLUSION
MAINSTREAMING THE MARGINALISED
www.inclusion.in

Cataloging in Publication Data--DK
Courtesy: D.K. Agencies (P) Ltd. <docinfo@dkagencies.com>

An agenda for India's growth: Essays in honour of P. Chidambaram / editor, Sameer Kochhar.
p. Cm.
Includes index.
ISBN 9789332700093

1. Economic development--India. 2. India--Economic conditions--1991- 3. India--Economic policy--1991- I. Kochhar, Sameer.

DDC 338.954 23

Typeset by Italics India, New Delhi.

Printed and bound by The Book Mint, New Delhi
www.thebookmint.in

Contents

About the Editor/ Contributors

Editor:

Sameer Kochhar is Chairman of Skoch Group and a passionate advocate of social, financial and digital inclusion of Indian society. Born in 1964, he was raised in a below poverty line background and after higher secondary, his education had to be cut short to support the family. Later on, while working, he completed his degree and professional courses through distance education. In 1997, after spending 15 years in pursuing careers in hospitality and IT sectors in India and abroad, he decided that it was time to move on and pursue one's own dream. At a time when the economic liberalisation process started gathering pace, Sameer decided to be what inner calling was—to be a development thinker, even though he had no academic credentials to become one. Ever since, Sameer has doggedly and single-mindedly applied himself to the rigours of self-education, academic research and field tours in order to broaden his horizon. The Skoch Group was born out of this ideal. The first venture of the Group, Skoch Consultancy Services, was formed in 1997. Later on, he launched the Skoch Development Foundation as a think-tank and Skoch Media as a platform to build robust discourses on development and inclusion issues in the public domain. The consultancy wing provides India strategy and management advice to several Fortune 500 and large Indian corporates. The development think-tank works with a goal of promoting inclusive growth, participatory democracy, empowerment, good governance and transparency. The quarterly magazine *Inclusion* brought out by Skoch Media, of which Sameer is Editor-in-Chief, enriches the public knowledge base and enables better policy-making with its sharp focus in these areas. In Sameer's thinking, writings and activities, his profound admiration for India's economic reforms—and in extension, those outstanding personalities who strive to make these reforms more meaningful and broad-based—comes out clear and unambiguous. That admiration is rooted on the belief that he is a direct beneficiary of these reforms in terms of helping him come up in life, given the underprivileged background in which he was born and brought up. It's remarkable that for a man with no academic training, his opinion continues to be actively sought by the government in crystallising development-related polices. He has been a member of several committees and expert groups constituted by the government of India. He is also the moving spirit behind the research studies and articles produced by Skoch Group on its platforms, which have also been highly valued in policy-making circles, journalists and the academia. Sameer writes extensively. In addition to authoring highly acclaimed *Speeding Financial Inclusion* (2009), he has edited *Infrastructure and Governance* (2008), *Financial Inclusion* (2009), *Urban Renewal: Policy and Response* (2009). He has also edited three festschrifts in honour of Vijay Kelkar (*India on the Growth Turnpike*, 2010), C. Rangarajan (*Growth and Finance*, 2011) and Montek Singh Ahluwalia (*Policymaking for Indian Planning*, 2012), all published by Academic Foundation, New Delhi. This volume, the fourth festschrift, is in keeping with the spirit of Sameer's appreciation for some of the key architects of India's economic liberalisation programme.

Contributors:

Isher Judge Ahluwalia is Chairperson, Board of Governors, the Indian Council for Research on International Economic Relations (ICRIER). She was awarded Padma Bhushan by the President of India in the year 2009 for her services in the field of education and literature. Dr Ahluwalia was Chairperson of the High Powered Expert Committee on Urban Infrastructure Services during 2008-2011. She is currently leading a major research and capacity building programme on the challenges of urbanisation in India at ICRIER. She is Member, National Manufacturing Competitiveness Council and is on the Boards of a number of premier research institutes in India. Dr Ahluwalia was Vice Chairperson of the Punjab State Planning Board from 2005 to 2007. She is on the Boards of CYMMIT, Mexico, the International Water Management Institute (IWMI), Sri Lanka, and Global Development Network, New Delhi. She was Chairperson,

Board of Trustees of the International Food Policy Research Institute (IFPRI), Washington D.C., from 2003 to 2006. She was a Member of the Eminent Persons Group (EPG) of the Asian Development Bank, which submitted its report, *Towards a New Asian Development Bank in a New Asia* in May 2008, and of the Commission on Macroeconomics and Health, which submitted its report to the Director General, WHO in 2002. Dr Ahluwalia's research has focused on urbanisation, industrial development, macroeconomic reforms, and issues in social sector development in India. She is author/co-author/editor of several books including *India's Economic Reforms and Development: Essays for Manmohan Singh* (1998), which she co-edited with Prof I.M.D. Little.

Montek Singh Ahluwalia is Deputy Chairman, Planning Commission, Government of India. He has been a key figure in India's economic reforms from the mid 1980s onwards. For his outstanding contribution to economic policy and public service, he was conferred the prestigious Padma Vibhushan by President of India in 2011. He received his Bachelors degree from St Stephens College, Delhi University. Later he received an MA and an MPhil degree in economics from Oxford University, where he was a Rhodes Scholar. After completion of studies, he joined the World Bank in 1968, as a Young Professional and then held various positions including Chief of the Income Distribution Division. He joined Government of India in 1979, as Economic Adviser in the Ministry of Finance, after which he held a series of positions including Special Secretary to the Prime Minister; Commerce Secretary; Secretary in the Department of Economic Affairs; Finance Secretary in the Ministry of Finance; Member of the Planning Commission and Member of the Economic Advisory Council to the Prime Minister. In 2001, he was appointed as the first Director of the newly created Independent Evaluation Office of the International Monetary Fund. He resigned the position in 2004 to take up the position of Deputy Chairman of the Planning Commission, which he holds at present. He has written on various aspects of development economics, including Indian economic policy and his articles have been published in a number of prominent Indian and international journals and books. He co-authored *Re-distribution with Growth: An Approach to Policy*, published in 1975. He also wrote

"Reforming the Global Financial Architecture", which was published in 2004 as Economic Paper No. 41 by the Commonwealth Secretariat, London. He has received several honorary degrees including an honorary doctorate in Civil Law from the University of Oxford. He is an honorary fellow of Magdalen College, Oxford, and a Member of the Board of Directors of the Global Green Growth Institute, South Korea.

Tarun Das has spent his professional career in the development and promotion of Indian Industry. Starting in November 1963 with the predecessor body of Confederation of Indian Industry (CII), he was the Director General and Chief Executive of CII from April 1967 to May 2004 and Chief Mentor from June 2004 to October 2009. His leadership of the organisation over three decades has led to strengthening business and strategic ties between India and the world. He is Member, Advisory Group for G-20, Ministry of Finance; Member, Expert Group, Government-Industry Consultations, Planning Commission; Member, Working Group on Business Regulatory Framework for the 12th Five Year Plan (2012-2017), Planning Commission; Member, Council of IITs, Ministry of Human Resources Development; Member, Round Table on Skills Development, Ministry of Human Resources Development; Member, National Culture Fund, Ministry of Culture; Member, Kerala State Planning Board, Kerala Government; Member, Indo-UK Round Table, Ministry of External Affairs. He is Founding Trustee, Council on Energy Environment and Water (CEEW); Vice President and Treasurer, World Wildlife Fund-India (WWF); Member, Board of Trustees, Public Interest Foundation (PIF); Trustee, Sasakawa India Leprosy Foundation (SILF); Member, Board of Governors, Indian Council for Research on International Economic Relations (ICRIER); Member, Executive Committee of the Board, ICRIER; Member, Apex Council on India@75, Confederation of Indian Industry (CII); Trustee, India@75 Foundation; Member, Singapore India Partnership Foundation (SIPF); Founding Trustee, Aspen Institute India; Lifetime Trustee, The Aspen Institute, USA; Member, Board of Governors, East West Center. He is Co-Chair of the US–India Strategic Dialogue; Co-Chair, Indo-US-Japan Strategic Dialogue; Co-Chair, India-Israel Forum; Member, India-Singapore Strategic Dialogue; Member, India-China Strategic Dialogue; Member,

India-Turkey Forum. He is Member, Board of Directors, John Keells Holdings PLC (Sri Lanka); Member, International Advisory Board of ACE Insurance (USA); Member, India Advisory Board of VOITH (Germany); Member, India Advisory Board, JCB (UK); Chairman, Haldia Petrochemicals Ltd (2001-2011).

Gursharan Dhanjal, MPhil, PhD from Delhi University and an expert in strategic affairs, is Editor & COO, Skoch Group. He is also Editor of *Inclusion*—a quarterly publication that focuses on development and addresses inclusive growth related issues. He has over 20 years of work experience ranging from academics to research and business journalism to consulting. He started his career as a Lecturer and taught at Delhi University for five years before joining Asia Business News (India)—Dow Jones, a premier broadcaster of business and financial news during mid-90s. He also worked for CNBC for over three years. He has led various research projects, impact assessments and field studies in financial inclusion, e-governance and ICT for development that included traversing across the country, interacting with stakeholders, collecting citizen voices for over a decade now. His areas of expertise include research and rich media content. A prolific writer, Dr Dhanjal has contributed over 200 columns in leading national dailies including *Hindustan Times*, *Times of India*, *Financial Express* and *The Pioneer*. He has published research papers in several journals of repute in addition to authoring a widely acclaimed book entitled *Tarapur: The Politics of Nuclear Age*. He has recently published another book in association with Sameer Kochhar entitled *Infrastructure and Governance*. He has contributed papers that have been published in various books, e.g., *Policymaking for Indian Planning: Essays in Honour of Montek Singh Ahluwalia* edited by Sameer Kochhar; and *Building from the Bottom: Infrastructure and Poverty Alleviation*, edited by Sameer Kochhar and M. Ramachandran. He is member of the Working Group on ICT in Higher Education constituted by Planning Commission for the 12th Five Year Plan. He is Member, Course Preparation Team for Master's Programme, School of Social Sciences, Indira Gandhi National Open University (IGNOU). He is a regular speaker at various public fora and institutions including IIT-Delhi and Delhi University, where he is also a visiting faculty. His research interests include: nuclear non-proliferation, political systems, ICT for development, financial inclusion, education, public administration, urban development, conflict resolution and peace building.

Ashok Jha, an IAS officer of the 1969 batch, has had a 38 years stint in the civil services and had held crucial positions in India's state and central government apparatus. He is one of the very few civil servants to have extensive work experience in foreign policy, industrial promotion, international trade as well as economic affairs and finance. His appointment as the Finance Secretary, Government of India, was a fitting culmination of an illustrious career. For about two years, he was in the finance ministry first as Secretary, Economic Affairs and later as Finance Secretary in addition to continuing as Secretary, Economic Affairs. Apart from preparing the Union Budget for two years—the years when GDP growth in India clocked about 9.5%—he was instrumental in formulating macroeconomic policies. These included issues relating to fiscal policy and public finance, inflation, public debt management and the functioning of capital markets. He was India's alternate Governor in the World Bank and the Asian Development Bank. Prior to the finance ministry, he was Secretary, Department of Industrial Policy and Promotion, in which capacity he promoted foreign direct investment into India besides ushering in a patents regime to conform with international obligations. He was also Advisor—International Affairs, Federation of Indian Chambers of Commerce & Industry (FICCI). After retiring from Government, he had two-year stint with Hyundai Motor India as its Executive President. He graduated from St Stephen's College in Economics and went on to do his Masters from the Delhi School of Economics. He has another Masters Degree in Development Economics from the Australian National University, Canberra, and was also a Visiting Fellow at Oxford University, UK. He is currently the Chairman of the Advisory Board of a Stock Exchange and also advises some other companies apart from being a Director on the Board of a few others.

Vijay L. Kelkar is Chairman, India Development Foundation, New Delhi and Chairman, Forum of Federations, Ottawa. He was the Chairman of the Finance Commission in the rank of an Union Cabinet Minister until January 2010. He was earlier Advisor to the Minister of Finance in the rank of a Minister of State from 2002 to 2004. Prior to this, he has held various senior level positions in Government of India (GoI) as well as in international organisations including Executive Director for India, Sri Lanka, Bangladesh and Bhutan at the IMF from August, 1999 to August, 2002; Finance Secretary, GoI, 1998–1999; Chairman, Tariff Commission, GoI, 1997–1998: Secretary, Ministry of Petroleum & Natural Gas, GoI, 1994–1997; Director & Coordinator, International Trade Division, UNCTAD, Geneva, Switzerland, 1991–1994; Chairman, Bureau of Industrial Costs & Prices; Secretary to the GoI, 1987–1991; Secretary, Economic Advisory Council to the Prime Minister, GoI, 1985–1988; Advisor, Economic Policy & Planning, Ministry of Petroleum & Natural Gas, GoI, 1982–1987; Economic Advisor, Ministry of Commerce, GoI, 1977–1981. In January 2011, the President of India awarded him Padma Vibhushan. Dr Kelkar chaired Task Force for Implementation of the Fiscal Responsibility and Budget Management Act, Ministry of Finance, Government of India, 2004; Task Force on Direct Taxes, Ministry of Finance, Government of India, 2002 as well as Task Force on Indirect Taxes, Ministry of Finance, Government of India, 2002. He recently chaired the Committee appointed by the Finance Minister to outline a roadmap for fiscal consolidation. Dr Kelkar has been member of Board of Directors, Advisory Council and Board of Governors of various global companies and organisations including Tata Consulting Services, CITI Group, Hero Honda Motors, Indian Council for Research on International Economic Relations, Administrative Staff College of India, Hyderabad, India National Innovation Foundation, Ahmedabad, Indian Society of Energy and Environment Economics, New Delhi, and Indian Institute of Technology, New Delhi, among many others. Dr Kelkar holds B.S., from University of Pune, India, 1963, M.S., from University of Minnesota, USA, 1965 and Ph. D from University of California at Berkeley, USA, 1970.

C. **Rangarajan** is a leading economist of India, who has played a key role both as an academic and a policy maker. He has held several important positions, which include Governor, Reserve Bank of India (RBI) and Governor of Andhra Pradesh. He is currently Chairman,

Economic Advisory Council to the Prime Minister in the rank of Cabinet Minister, a position he has held since January 2005, except during 2008-09 when he was a Member of Parliament (Rajya Sabha). Prior to this, he was Chairman of the Twelfth Finance Commission, a Constitutional commission set up every five years to determine the sharing of tax revenues between the Centre and the state governments. Dr Rangarajan was Governor, RBI during 1992-1997 at a time when India embarked on wide-ranging economic reforms, which fundamentally altered the structure of the Indian economy. He was actively involved in the design and implementation of the reform agenda. He gave a major thrust to financial sector reforms, which included simplification and deregulation of interest rate structure, reduction of reserve requirements with a view to improving banks' lendable resources, strengthening the soundness of banks through the institution of internationally accepted prudential norms and an improved supervision system, and imparting a greater element of competition in the financial system. After taking his Honours Degree from Madras, he obtained his PhD from the University of Pennsylvania. He has published extensively in professional journals and also has several books to his credit. He was President, Indian Economic Association in 1988 and President, Indian Econometric Society in 1994. In recognition of his distinguished service to the nation, Dr Rangarajan was awarded Padma Vibhushan in 2002.

M. Govinda Rao is Member, Fourteenth Finance Commission, Government of India. His past positions include Director, National Institute of Public Finance and Policy (2003-2012) Member, Economic Advisory Council to the Prime Minister of India (2004-2012), Director, Institute for Social and Economic Change, Bangalore and Fellow, Research School of Pacific and Asian Studies, Australian National University, Canberra, Australia. Dr Rao has held a number of advisory roles in India. He was Member, Financial Sector Legislative Reforms Commission (FSLRC); Member, High Level Expert Committee on Universal Health Coverage; Member, High Level Expert Committee on Efficient Management of Public Expenditure; Member, Advisory Group of Eminent persons to advise the Finance Minister on G-20 matters. His research interests include: macro-fiscal policy, tax policy and reforms, public expenditure management, state and local finances, fiscal decentralisation and federalism.

Parthasarathi Shome is Adviser, at the level of Minister of State, to Indian finance minister from January 2013. Earlier, he was Director & Chief Executive, Indian Council for Research on International Economic Relations (ICRIER), New Delhi (2011-12). He was Chief Economist, Her Majesty's Revenue & Customs (HMRC), United Kingdom (2008-2011) and Adviser, at the level of Secretary, to Indian finance minister (2004-2008). He served at the IMF (1983-2004) in various capacities, including as Senior Economist, Office of the Managing Director, 1989; Chief of Tax Policy (1992-1995); and Director, IMF Singapore Institute (2001-2003). He was RBI Chair, ICRIER (1999-2001) and Director, National Institute of Public Finance and Policy (1995-1997), and Professor of Economics at American University Washington D.C. (1975-83). In 2000, he was awarded the highest civilian honour of the Brazilian government, Commander of the Order of the Southern Cross, for his contributions to Brazilian tax reform. He was among the 2012 Global Tax 50 of the *International Tax Review*. A prolific writer, he has authored many books. He has published in the *Asia-Pacific Tax Bulletin, Bulletin for International Fiscal Documentation (IBFD), IMF Staff Papers, Journal of Economic Theory, Journal of Public Economics, Oxford Economic Papers, Oxford Review of Economic Policy* and other international and national journals of Argentina, the Basque Region, India, Japan, Malaysia, Philippines, Singapore, and the United States. He has given fiscal technical assistance to over 30 countries in Africa, Asia, Europe and Latin America. He chaired India's Ninth Five Year Plan and Tenth Five Year Plan Task Forces on Tax Policy and Administration. He did his PhD from Southern Methodist University in 1975. For his doctoral thesis on the burden of the corporation income tax, he received the National Tax Association of America award as an "outstanding student of taxation and public finance". He has Masters degrees from University of Rochester (1973) and Delhi School of Economics (1972). He graduated with a BA Honours degree from Presidency College, Calcutta University (1970) and high school matriculation from Madras University (1966).

N.K. Singh is a renowned politician, economist and former top bureaucrat. Presently, he is a member of the Rajya Sabha from the state of Bihar. He serves on the Parliamentary Standing Committee on External Affairs and the Committee on Local Area Development Scheme, the Public Accounts Committee, the Consultative Committee on Finance, the Committee on Rules, the Housing Committee and the Parliamentary Forum on Global Warming and Climate Change. He was also on the Standing Committee on Human Resource Development and the Committee on Public Undertakings. He has been among the country's top bureaucrats and handled important portfolios such as India's Expenditure and Revenue Secretary, a Member of the Planning Commission as well as Secretary to the Prime Minister. He was the principal interloculator with multilateral institutions during India's balance of payment crisis. Since then, he has served in important advisory roles and headed several task forces on telecom and electricity and keenly engaged in the economic reforms strategy over the last 20 years. He is on the governing bodies of research organisations like, Indian Council for Research on International Economic Relations (ICRIER), International Management Institute (IMI) and National Institute of Fashion Technology (NIFT). He has a wide-range of national and international experience having interacted closely with multilateral organisations like World Bank, IMF, ADB, UNCTAD, GATT, WTO, UNDP and OECD. Additionally, he has taken up various international responsibilities in the UN, World Economic Forum, Indian Embassy (Tokyo), IMF, etc. He has a Master's Degree in Economics and was teaching Economics at the prestigious St Stephen's College, Delhi, prior to joining the Civil Service, and has lectured widely at eminent universities like Columbia, Yale, Stanford and London School of Economics. He has authored two books entitled, *Politics of Change* and *Not by Reason Alone,* and has continuously been a repute of columnist in leading Indian dailies, *Financial Express, Hindustan Times, Hindustan* and *Indian Express*.

U.K. Sinha is Chairman, Securities & Exchange Board of India (SEBI) since 2011. Formerly from the Indian Administrative Service, he brings with him rich experience in the financial markets for more than a decade. He has held several responsible positions with distinction in the State and Central Governments. He was Joint Secretary (Banking) and Joint Secretary (Capital Markets), Ministry of Finance, Government of India. He was also Chairman, Working Group on Foreign Investment in India formed by the Government of India. He was a member of several committees set up by the Government of India including the Committees on Liquidity Management, Foreign Institutional Investors, Corporate Bond Market and Investor Protection. Prior he was Chairman and Managing Director, UTI Asset Management Company Limited and Chairman, Association of Mutual Fund in India. He has actively contributed to the financial sector reforms in the country. He is also credited with starting the micro-pension movement in India. He is also currently Chairman, Asia Pacific Regional Committee of International Organization of Securities Commissions (IOSCO).

Duvvuri Subbarao assumed office as the twenty-second Governor of the Reserve Bank of India on 5 September 2008. Earlier, he served as Finance Secretary, Government of India from April 2007 to September 2008 and as Secretary, Prime Minister's Economic Advisory Council from March 2005 to March 2007. As a member of the Indian Administrative Service (IAS), Dr Subbarao has been a career civil servant. Over the years of 1988-1998, he worked in various positions in State government of Andhra Pradesh and Government of India. He was a Lead Economist in the World Bank (1999-2004), where he also task managed a flagship study on decentralisation across major East Asian countries, which was acknowledged as innovative policy work. Dr Subbarao received BSc (Hons) in Physics from the Indian Institute of Technology, Kharagpur and MSc in Physics from the Indian Institute of Technology, Kanpur. Subsequent to joining the civil service, he received an MS in Economics from Ohio State University (1978) and was a Humphrey Fellow studying public finance at MIT during 1982-83. He earned his PhD in Economics from Andhra University (1998). Dr Subbarao maintains a strong commitment to academic pursuits, and has written and lectured extensively on issues in public finance, decentralisation and political economy of reforms.

Y.S.P. Thorat is CEO, Rajiv Gandhi Trust, New Delhi. He obtained PhD in Economics, 2006, from Shivaji University, Kolhapur on "Rural Financial Services Market in Kolhapur District". He is pursuing another PhD from University of Reading, UK, on Provision of Micro Finance Services through Path Sansthas (Non-Agricultural Cooperative Credit Societies). He joined RBI in 1972 as a Direct Recruit in Grade 'B'; promoted as Executive Director RBI in 2003; left in 2004 to take up appointment as Managing Director, NABARD. In addition to discharging the duties of CEO (2004-05), he was associated at the policy level with Vaidyanathan Committees on the ST & LT Cooperative Credit Structure as Member Secretary, and as Chairman of the Expert Groups on Credit Deposit Ratio and Investment Credit appointed by the GoI and RBI respectively. Earlier he was Chairman, Micro Finance Development and Equity Fund, GoI, with the responsibility of suggesting a legislative framework for MFIs. He was appointed Chairman, NABARD in 2006 and served until November 2007. Dr Thorat has been a regular visiting Lecturer at the University of Reading since 1998 and have lectured there on various subjects including agriculture, rural credit, microfinance, poverty alleviation, etc. This, in addition to University of Manchester, (1998, 1999); University of Geneva, Switzerland (1998, 2005); University of Zurich, Switzerland (1998, 2005) and so on. He has contributed several research papers, monographs on areas like, agriculture credit, cooperatives, microfinance and rural credit. He has also chaired several committees like Group of Experts on Sugar Policy; Committee to Formulate a Comprehensive Human Resource Policy for RRBs; and Advisory Board for Micro Finance Development & Equity Fund.

1 Introduction

Sameer Kochhar

The story goes that as India's economic liberalisation gathered steam in the summer of 1991, Union Commerce Minister P. Chidambaram asked his ministry's officials to come up with the maximum number of changes they would like to see in the existing foreign trade policy. All top officials tried their best to redraw the rules of the game with their own ideas. However, when he realised that what his officials had to offer was woefully inadequate in sum and substance for the brave new world he envisaged, Chidambaram—known for his broad, systematic and methodical approach—told them to report back with a fresh draft that was literally dictated by none other than himself! Nothing was left to chance too. Some days, he was in office till about 3 in the morning trying to rework the trade regime so that the new one could be rolled out within the timeframe that he had in mind. Within few days, history was made as independent India put in place a radically liberalised foreign trade policy regime widely heralded as a game-changer in the country's economic history.

India's policymaking has an uncanny tendency to be tied in knots of red-tape obfuscation, complexity, mis-steps and political point-scoring. Yet, whatever the odds, there is one unmistakable message Chidambaram always likes to deliver when he is at the helm of a ministry: it is no longer 'business as usual'. The ability to bring considerable change to policymaking has become so built into his persona that whenever he assumes charge of a ministry, one can immediately sense Chidambaram working overtime to shake off the lethargy and dithering associated with traditional government functioning.

This is the reason why, for his admirers and detractors alike, he comes across as a no-nonsense man who constantly questions, is hands-on and meticulous, and intolerant of people who do not manage their time well. Among India's current crop of politicians, Chidambaram is outstanding for his gifted ability to work around bickering politicians, enliven the spirit of colleagues and cut through all the haze and clutter that surrounds political rhetoric, ideological rigidity and policy inaction. In fact, it appears these qualities come naturally to him, drawing upon his immense reservoir of sharp intellect, attention to detail and highly-refined articulation and persuasion skills. His eloquence—of which brevity is a great charm, as Marcus Cicero would have it—and clarity of vision to see what Zen gurus call "the next horizon"—the wisdom ordinary people miss—have made him arguably the most effective spokesman for change within the Congress party.

In an interaction with me in 2012, C. Rangarajan, who has known Chidambaram since the beginning of economic reforms in 1991, characterised him as "wherever you put him [Chidambaram], he is sure to shine well." People who know Chidambaram well will readily concede that the *sine qua non* to forging rapport with him is that one has to be alert intellectually. "He has great confidence in what he does and he also understands the problems posed to him and therefore when you are dealing with him as a minister, you are dealing with a person who understands a problem, who can analyse the problem. Therefore, in some way, you have to match his brilliance. Those who fall short of that may find it difficult to work with him," as Rangarajan put it to me.

There are no two opinions about this. Chidambaram is blessed with a very sharp mind and unlike a lot of people who waste their intellectual edge, he has built upon it through a cultivated sense of hard work, unflinching dedication and a sense of mission to produce very good results in whichever sphere he has been asked to operate.

Like all trained lawyers, which Chidambaram is, he is able to look at any puzzle put up to him analytically and tenaciously to come to logical conclusions. But, at the same time, he has the political sensibility to determine which solution works and which does not. "Therefore he is a combination of political maturity with intellectual brilliance, a combination which is very rare among Indian politicians. I think this is the hallmark of Chidambaram," says Rangarajan.

Chidambaram is a committed moderniser and reformer. Political sagacity that complements the intellectual brilliance enables him untangle policy muddles.This has become his hallmark and contributed to his reformist zeal in overhauling the system to make it forward-looking and well-oiled.

An inescapable element in Chidambaram's handling of any central government ministry is the perceptible improvement in the policy environment, which becomes apparent as soon as he assumes office. When he was Finance Minister during 2004-2008, the country's growth was motoring along at a near double-digit clip. The growth momentum slowed after he was shifted to the Home Ministry in the aftermath of the 26/11 Mumbai terrorist attacks.

In July 2012, Chidambaram was appointed Finance Minister again when Pranab Mukherjee resigned to be elected the President of India. His actions in the first few days were enough to drive home the point that he meant business. Soon after re-designating the finance ministry portfolio to Chidambaram, Prime Minister Manmohan Singh spoke of reviving "animal spirits" in the economy. As before, Chidambaram wasted no time in coming to grips with the new challenges as India's economy was in the grip of what seemed to be policy paralysis, which contributed to in slow growth, slackened foreign investment, worrisome fiscal and current account deficits, high interest rates and stubborn inflation. Within a few weeks, the government unveiled a slew of reform measures to revive growth—raising the price of subsidised diesel and easing foreign direct investment caps in multibrand retail, broadcasting and the airline industry. With India's economic policy-making landscape suddenly infused with fresh energy, the overall market sentiment lifted up.

To talk up market sentiments further, Chidambaram declared that he would remove irritants the investor faces. He promised a non-adversarial tax administration and hinted at the possibility of interest rate cuts. High interest rates raise costs for producers and buyers, curtailing demand. He also unveiled a five-year action plan to cut fiscal deficit in order to attain much-needed fiscal consolidation.

His statements, delivered in measured tones, do not mince words. "I am making this statement, so that everybody in India...acknowledges that the government is determined to bring about fiscal consolidation. I sincerely hope that everybody will read the statement and will take note of that," he declared on October 29, 2012 after the Reserve Bank of India's (RBI) Second Quarter Review of Monetary Policy for 2012-13 was announced. His plan is to restrict the budget deficit to 5.3 per cent of GDP in 2012-13 and 4.8 per cent in 2013-14. The larger aim of the fiscal consolidation plan announced by him is to slash the fiscal deficit to 3 per cent by 2016-17. The fiscal deficit was 5.8 per cent in 2011-12.

After emphasising the importance of winning back investors' confidence, Chidambaram went on to draw up a package of smaller measures to stop the rot, such as improving tax collection, fast-tracking stalled infrastructure projects and asking state banks to ease lending to small manufacturers. Reinforcing the message of change was the appointment of Raghuram Rajan, outspoken former chief economist of the International Monetary Fund, as Chidambaram's top adviser. Earlier in 2012, Rajan had critiqued the UPA-II government's economic policy paralysis at an event attended by Prime Minister Manmohan Singh.

One belief underlying Chidambaram's unwavering spirit of reform and change is the maxim "the buck stops here." In fact, the winds of change start blowing from the very office in which he sits. It is now folklore among central government officials that no sooner does Chidambaram assume the mantle of a ministry than a sudden change in staff behaviour becomes palpable—officials work longer hours, work even on weekends, and with a new sense of urgency and accountability.

The pattern repeated itself. As soon as he moved to North Block in July 2012, a news report quoted an official who attended Chidambaram's first meeting with senior staff, "His message is very clear. Either you have to perform or find a way to move out of the ministry." The report went on to say that since Chidambaram's arrival, senior ministry officials had been logging their arrival and departure each day using the fingerprint scanners located at the building's entrances. Earlier, only junior staff were required to do so. "What he has done is put everyone on their toes and made them accountable," quipped the unnamed official.

A stickler for work ethics, Chidambaram is intolerant of plain fools. Ashok Jha, former secretary of the Union finance ministry who has closely worked with Chidambaram, told me: "Basically, if you discuss something with him, after due preparation, there will be absolutely no problem....He has a razor-sharp mind and is quite quick to spot somebody who is trying to bluff their way out."

G.K. Pillai, who has worked closely with Chidambaram at both the commerce and home ministries, had something similar to say. "You realise that you have to really struggle to keep up with him [Chidambaram]. He studies the subject so well that unless you are prepared, he will make mincemeat out of you," he told me.

Chidambaram is an intellectual leader who listens to the arguments of others and is willing to abide by what somebody else says if he finds wisdom in it. This book is replete with essays of leading figures who scripted India's economic reform story who felt very easy and very comfortable working with Chidambaram because they were all bound together by the worthwhile goal of attaining financial inclusion by bringing all sections of Indian society into the orbit of the organised financial system in a commercially viable and sustainable manner.

Chidambaram established a reputation for being a moderniser from the very beginning of his government career. Although he was active in the Tamil Nadu Pradesh Congress Committee (TNCC), his passion was largely consumed by his successful law practice until 1985 when he was offered a ministerial role in the central government by Prime Minister Rajiv Gandhi. That time Chidambaram could hardly have foreseen the key role he would play in the nation's affairs in the following decades. In his first assignment, as Minister of State of Personnel Department, he pushed through some landmark changes none of his predecessors had even thought of. The reform of the civil services examination procedures and an overhaul of staff leave norms were notable among them. In 1986, when he was given additional charge as Minister of State of Home Affairs, he trained his attention on modernising the police/paramilitary recruitment process and training.

In many ways, the momentum towards economic and broader administrative reform had started building up during Rajiv Gandhi government's tenure from 1984 to 1989. However, what happened in 1991 was historic. With a dyed-in-the-wool reformist like Chidambaram in the Dream Team of 1991, a more perfect start to the economic reform story of 1991 could not have been made.

"The course of reforms has always been difficult, but never more difficult than at the very beginning," Chidambaram wrote in a column in *The Indian Express* in October 2003. "We have heard of the dictum 'Art for art's sake'. We have seen, and continue to see, 'Ministers for ministers' sake'. And now we have a new principle.... and that is 'Reforms for reforms' sake'," he wrote, criticising the disinvestment policy of the NDA government headed by Atal Bihari Vajpayee. Between August 2002 and March 2004, while he was in Opposition, Chidambaram wrote a weekly column for the newspaper, offering matter-of-fact and prescient commentaries on India's economy and polity.

A selection of those essays was published in a book form, titled *A View from the Outside,* in 2007. In his introduction to that book, Chidambaram wrote:

> Since 1991, I have been involved, in one manner or other, with India's economic reforms, and that is true even in respect of the period that I was not in government or in Parliament. Save that I read '101 Economics' taught by Professor Simon Kuznets at Harvard, I had no formal instruction in economics. Over the years, I have made a determined effort to educate myself by reading extensively and through discussions with qualified trained economists, and I continue to do so. I make no claim to be a trained economist. My strengths—if any—are that I bring an open and curious mind and a passion for change.
>
> There is no iron law that says that India shall remain a poor country or that most Indians shall remain steeped in poverty. Poverty is not a badge of honour; it is a stain that must be removed. We are the moving finger and we can write our collective fate.

Even though this firm conviction remains at the root of Chidambaram's worldview, the course of reforms has always been difficult. Political controversy dogged the reform process at every step, be it the rupee's devaluation, loosening of export/import controls, industrial delicensing, tax reforms, or India joining the WTO. But, as Chidambaram noted in another article in October 2002, "In 1991, we turned our back on the dirigiste model that we had followed for 40 years. As a consequence, the 1990s registered the highest decadal growth rate in the history of India. That decade also registered the sharpest reduction in the level of poverty."

Nevertheless, the reforms of 1991 did not happen by design alone; it had to occur by chance as well. Many still wonder that if India had not faced such a crippling balance of payments crisis, would anyone in the government have launched reforms at all. Some call it the moment of reckoning for the Indian economy, from where turning back was simply not an option. Apart from Prime Minister P.V. Narasimha Rao, Finance Minister Manmohan Singh, the other key player who helped steer the nation out of unchartered waters at that crucial moment in India's economic history was P. Chidambaram.

During the first year of Narasimha Rao's government, when India was confronted with its biggest economic crisis which stemmed from the foreign exchange crunch, the rupee was devalued in a two-step move by Finance Minister Manmohan Singh. As a raft of reforms were announced by the finance ministry in the early days of reforms, Chidambaram played an instrumental role as a supportive commerce minister. The commerce ministry was responsible for India's external trade, an area that bore the brunt of the far-reaching changes unleashed by reforms.

In fact, the Narasimha Rao government had to swing into action within weeks of taking office on June 21, 1991. The investor confidence had plummeted and resultantly, the foreign exchange reserves dipped to alarmingly low levels. India's credit rating had taken fatal knocks. All these forced the government's hands to do something to rescue the economy even before it could present its first Budget. The first measure the government adopted was devaluation of the currency. The rupee was devalued two times within a gap of as many days in the first week of July 1991. The 10 per cent devaluation announced on July 1 was not whole-hog; so, a second round of 12 per cent was called in on July 3.

However, the rub was that the devaluation had to be in tandem to a radical shift in the external trade policy, which was originally scheduled to be released some weeks later. After the second devaluation, that time window closed dramatically.

On cue of the July 3 devaluation move, Chidambaram and his team at the commerce ministry swiftly and decisively got into the act. On the same evening the devaluation was announced, Chidambaram unveiled the contours of the revised trade policy. In that, the negative import list was significantly reduced, a new instrument (the tradeable licence for exporters called Exim scrips) was introduced and the erstwhile cash compensatory support was withdrawn. The new trade policy set the stage for market-determination of the rupee's value.

As part of the trade policy reform, the licence-permit raj relics of Red Book and Blue Book were jettisoned and they were replaced by an export/import policy which was, as Chidambaram reminisced in a recent interview to me, "the first time a policy was written in simple English—in double space, 12 point font, and it was only 100 pages." It's a widely known fact that Chidambaram has zero-tolerance for prolix, complex and jargon-filled documents.

The reform of the external sector had several dimensions. The first was to dismantle controls over imports. Second, import duties had to be slashed drastically. Third, the currency needed to be tethered to a stable exchange rate mechanism. As a first step towards a marked-determined exchange rate change, the commerce ministry introduced the dual exchange rate system. But even before its introduction, Exim scrips were announced by which an additional premium was payable to exports so that the sector could be hedged against sudden unfavourable consequences. In a calibrated fashion, India was moving towards a reform of the exchange rate regime. The Exim scrips were followed soon by a dual exchange rate system and finally, in February 1993, India cemented the market-determined exchange rate system.

In the meanwhile, the commerce ministry under Chidambaram was eliminating a whole lot of export/import controls, giving space and opportunity for the business community to get on with its affairs instead of running to the ministry for arbitrary clearances at every turn. The import substitution policy was given up, thereby dispensing with various quantitative controls on imports, and work was in progress to pave way for a system in which India's exports could expand and effectively meet the requirements of balance of payments.

The most significant impact of import decontrol was that it unshackled industry from government controls so that when they needed raw materials or components or finished goods, they didn't have to seek government licences. Arbitrary licensing authority, in other words, amounted to rent-seeking. "Import licensing was a big control mechanism located in the commerce ministry and he was actually giving up his own licensing power in exchange for giving exporters a better deal by introducing Exim scrips. So, I call that a game-changer which essentially set the stage within two years to move to a flexible exchange rate," Montek Singh Ahluwalia, the then commerce secretary, told me in an interaction.

Trade reforms subsequently yielded a massive reduction in import licensing, except for consumer goods. This was made possible because Chidambaram recognised that when import duties are lowered, it allows the exchange rate to play its due market role, not hamstrung by government interventionism. The exchange rate depreciates and that is good enough to control imports and is very good for exporters. The logic of moving away from a system of excessive control with various export sops to a system where bulk of the trade supporting mechanism was really a market-determined exchange rate won the day.

When Chidambaram became Finance Minister in the United Front coalition government during 1996-1998, he carried forward the reforms introduced by Manmohan Singh, his predecessor at the ministry. His famous Union Budget for 1997-98 contained all the ingredients of a "Dream Budget", as it was dubbed. In this Budget, he ushered in a new chapter in India's taxation policy. Tax rates were fixed at just three slabs, compressing them to 10, 20 and 30 per cent.This rechristened the rates of personal tax in a manner which no Finance Minister since has ever thought to tinker with. Hence, Chidambaram pulled off a drastic reduction in the marginal tax rate in a single stroke—a bold step by coalition-era standards. Subsequent events have clearly shown that reduction in the rates did not affect the state exchequer because GDP growth has buoyed up the Indian economy ever since. In fact, this tax rationalisation led to best tax compliance in India. Even the tax-GDP ratio registered an upward kick as a consequence of these steps that he took.

Speaking of his "Dream Budget" once when I interviewed him, Chidambaram termed it as "path-breaking" because he succeeded in breaking a few moulds. "One of them was that high tax rates were a way to raise revenue. All my training told me that high tax rates do not bring more revenues; lower tax rates brings you more revenue." Clearly, for him, the Laffer Curve—representative of the relationship between government revenue raised by taxation and possible rates of taxation—proved to be alive and kicking.

During his second stint as Finance Minister in the United Progressive Alliance (UPA) government from 2004, Chidambaram once again carried forward the reform process in a calculated way. Major reforms having already been introduced earlier, he focused on the small steps within the spirit of liberalisation, in spite of the stiff resistance offered by Left parties. From 2004 to 2008, India's economy grew at the highest annualised rate—8.5 per cent average. Inflation average was only 5.5 to 6.0 per cent. As state revenues were bulging on the back of an economic boom that lasted until the Great Recession struck in 2008, the government introduced a gargantuan agricultural loan waiver programme, expanded the education loan programme, and launched financially-inclusive social welfare programmes like the Mahatma Gandhi National Rural Employment Guarantee Scheme (MGNREGS). Chidambaram also sought measures to curb the fiscal deficit, as per the Fiscal Responsibility and Budget Management (FRBM) Act introduced by his predecessor, Yashwant Sinha.

Chidambaram continued with the policy of ensuring a simple, straight forward tax system where three aims were paramount: the rates are low, the base is wide and exemptions are limited. To the extent coalition politics allowed, he made efforts to revive the public sector undertakings disinvestment process, which had been stalled under the NDA government.

His fiscal initiatives actually produced results. In 2003-04, the financial year before he took over as Finance Minister, the direct tax-GDP ratio was about 3.75 to 3.8 per cent, but that went up to close to 6.4 per cent in 2007-08, before he was moved out to the home ministry. "The sharp increase of 2.6-2.7 per cent presents one of the largest increases in such a short duration anywhere in the world," Rangarajan pointed out to me.

Financial inclusion is a theme that features prominently in this book. In fact, Chidambaram is considered one of the early votaries of financial inclusion in the government. He set up the Committee on Financial Inclusion in 2006 under the chairmanship of Rangarajan. The Finance Minister, Rangarajan noted, was particularly keen to see that the Indian financial system, particularly the banking system, was able to fulfill the needs and requirements of all sections of Indian society.

In February 2008, the government constituted a Financial Inclusion Fund (FIF) and Financial Inclusion Technology Fund (FITF) which has been announced by Chidambaram in his 2007-08 Budget speech. The FIF was meant for training inputs, especially to business facilitators and correspondents, who would ensure institutional credit as representatives of banks, especially among weaker sections and low-income groups. The FITF was mandated to provide user-friendly technology to ensure affordable financial services to disadvantaged sections. The fund was also intended to create a common technology infrastructure with comprehensive credit information, and provide viability gap funding for unproven, but potential, technological interventions.

In my interview with him, Chidambaram outlined his view on financial inclusion. "A large number of programmes, where we reached out to the poor directly, were possible because of high growth. Within the government, I was the one who continued to emphasise that growth is a pre-requisite for inclusive growth. You cannot have inclusive growth without growth. Where is the money going to come from for all these grand sweeping schemes that we are introducing? You need money. That cannot come from borrowing; it has to come from government's own resources. And government's resources are only tax and non-tax revenues, mainly tax revenues, and that will come only if we continue to grow at a clipping pace. I think, by and large, that is accepted. Once the monies were visible, then of course the demand for inclusive growth became quite vocal and we responded to it."

Certainly, Chidambaram believes that for financial inclusion to work, India must have a banking system that is commercially viable. He believes in a banking system that has to be efficient and any scheme introduced has to be commercially balanced rather than being a subsidised programme. In other words, the banking system must be at the forefront of coordinated and sustained efforts to cover all sections of society.

Rangarajan calls the Direct Taxes Code (DTC) "a child of Chidambaram's imagination and work." Of course, there have been subsequent changes, which are being introduced in the light of discussions with stakeholders, but he entirely rewrote the tax code and made it simpler and easier to understand. This reform is in lockstep with his three major aims of tax reforms: widening the base, reducing rates and curtailing exemptions.

A lot of work remains to be done on fiscal consolidation, and that is why Chidambaram attaches so much importance to it after he became Finance Minister again in 2012. The fiscal consolidation plan he unveiled in October 2012, as noted earlier, has set as its goal paring the fiscal deficit down to 3 per cent by 2016-17.

Chidambaram was India's home minister from November 2008 to July 2012. One of his signal achievements during this tenure was the fresh focus on what is broadly called police reforms: merit-based, transparent recruitment and modern training of the country's police force. He implemented the Integrated Action Plan in about 60 Naxal-affected districts of the country. Notable other achievements are the formulation and implementation of the National Intelligence Grid (Natgrid), the Crime & Criminal Tracking Network & Systems (CCTNS), the Multi Agency Centre (MAC), the Mission Mode Project on Immigration, Visa and Foreigners Registration & Tracking (IVFRT) and the idea of a National Counter Terrorism Centre (NCTC).

According to a meticulous cover story in the special issue of *Inclusion* in 2011, Chidambaram achieved in just 45 days what his predecessor, Shivraj Patil, achieved in four-and-half years. "Chidambaram personally monitors work, conducts fortnightly and monthly reviews and never shies away from pulling up slow movers. Once he says it will be done, he sees to it that it is actually done," the article said, commenting on his no-nonsense style of work at the ministry.

In one of the thought-provoking essays he penned for *The Indian Express* in October 2002, Chidambaram's opening sentence runs: "If a man is known by the company he keeps, I suppose that a nation can be known by the issues that engage its attention." Certainly, one thing Chidambaram has established in his political life is that he has got the issues that engage his attention right.

He concludes his critique of the NDA government's economic policies in an article published in July 2003 with quote of Jonathan Swift: "Whoever would make two ears of corn or two blades of grass to grow upon a spot of ground where only one grew before would deserve better of mankind and do more essential service to his country than the whole race of politicians put together." Again, judging from his political career, it's a cardinal principle Chidambaram has taken to heart.

Make your point, shut up and then quietly do your work: if you follow this dictum, they say, you are bound to stand out in a crowd. Chidambaram has the unique ability to blend excellence in eloquence with single-minded focus on the task at hand.

It is said that Chidambaram often stands out among other distinguished speakers at the World Economic Forum (WEF) meetings in Davos, for he finishes his speeches within the 10-minute time limit after clinically making his point, whereas many others struggle to do so and end up overshooting the time limit.

An Agenda for India's Growth is then as much a tribute to Chidambaram's eloquent advocacy of policy reform—and the courage he displayed in implementing them—as much as a tribute to his capacity to ruthlessly focus on the essentials. In short, crisp essays, the contributors in this book describe Chidambaram's role as a key architect in catapulting India's growth story and dilate the areas where the spirit of the reform process needs to be rekindled.

Almost all the contributors have known Chidambaram far longer than I have. I am indeed glad that they agreed to contribute essays to felicitate his remarkable political career and public policy advocacy and implementation. Each contributor reminisces about their association with him and then goes on to flesh out the agenda as to, borrow from what Vijay L. Kelkar said on another occasion, "India embarks on this growth odyssey."

Monetk Singh Ahluwalia's association with Chidambaram dates back to 1991 when he served as commerce secretary. In Montek, Chidambaram had a staunch supporter in pushing through his economic vision. That camaraderie continues to this day, with Chidambaram as Finance Minister and Montek as Deputy Chairman of the Planning Commission. At the outset of his paper, "Policies for Strong Inclusive Growth", Montek says:

> When the history of India's economic reforms post 1991 is written, Chidambaram will undoubtedly figure as the second most important political personality, after Manmohan Singh, pushing the reform agenda forward. He has a strong conviction that India has the capacity to grow rapidly and compete successfully in an increasingly integrated and competitive world economy and also that this growth can be made sufficiently inclusive to transform the lives of the mass of our people. He recognises that the private sector and markets have a major role to play in India's development, but he also believes the government must proactively support the process, intervene when necessary to regulate markets and deal with market failure.

Montek covers five sections in his chapter. Section I recounts how the trade policy reforms of 1991 were enforced. The story is of special relevance for this volume as it describes as insider's account on critical role played by Chidambaram himself in the first year of reforms, and also because it provides important pointers for policy formulation at the current juncture. Section II deals with inclusive growth, "and especially the relationship between the two objectives of rapid growth and inclusiveness." Section III outlines the macroeconomic constraints on achieving faster growth, while the next section discusses constraints posed by three sectors, energy, water and land, and the policy action required to fix these constraints. Section V explores how rapid growth can be made inclusive.

Referring to the lessons of 1991, Montek argues: "First and most important, Chidambaram's readiness to give up discretionary power in support of a system with much less discretion was absolutely critical. A similar willingness to give up discretionary power in favour of more transparent market-driven processes is needed in many areas, not only in the Centre but even more so in the states."

An interesting conclusion Montek draws from the experience of 1991 is that India can deliver results very fast when necessary. "I cannot recall any other occasion when such a major restructuring of established policy, involving more than one ministry, and actually requiring the approval of the prime minister, was taken in the short space of about ten hours!"

Montek's paper analyses some of the key challenges in achieving the Twelfth Plan goal of strong inclusive growth. He calls for wide-ranging reforms in the agriculture and manufacturing sectors, two key pillars of the Twelfth Plan growth strategy that sets an average of 8 per cent growth over the Plan period. In conclusion, he says,

> These reforms will contribute to the growth of total factor productivity which, together with growth of primary inputs, mainly capital and human resources, provide the impetus for growth from the supply side. A comprehensive discussion of these reforms is beyond the scope of this paper. The paper has attempted to highlight a number of critical policy challenges which need to be addressed if we are to achieve the objective of strong inclusive growth. A credible response requires actions by the central government and also by the state governments. Business as usual, with incremental change here and there, will not do.

Rangarajan, in his essay "Reforms: Past, Present and Future", says what impresses him most about Chidambaram is his intellectual brilliance. "With his sharp analytical skills, he is able to cut through the maze of facts and arguments relating to any problem and arrive at rational and economically sensible decisions. At the same time, he has a feel for what will work at the ground level. This is indeed a rare combination. He has provided the intellectual support to the liberalisation programme. He has articulated with conviction the need for India to take a different path."

"India's economic reforms are unique in two important respects—not because of the content of the reforms but because of the context in which we are pursuing them. First, we are implementing reforms in a democratic context, no matter that it has many flaws. Second, we are pursuing reforms in a decentralising context. This democracy-federalism context oftentimes has meant restraint, even compromise, deliberate decision-making and slow progress. While there are many respects in which we can make our approach to reforms more efficient and purposeful, in an overall perspective it must be acknowledged that making haste slowly...has a lot of merit. The participatory and consultative processes inherent in our institutions of meditation and restraint have added to the credibility and robustness of our reforms," he says.

Reviewing the progress of the country's economic movement, Rangarajan notes that the three important tasks before the Indian economy now are to tame inflation, and to contain the fiscal and current account deficits. However, reforms form part of a continuing agenda and a road map for the future must take a much more broader view of development.

"Development has many dimensions. It has to be inclusive; it must be poverty reducing and it must be environment-friendly. We need to incorporate all these elements in the growth process. Strong and balanced growth will enable the economy achieve multiple goals, including lowering inflation. Reforms will help us to achieve growth with equity," Rangarajan argues.

My essay, titled "Banking for the Last Mile", examines the ground covered by the government's financial inclusion plan under Chidambaram's watch. My research has found that since Chidambaram's departure from the finance ministry (December 2008 to July 2012), Mission Financial

Inclusion had veered off-course and the results are far from encouraging. "While his vision of financial inclusion was very clear, somehow, during the time that he was not at the helm of Finance Ministry, implementation got diluted and remained limited to opening no-frill accounts."

Now that Chidambaram is back at the finance ministry, hopes are rekindled about giving a new policy thrust to financial inclusion. It is my firm belief that Chidambaram has what it takes to be a transformational figure in India's economic scene. I am, in fact, reassured by his actions after he returned to the ministry in July 2012. The Direct Benefit Transfer (DBT) scheme, despite its many teething troubles, can prove to be a masterstroke because it is the first time the government is attempting to converge all social benefit schemes onto the financial inclusion platform. Since 2011, many new plans have been conceived. The Swabhimaan plan and the push for new private sector bank licences are good omens. The amendments to the Regional Rural Banking Act approved by the Union cabinet in January 2013 that seeks to shore up the capital of regional rural banks can have a salutary effect, too. Yet, I argue, every good intention could come to grief if India's financial inclusion plan is not given a new pivot.

Therefore, the paper chalks out a path to make the financial inclusion plan 'inclusion by design' as opposed to 'exclusion by design', which is the picture obtained by my research and available indicators. The business correspondent/banking facilitator methods have virtually collapsed because of flawed design and an inappropriate business model. A majority of no-frills accounts are inactive. Mobile phone banking is overridden by regulatory curbs. Priority sector lending has shown a decelerating trend over the years. Self-help groups are starved of funding. No financial literacy programme worth the paper it's written on has bridged the wide gulf of financial and digital literacy. The list, unfortunately, does not end here.

The paper mulls on what meaningful action needs to be undertaken to revive the business correspondent/banking facilitator model and to ensure realistic, need-based microcredit delivery. "Financial literacy is still a huge challenge. All financial inclusion initiatives in the country have been undertaken from the supply side. Therefore, livelihood promotion and credit needs of the people at the grass roots have largely remained unmet. Even the growth of self-help groups has suffered in the last couple of years," the chapter observes, flagging these as some other areas that cry out for urgent attention by the government.

The chapter draws upon Skoch's *State of the Sector* reports and the experience of its Samavesh pilot project, an idea that was born to spread financial and digital literacy among villagers. In the concluding part of the chapter, I have settled for no less than a paradigm shift in developmental banking parameters. I remain convinced that such a change is essential for financial inclusion to become a reality in India, and Chidambaram has the vision and administrative capability to make it possible.

In roughly three years when Chidambaram was India's Home Minister, the changes he had wrought in India's internal security front were so wide that they merit a separate chapter to take a full-spectrum view of the legacy he left behind the ministry. Therefore, I have co-authored with my colleague, Gursharan Dhanjal, the chapter, "Security: What Chidambaram Changed?"

The setting in which Chidambaram became the home minister was unfortunate in many respects. The outrageous terrorist audacity of the 26/11 attacks in Mumbai had thoroughly exposed loopholes in India's overall internal security thinking and preparedness. Intelligence agencies often worked at cross-purposes and the need for a central counter-terrorism agency became all the more pronounced. Border, especially coastal, security was in doldrums. Raging Left-Wing Extremism (LWE) in many parts of the country constituted a direct challenge to the state's authority. Counter-militancy in Jammu & Kashmir needed a new approach. Lack of modernisation had sapped the morale of India's police forces. The use of technology was at a pretty nascent stage in law-enforcement.

Many of the reforms and policy initiatives Chidambaram pulled off—from reviving the Multi Agency Centre, Integrated Action Plan to combat LWE to NATGRID and CCTNS—in rather a short span of time were *sui generis*. The results are already apparent, from containing LWE to establishing robust technological interfaces and tools to combat crime and terrorism.

"All in all, most of the tasks Chidambaram initiated within the first six months of taking over as Home Minister have either been achieved or were on track to being accomplished by the time he left office on July 31,

2012.... Having seized the moment and crafted a brand-new philosophical, technological and operational framework for internal security, the legacy that Chidambaram has left behind at the Ministry of Home Affairs is impressive. It is for his successors to build on it," our chapter concludes.

In "Urbanisation and India's Economic Development", Isher Judge Ahluwalia states that the reason she has chosen this topic is because India's growth momentum cannot be sustained if planned urbanisation is not actively facilitated. "As Finance Minister of India, Chidambaram can provide effective leadership in facilitating urbanisation for sustained growth," she adds.

She maps out the challenges facing the Jawaharlal Nehru National Urban Renewal Mission (JNNURM) implemented since 2005, the first time the government of India "proactively engaged in the process of urban development." The main challenge relates to enforcing the conditionality of reforms in a project-based financing approach, she says, adding that slow and uneven progress on reform has been a major weakness under JNNURM. Then there is lack of capacity to prepare and implement projects in urban infrastructure within the framework of a development plan. "The challenge of urban development not only requires skills in planning, engineering, finance and management but a stable manpower which can learn from experience and training and put it to effective use," she says.

Another challenge is the need for a legislative framework which will facilitate land acquisition for urban development. "Finally, a city development plan could not be backed by a financial plan from the urban local bodies (ULBs) because of their weak and vulnerable finances and unwillingness to raise user charges or use land-based instruments of finance. The government of India and state governments can help in responding to the financing challenge by working towards an effective devolution of funds to ULBs," she suggests.

"It is also very important to shift focus from bridging the deficit in infrastructure investment to ensuring service delivery on a sustainable basis. This will compel urban planners and city managers to build economic viability and sustainability into the process of planning and managing infrastructure projects. Only then can we ensure quality of life for India's urban population, while also realising our potential for economic and social development by pushing cities as engines of growth," Isher argues.

In his essay titled "Rejigging the Elephant Dance", Duvvuri Subbarao ponders the question if India is still capable of embarking on the double-digit growth trajectory. If the government can do so, he avers, if the country will be able to successfully address many challenges. "The first challenge is to step up agriculture production and productivity," he notes, and cautions that the quest for inclusive growth is in jeopardy if the root causes of structural food inflation are not addressed. The second major challenge to inclusive growth is employment opportunities. The answer lies in stepping up growth; "more importantly, stepping up the employment intensity of growth." Till that happens, he warns that India's "demographic dividend" will remain an illusion.

Subbarao then turns his focus on the imperative of enhancing productivity to make inclusive growth possible and argues that, "Productivity improvement entails managing factors of production as well as factor productivity better." He argues in favour of the rate of urbanisation picking up so as to move people up the productivity ladder and managing the pressures of urbanisation proactively. Emphasising the role of infrastructure development, he says the deficit on this score is "the most binding constraint to accelerating growth."

"Good governance is at the very heart of economic growth and poverty reduction, and even political legitimacy. In the ultimate analysis, it is the quality of governance that separates success and failure in economic development," he stresses.

In "Financial Inclusion: An Insider's View", another essay that contemplates the question of inclusive growth, Ashok Jha explores financial inclusion through banks and microfinance institutions (MFIs), as well as through stock exchanges. He pieces together data and concludes that banks are, however, only one instrument for attaining financial inclusion.

His examination of the roles these institutions play in safeguarding inclusion has proved that over-emphasis on bank accounts is not an adequate yardstick to measure financial inclusion. "It is not generally recognised that MFIs can play a pivotal role in taking care of the credit requirements of both rural and urban households which have no collateral to offer. Stock exchanges also can function as effective supplements to banks in channelising savings for productive investment," he notes.

In his essay "Reformer by Instinct and Choice", N.K. Singh highlights the importance of trade reforms and details how the broad-based trade liberalisation programme initiated in response to the balance of payments crisis of 1991 marked a significant turnaround in India's highly protected trade regime. He traces the history and explains that Chidambaram was instrumental in pushing through reforms in the trade and external sectors through deregulation of trade, removal of trade barriers, rationalisation of tariffs and putting an end to the license permit *raj*. Singh also reviews Chidambaram's record as Finance Minister—especially the 'Dream Budget' of 1997—and notes how that one budget revolutionised the taxation system in the country.

"The Indian economic story has and will go through many ups and downs. The current stagnant phase of both policy and outcomes should not blind us to accept that not only has India seen better days but also experienced a period of high noon of economic growth unprecedented in recent times. Chidambaram has been a key architect in catapulting the India growth story—a story widely acclaimed as India's long awaited arrival on the global scene," Singh concludes.

Chidambaram employed cricketing metaphors when summing up to me how he felt when preparing his 'Dream Budget'. He said he felt as if he was at the crease, allowed to bat freely, or in other words, allowed to do the things that he wanted to do so that "for the first time people recognised that the Budget was a powerful platform to canvas ideas." No doubt people recognised it, and as he himself foresaw, it set a precedent for succeeding finance ministers to use the Budget speech as a platform to harness and canvas new ideas.

It is noteworthy that on inclusive development Chidambaram believes that if there is all-round growth and growth is sustained over a period of time, even the very poor will come out of poverty. "If we simply apply ourselves to promoting and sustaining high growth over a long period of time, even the poorest in India will come out of poverty. A rising tide lifts all boats," he told me in the interview.

In "Second Decade of Securities Market Reforms: An Evaluation", U.K. Sinha spells out the second level of stock market-related reforms that have been undertaken in light of the shortcomings brought to the fore by a few high-profile scams. He identifies three areas for reform: first, making the domestic market more attractive for capital-raising; second, drawing domestic household savings and foreign investors into the market; and third, managing risk in order to make the market safe and protecting interests of investors. He, however, calls the gains from the second wave of reforms "modest".

Charting out the tasks ahead, he says that after the global financial crisis of 2007-08, systemic stability of financial markets has attracted renewed attention of regulators and policy makers worldwide. "It is now well recognised that securities regulators also have to contribute to the monitoring and prevention of systemic risks," he says. In conclusion, he adds: "Securities market regulators need to supplement legal expertise far beyond strong technological infrastructure to also include expertise in the area of financial technology, forensic, behavioural science, financial economics, financial education, human resource development, etc."

In his essay on the same topic, titled "Indian Exchanges at a Crossroads", Vijay L. Kelkar elaborates the role India's stock exchanges played in capital markets to bolster the pace and pattern of economic growth. Viewing the current stock exchange system in the country at a crossroads, he lists policy decisions regarding its governance and ownership as imperative issues in India.

He cites two reasons to underline the need for reforms in this context. "First, in the recent global financial crisis, it has been seen that 'conflict of interest' in systemically important financial institutions can be potentially very disruptive. Since exchanges play both a commercial and regulatory role, there is an inherent 'conflict of interest' in the exchange business. Second, it is being increasingly argued that not allowing exchanges to get listed would hurt their natural evolution as for-profit organisations and the full benefits of demutualisation may not be recognised. It is also suggested that listing would not only mean easier financing for exchanges but also more nimble decision making."

Kelkar's essay addresses questions like managing the conflict between commercial and regulatory roles, listing of exchanges, reforms in the ownership structure and ends with a warning against any judgement error in introducing exchange reforms, because that has the potential to blot out decades of progress made in a short duration of time. He cautions policy-makers to make sure that no incentives are created at the micro level which do not sit well with the macroeconomic role that exchanges are expected to play.

Chidambaram, for sure, is mindful of the factors that could derail growth. "If investments collapse, growth will derail. If savings collapse for some reason, growth will be derailed. I think we have to keep a watchful eye over every factor that fosters and promotes and sustains growth," as he put it to me recently.

In "Goods and Services Tax: Challenges of Ensuring an Acceptable Structure", M. Govinda Rao says that in India a leader who implements reforms in a systematic manner requires more than political skills; "he should be a statesman and Chidambaram has shown statesmanship in adopting a modern approach to tax reforms in the country."

In his paper, Rao lists the challenges of reforming the consumption tax system by introducing the goods and services tax (GST). "The two major tax reform initiatives on the agenda which Chidambaram as finance minister will have to address in the short and medium term are the Direct Taxes Code (DTC) and the introduction of GST. In both cases, the attempt is to broaden the base, reduce the rates, minimise rate differences and ensure a simple and transparent tax system," he says.

"The reform of the consumption tax system to levy GST is not just an option but imperative. The reform is necessary not only for minimising the collection, compliance and resource allocation costs but also to raise significant additional revenue over the medium term. The much needed resources for universalising healthcare, augmenting expenditures on education and, above all, to contain the fiscal deficit at the level recommended by the Finance Commission which has been accepted by the Centre would require additional resources amounting to almost 6 per cent of GDP and a significant volume of that will have to come from raising additional taxes. Introduction of GST will be a win-win strategy for both the Centre and states and there is every reason to embrace it. However, reform of this nature involving both Centre and states is an experiment in cooperative federalism and requires stewardship by statesmen," he concludes, saying that Chidambaram fits the bill to take up this task.

In his essay, "Agriculture Growth in India: The Hope and Despair Syndrome", Y.S.P. Thorat recalls his NABARD days of working together with Chidambaram and says that his [Chidambaram's] approach was a breath of fresh air. "He neither generalised nor minced his words and would inevitably pin the participants to specific answers, specific action points and specific timeframes," Thorat remembers. His choice of agriculture as the topic of his article is because it is "not only an area closer to Chidambaram's heart but also because the sector is in need of serious reform."

"There are several areas of importance for growth of the agriculture sector including enhancing public sector investment in research, effective transfer of technology, institutional reforms in the research set up to make it more accountable and geared towards delivery, conservation of land, water and biological resources, the development of rainfed agriculture, development of minor irrigation, timely and adequate availability of inputs, support for marketing infrastructure and an increase in flow of credit particularly to small and marginal farmers," he says. "Foreign direct investment—through technology transfer, productivity gains and capacity-building in key areas—will have multiplier effects on India's agriculture sector," he adds.

In "An Agenda for Nine per cent Growth, Tarun Das discusses the prospects for achieving what he calls the "turnaround job"—to get back to nine per cent growth rate. Calling the task "not impossible", he enumerates certain policy fillips needed to make the turnaround possible. First, he argues for a stronger role for public sector undertakings so that they continue to play a major role in the national economy. He favours continuation of the disinvestment process in order to allow Indian citizens to buy shares in public sector enterprises and to shore up strong corporate governance practices and accountability among these enterprises.

Second, Das sees higher investment in physical infrastructure development as a key area that could act as the force multiplier for economic activity and employment. Third, he advocates incentives for the private sector to do its bit to attain nine per cent growth and argues that the present policy climate does not induce private sector investment to the level desired. He also sees a big role for defence production and says that the impact of rapid growth of the public and private sectors in manufacturing and defence production would catalyse the birth of new enterprises in the small and medium industry sector. Although he anticipates agriculture not to add to the GDP growth rate in a major way, he flags its steady growth as an important benchmark for higher growth.

"The agenda for nine per cent growth is neither unreal nor unachievable. Practical, steady policies, management and implementation, which are already in evidence under the leadership of Chidambaram, are showing the way to a renewal of the nine per cent legacy," he writes.

In his essay "India: From Value Added Tax to Goods and Services Tax", Parthasarathi Shome identifies the measures to be taken towards taxation reforms in India. He dwells at length on the reforms to be made in value added tax (VAT) and the proposed GST in order to broad-base them and bring them up to global best standards.

"Examining global experience among fiscal federal countries, India has accomplished more in terms of VAT uniformity and in ameliorating possible deleterious distortions for economic decision-making," he says. At the same time, he calls for reformulating the GST Bill to facilitate a low rate structure and ample base with few rational exemptions. Effective and transparent administrative organisation and rules are another pre-requisite, he adds.

In presenting this festschrift as a tribute to Chidambaram's service to the nation, I'm overcome by some personal emotions. I had a humble beginning in life. As I look back and reflect on the course my life has taken, I can vouchsafe that but for the long-term vision transformational personalities like Chidambaram, Manmohan Singh, Montek Singh Ahluwalia and C. Rangarajan—in various capacities in different points in time—I would not have realised the India Dream myself, like multitude of our countrymen. In fact, they have given birth to a new Indian nation, forward-looking and confident.

They bear out Miguel de Cervantes's observation in *Don Quixote*: "Great persons are able to do great kindnesses."

2 Reforms: Past, Present and Future

C. Rangarajan

P. Chidambaram is one of India's outstanding politicians. What impresses one most about him is his intellectual brilliance. With his sharp analytical skills, he is able to cut through the maze of facts and arguments relating to any problem and arrive at rational and economically sensible decisions. At the same time, he has the feel for what will work at the grass roots level. This is indeed a rare combination. He has provided intellectual support to the liberalisation programme. He has articulated with conviction the need for India to take a different path. First, as commerce minister, he was responsible for opening up the external trade sector. Later, as finance minister, he became instrumental in reforming India's fiscal sector, more particularly the tax structure. He continues to play the role of a catalyst of reforms in our country.

1991 Reforms: Genesis

In the post-independence economic history of India, 1991 stands out in bold relief as a watershed year. This was the year in which the economy was faced with a severe balance of payments (BoP) crisis. In response, we launched a broad-ranging economic programme, not just to restore the BoP but to reform, restructure and modernise the economy. This was an appropriate move, for the external payment crisis was just the proximate manifestation of a policy regime that has, over the years, tended to give precedence to command and control over productivity, efficiency and entrepreneurship. In the event, the 1991 reforms signalled a shift away from the earlier paradigm.

Economic Reforms: Break with the Past

This break with the past came in three important directions. The first was to dismantle the complex regime of licences, permits and controls that dictated almost every facet of production and distribution—what to produce, where to produce, how to produce and how much to produce. The entrepreneur now had greater freedom to decide on all these choices. The second change was to reverse the strong bias towards state ownership of means of production and proliferation of public sector enterprises (PSEs) in almost every sphere of economic activity. Areas once reserved exclusively for the state were now thrown open to private enterprise. The final change was to abandon our inward-looking trade policy. This elusive, and in hindsight ill-advised, quest for self-sufficiency was driven by a belief that there was a value in minimising the economy's external dependence and producing what we need ourselves even if it meant high costs and low efficiency. By embracing international trade, India signalled that it was boldly abandoning its export pessimism and was accepting the challenge and opportunity of integrating into the world economy to leverage the well and long known gains arising from the welfare and efficiency benefits of free trade.

Rationale Underlying Reforms

Although the various elements of the reform agenda may look disparate, there is an underlying rationale running across the broad swathe of economic reforms. This was to give a greater market orientation to the economy and to let the competitive forces and growth impulses that are the bedrock of a modern, dynamic economy to come into fuller play. Liberalisation removed the barriers to entry, and relaxed the plethora of restrictions on production and distribution. It brought about a more competitive domestic environment while the liberalised trade and foreign investment policy sought to improve international competitiveness. By reducing its entrepreneurial role, the government was yielding economic space to the private sector, while also redefining the role of the state.

Stabilisation and Structural Adjustment

Conceptually, the economic reform agenda can be divided into two strands—stabilisation aimed at redressing the internal and external imbalances in the economy, and structural adjustment aimed at removing the rigidities and inefficiencies in the system and improving its competitiveness. Thus, stabilisation can be attempted and completed quickly, while structural adjustment is a medium to long-term process. Stabilisation is macroeconomic in content while structural adjustment encompasses both macro and microeconomic aspects. While stabilisation could be managed by the government acting on its own, structural adjustment is much broader and deeper in scope, requiring the proactive involvement of the government at various levels and the people at large.

Uniqueness of India's Reforms

India's economic reforms are unique in two important respects—not because of the content of the reforms but because of the context in which we are pursuing them. First, we are implementing reforms in a democratic context, no matter that it has many flaws. Second, we are pursuing reforms in a decentralising context. This democracy-federalism context oftentimes has meant restraint, even compromise, deliberate decision-making and slow progress. While there are many respects in which we can make our approach to reforms more efficient and purposeful, in an overall perspective, it must be acknowledged that making haste slowly—'crossing the river by feeling the stones', as the Chinese say—has a lot of merit. The participatory and consultative processes inherent in our institutions of meditation and restraint have added to the credibility and robustness of our reforms.

Thus, there is a common thread running through all the measures introduced since July 1991. The objective is simple and that is to improve the efficiency of the system. The regulatory mechanism involving multitudes of controls had fragmented capacity and reduced competition even in the private sector. The thrust of the new economic policy is towards creating a more competitive environment in the economy as a means to improving the productivity and efficiency of the system. This is to be achieved by removing the barriers to entry and the restrictions on growth of firms. While changes in industrial policy, such as the dismantling of licences seek to bring about a greater competitive environment domestically, the trade policy seeks to improve international competitiveness subject to the protection offered by tariffs which are coming down. The private sector is being given a larger space to operate as some of the areas earlier reserved exclusively for the public sector are also now allowed to the private sector. In these areas, the public sector will have to compete with the private sector, even though the public sector may continue to play a dominant role. What is sought to be achieved is an improvement in the functioning of the various entities, whether they are in the private or public sector, by injecting an element of competition. There is, however, nothing in the new economic policy which takes away the role of the state or the public sector in the system. The new economic policy of India has not necessarily diminished the role of state; it has only redefined it, expanding it in some areas and reducing in some others. It is sometimes said, somewhat paradoxically, 'more market' does not mean 'less Government' but only 'different Government'.

Trends in Growth

That our economic reforms are on the right track is vindicated by the performance of the economy since the launch of reforms. India's economic growth in the first three decades after independence was low. The annual growth rate of the economy was around 3.5 per cent. With population growing almost at 2 per cent, the per capita income grew at only 1.5 per cent per annum. Subsequently, there was some pick-up in the 1980s when the average annual growth rate was 5.7 per cent (Table 2.1). However, the economy collapsed in 1991-92 when the growth rate fell to 1.6 per cent and the country ran into severe BoP and fiscal problems, pointing to the inappropriateness of the policies followed in these areas. In the post-reform period beginning 1992-93, the economy has grown at an average rate of 6.9 per cent per annum, a significant improvement over the pre-reform period.

Coming to the more recent period, economic growth in the seven-year period beginning 2005-06, despite the crisis affected year of 2008-09, was at an average of 8.3 per cent. This clearly represented an acceleration in the

Table 2.1

Growth in GDP at Factor Cost and its Components at 2004-05 Prices

(Per cent per annum)

	Agriculture Forestry & Fishing	Mining & Quarrying	Manu-facturing	Construction	Electricity, Gas, and Water Supply	Trade, Hotels, Storage, Transport and Communi-cations	Finance, Insurance, Real Estate & Business Services	Community, Social and Personal Services	GDP at Factor cost
1980-81	12.9	12.2	0.2	13.2	5.7	5.7	1.9	4.1	7.5
1981-82	4.6	13.7	8.2	5.5	9.5	6.2	8.1	2.1	5.7
1982-83	-0.3	11.9	3.3	-7.0	6.6	5.4	9.5	7.7	2.9
1983-84	10.1	2.9	10.2	5.4	6.9	5.1	9.8	3.7	7.8
1984-85	1.6	1.2	4.2	3.5	10.8	4.8	7.5	6.9	4.0
1985-86	0.3	5.5	3.2	5.7	7.9	7.9	9.8	5.7	4.3
1986-87	-0.4	12.2	5.5	2.4	10.3	6.0	10.5	7.5	4.5
1987-88	-1.6	3.8	5.6	5.7	7.8	5.3	7.3	7.2	3.7
1988-89	15.6	16.2	8.5	7.0	9.7	5.8	9.8	6.0	10.1
1989-90	1.2	7.6	8.8	7.0	9.7	7.4	12.4	7.9	6.3
1990-91	4.0	10.5	4.8	11.8	6.7	5.1	6.2	4.4	5.4
1991-92	-2.0	3.4	-2.4	2.1	9.7	2.6	10.8	2.6	1.6
1992-93	6.7	0.9	3.1	3.5	6.9	5.6	5.4	6.0	5.3
1993-94	3.3	1.4	8.6	0.6	7.5	6.9	11.2	4.5	5.7
1994-95	4.7	9.3	10.8	5.4	9.4	9.9	3.9	2.3	6.4

contd...

...contd...

	Agriculture Forestry & Fishing	Mining & Quarrying	Manu-facturing	Construction	Electricity, Gas, and Water Supply	Trade, Hotels, Storage, Transport and Communi-cations	Finance, Insurance, Real Estate & Business Services	Community, Social and Personal Services	GDP at Factor cost
1995-96	-0.7	5.9	15.5	6.0	6.8	13.2	8.1	7.3	7.4
1996-97	9.9	0.6	9.5	1.9	5.4	8.1	6.2	8.1	7.8
1997-98	-2.6	9.8	0.1	10.5	7.7	7.5	11.7	8.3	4.5
1998-99	6.3	2.8	3.1	6.3	7.0	7.6	7.8	9.7	6.6
1999-00	2.7	3.2	3.2	8.4	5.5	8.2	9.2	11.5	6.5
2000-01	-0.2	2.4	7.7	6.2	2.1	7.3	4.1	4.7	4.4
2001-02	6.3	1.8	2.5	4.0	1.7	9.2	7.3	4.1	5.7
2002-03	-7.2	8.8	6.8	7.9	4.7	9.4	8.0	3.9	4.0
2003-04	10.0	3.1	6.6	12.0	4.8	12.0	5.6	5.4	8.4
2004-05	0.18	7.9	7.4	16.3	7.9	9.7	8.7	4.9	7.0
2005-06	5.1	1.3	10.1	12.8	7.1	12.1	12.6	7.1	9.5
2006-07	4.2	7.5	14.3	10.3	9.3	11.6	14.0	2.8	9.6
2007-08	5.8	3.7	10.3	10.8	8.3	10.9	12.0	6.9	9.3
2008-09	0.1	2.1	4.3	5.3	4.6	7.5	12.0	12.5	6.7
2009-10	0.8	5.9	11.3	6.7	6.2	10.4	9.7	11.8	8.6
2010-11	7.9	4.9	9.7	10.2	5.2	12.3	10.1	4.3	9.3
2011-12	3.6	-0.6	2.7	5.6	6.5	7.0	11.7	6.0	6.2
2012-13	1.8	0.4	1.9	5.9	4.9	5.2	8.6	6.8	5.0

Note: For years prior to 2004-05, the 1999-2000 base series is taken backwards based on splicing.

Source (Basic data): National Income Accounts, CSO.

pace of growth. Per capita GDP grew at an average of 7.0 per cent in these seven years.

Under the severe impact of the global crisis, the Indian economy registered a growth of 6.7 per cent in 2008-09 after having registered a growth rate exceeding 9 per cent for three consecutive years. By any standard, the Indian economy was able to protect itself reasonably well in the turbulent conditions of financial crisis.

The growth rate picked up soon and the economy achieved a growth rate of 8.6 per cent in 2009-10, despite a severe drought.

The growth rate rose further to 9.3 per cent in 2010-11 as well. There was a substantial jump in agricultural production. The monsoon was good and, therefore, the agricultural GDP grew at 7.9 per cent. The manufacturing sector grew by 11.3 per cent and the services sector by 9.4 per cent.

Economic activity moderated quite substantially in 2011-12. The overall growth rate was 6.2 per cent. Growth in the last quarter was a low 5.3 per cent. While agriculture grew at 3.6 per cent, which came on top of a sharp increase in the previous year, the performance of the manufacturing sector was a great disappointment. It grew at 2.7 per cent. The service sector also showed some deceleration. The low growth was caused by supplyside bottlenecks, price shocks and weak investment demand. Coal output fell. So also did several other minerals. The investment sentiment was affected by various factors including non-economic. The external environment was also not hospitable.

In the current fiscal, the monsoon was disappointing to begin with. But rains were normal in the months of August and September 2012. Manufacturing is yet to pick up, even though there are some signs lately. During April-November, manufacturing sector showed a growth of 1.0 per cent. We can see an improved performance in the coming months. Some recent decisions relating to FDI as well as pricing of petroleum products should help to change the investment sentiment. On the whole, the growth rate in the current year may stay around 5.5 per cent.

As I look ahead, the next fiscal 2013-14 may turn out to be better. The growth rate can be 1 per cent higher than this year. The full impact of the change in investment sentiment may be reflected through the year resulting in higher growth in manufacturing. There will also be a special emphasis on achieving the production and capacity creation targets in the key infrastructure sectors that lie in the public domain such as coal, power, roads and railways.

The Indian economy is currently passing through a difficult phase. Growth has slowed and inflation remains high. The fiscal and current account deficits also remain high. We need to address these issues if we have to achieve a sustained high growth rate. India's savings and investments rate, after having reached peak at 36 and 38 per cent of GDP respectively, in 2007-08, have fallen rapidly. We need to reverse this trend. The three important tasks before the Indian economy now are to tame inflation, and to contain the fiscal and current account deficits. We need a well laid out road map to bring down the twin deficits.

Road Map for Future Reforms

In the first phase, reforms were introduced in the industrial sector, external trade and investment sectors, exchange rate management, fiscal policy and financial sector. Later, communications and other key infrastructure sectors were covered. We need to extract the full potential of the reforms we have already introduced. However, reforms form part of a continuing agenda. As we look ahead, the road map for reforms must include the following:

1. The basic principle of liberalisation of creating competitive markets with minimal barriers to entry and exit should be extended to all sectors. There are still some sectors which are subject to production and distribution controls. Coal, for example, is a sector in which private initiative is still restricted only to power plants for their use. In fact, until the sector is opened up for private sector, public sector coal companies can engage private sector firms to open up new fields as their agent through a management contract. Another example of a sector which is still subject to various controls is sugar.
2. Pricing of natural resources has become an issue. In certain areas, competitive forces may not be adequate to determine price. In

such situations, transparent mechanisms for fixing price must be followed which will be fair to producers and end-users.

3. Subsidies require a second look. If the process of fiscal consolidation is to move along a clear road map, subsidies as a proportion of GDP must be brought down. In fact, there is need for clear prioritisation as far as subsidies are concerned. If, for example, food subsidies are considered to be paramount, we can provide for them fully. But this will demand that other subsidies such as those on fuel and fertiliser must be reduced substantially. Cash transfers are a good mechanism for delivering subsidies. However, the key question is the extent of subsidies. There must be clarity on it.

4. The issue of subsidies is also linked to pricing of products. As mentioned earlier, pricing must largely be left to the market. State intervention must be limited to as few areas as possible. Also, if the benefit is to accrue to certain vulnerable sectors of the society, it is best done through cash transfers than altering the pricing mechanism.

5. Among the sectors that have remained untouched by reforms, the most important is agriculture. Even as much remains to be done to improve the productivity of agriculture through scientific research and improved dissemination of knowledge, there are areas like marketing where reforms are badly needed. We need to create a single market for all agricultural products and all barriers to movement of agricultural crops must go. Equally important are the modifications to Agriculture Produce Marketing (Regulation) (APMC) Act to facilitate procurement of agricultural products, particularly perishables, directly from agriculturists. We should also move towards a more liberalised trade policy with respect to agricultural products (other than food grains where food security concerns are relevant) with no quantitative restrictions, and with minimal duties on exports and imports.

6. Cutting across various sectors, land acquisition and environmental clearances have become critically important for expediting the time taken for translating investment decisions into

investment on ground. The law relating to land acquisition and compensation needs to be passed as early as possible. In the case of environmental clearances, speed is the essence without sacrificing the basic requirement.

7. We need to make our labour markets more flexible while strengthening the social safety nets. This will facilitate greater investment in labour-intensive manufacturing.
8. The governance system must be improved to ensure that where approvals are still needed by the government, they are given speedily and in a transparent manner. At least in the case of large projects, an integrated view is required to be taken, as an integrated approval will help speedy implementation of projects. This is particularly true of projects in the infrastructure areas.
9. Government's role in the economy has changed. It is the major provider of public goods and services such as health and education. Greater focus on the improvement of the machinery for delivering these services is required.

Need for High Growth

As we look ahead, growth is an important factor in generating employment and reducing poverty. Obviously, the composition of growth is equally important. If we grow at 9 per cent per annum, India's per capita GDP will increase from the current level of $1,600 to $8,000-10,000 by 2025. Then we will become part of the middle income group of countries. Without a strong growth, we will not be able to provide employment to the growing number of young people who will join the labour force. Continued strong growth will help to accelerate the declining trend in the poverty ratio. In the recent period, we have launched a number of schemes aimed at broadening the base of growth. These include employment guarantee scheme, universalisation of education, expansion of rural health, and food security. All these programmes have made a substantial demand on public expenditure. This has been made possible only because of the strong growth that we have seen in recent years. Growth has facilitated raising more resources by the government.

Development has many dimensions. It has to be inclusive; it must be poverty reducing and it must be environment-friendly. We need to incorporate all these elements in the growth process. A strong and balanced growth will enable the economy to achieve multiple goals, including lowering inflation. Reforms will help us to achieve growth with equity.

3 Policies for Strong Inclusive Growth

Montek S. Ahluwalia

I have been privileged to have a close association with P. Chidambaram, in various capacities over the past two decades, beginning in 1991 when I served under him as Commerce Secretary and he was the Commerce Minister. When the history of India's economic reforms post 1991 is written, Chidambaram will undoubtedly figure as the second most important political personality, after Dr Manmohan Singh, pushing the reform agenda forward. He has a strong conviction that India has the capacity to grow rapidly and compete successfully in an increasingly integrated and competitive world economy and also that this growth can be made sufficiently inclusive to transform the lives of the mass of our people. He recognises that the private sector and markets have a major role to play in India's development, but he also believes the government must proactively support the process, intervene when necessary to regulate markets and deal with market failure. It is a pleasure to contribute this paper to a volume in his honour as he entered an unprecedented third term as India's Finance Minister.

The paper focuses on some of the key challenges in achieving the Twelfth Plan scenario of 'Strong Inclusive Growth' which targets an average of eight per cent growth over five years. This implies an acceleration from under six per cent growth in 2012-13, to slightly higher than nine per cent in the last two years. The economy did achieve nine per cent growth for five years prior to 2008, but that was when the global economy was booming; it will be much more difficult in a period when the global economy is projected to remain weak. The Plan itself emphasises that it is feasible only if bold and difficult policy decisions can be taken in many areas and this paper discusses some of these decisions.

The paper consists of five sections. Section I takes the reader back in time to recount how the trade policy reforms of 1991 were implemented. The story is of special relevance for this volume since it describes the critical role played by Chidambaram himself in the first year of reforms, and also because it provides important pointers for policy formulation at the current juncture. Section II briefly outlines what is meant by strong inclusive growth, and especially the relationship between the two objectives of rapid growth and inclusiveness. Section III discusses the macroeconomic constraints on achieving faster growth. Section IV discusses the constraints posed by three critical sectors, energy water and land, which call for bold policy action. Section V discusses how rapid growth can be made inclusive.

The Trade Policy Reforms of 1991: Some Lessons

The Congress Government under Prime Minister Narasimha Rao, which took office on June 21, 1991, inherited a crisis situation. A loss of confidence had caused capital flows to dry up, and foreign exchange reserves had plummeted to rock-bottom levels. The new government had to take action even before the Budget could be presented. A modest devaluation of 10 per cent was announced on July 1, but it was clear that this was not enough and a further adjustment would be needed.

Chidambaram had just taken charge as the commerce minister and we were busily engaged in briefing him on the need for radical changes in trade policy. I was deeply impressed, as were others, by his razor-sharp mind and the speed with which he grasped complex issues and mastered details without losing sight of the big picture. An important initiative we were considering at the time was the replacement of the old REP licence system with a new tradable incentive licence for exporters to be called Exim scrips. These would be issued for a face value of 30 per cent of the value of exports (40% for some products), and could be used to import any item up to this value from the restricted imports list. Being tradable, exporters could sell the licence and the price received would reflect the premium people were willing to pay to import restricted items. The sales proceeds would improve export profitability without imposing a direct burden on the budget.[1] Since the total value of Exim scrips would be linked to exports, there was no danger of a flood of imports—excess demand for imports would simply lead to a higher premium on the licence. The move constituted a genuine import liberalisation since it would eliminate the need to issue import licences for items on the restricted list.

The trade policy was scheduled to be unveiled some weeks later, but on July 3, Finance Minister Dr Manmohan Singh, telephoned me to say that a second devaluation would be announced that very evening, and it was necessary simultaneously to announce the withdrawal of cash compensatory support (CCS) for exports. He said he would explain this to Chidambaram a little later, but I should brief him in advance. In briefing Chidambaram, I explained that the finance ministry felt that the second exchange rate adjustment would amount to a cumulative devaluation of 24 per cent, making continuation of the CCS unnecessary. Abolishing the CCS would also be a signal of seriousness in reducing the fiscal deficit, which was very important for restoring confidence internationally. CCS was a long established instrument for export promotion, and its abolition was bound to provoke criticism from exporters. However, I pointed out that we would avoid this criticism if we could announce the new trade policy we had been discussing, including especially the Exim scrips, and present the abolition of the CCS as part of the new trade policy. Since in those days any change in import policy needed the approval of the Commerce Minister, the Finance Minister and the Prime Minister, this would require exceptionally fast decision-making.

Chidambaram agreed to try to persuade Dr Manmohan Singh to agree to the trade policy reforms being announced that very evening. We trooped off to meet the Finance Minister and Chidambaram explained the proposal in detail to Dr Singh and his key officials. The officials had doubts about the proposed liberalisation, but Dr Singh readily agreed. He asked

1. Exporters were familiar with tradable licences because the REP licenses, which allowed duty-free imports of the imports needed for exports, were freely tradable. The difference was that REP licences were designed to allow imports of items actually needed for exports and they were allowed duty-free whereas the Eximscrip only allowed free imports of restricted items without any licence but on full payment of duty.

only how long it would take to work out the proposal and obtain the PM's approval, since the announcement of the devaluation could not be delayed. Chidambaram promptly assured him that we would have the file ready in a few hours.

We returned to the Commerce Ministry and worked feverishly to outline the proposals, with Chidambaram personally finalising all the details. The file was signed by the two Ministers, in quick succession, and then taken by them that very evening to the Prime Minister Narasimha Rao. Chidambaram explained the proposal to the Prime Minister who asked Dr Singh whether it had his approval. On receiving confirmation, the Prime Minister promptly signed the file (there was no detailed examination by the PMO). Jairam Ramesh, then a consultant in the PMO, was asked to ensure that it received wide publicity.

The second devaluation was duly announced on the evening of July 3 and Dr Manmohan Singh indicated that a supporting package of trade policy reforms would be announced separately by the Commerce Ministry later that evening. On July 4, Chidambaram held a Press Conference to explain the wide-ranging trade policy changes. He highlighted the star role of the Eximscrip and also outlined his vision of trade policy in future, stating that it was the intention of the government to reduce tariffs over time and also to move to "full convertibility of the rupee on trade account" in three to five years.[2] The policy was extremely well received. The *Times of India*, in its editorial on July 5, had this to say: "The new trade policy is a commendable example of thinking big. Instead of being a scratch here and fiddle there, it outlines a strategy to make the rupee convertible in three to five years. Its importance lies not in its many individual clauses but in the vision of a new India that stands on its own feet and pays for its imports through exports that do not need artificial props and never ending subsidies." The editorial concluded by approvingly quoting Chidambaram's words to the Press, "We have always had wings, but suffered a fear of flying" and went on to urge, "We should now soar in the high skies of trade."

As it happened, events moved even faster than Chidambaram had anticipated. Exim scrips proved so successful that in less than a year they

2. What was meant by convertibility on 'trade account' was that rupees could be freely exchanged for foreign currency to import goods leaving the pressure of excess demand foreign exchange on this account to be reflected in the exchange rate.

were replaced by a dual exchange rate. I had moved to the Finance Ministry in late 1991 and in March 1992 we introduced a system in which exporters were required to surrender a portion of their foreign exchange earnings at the official exchange rate selling the rest in the market at a market determined exchange rate.[3] The system worked so well, that one year later in 1993, we moved to a unified exchange rate. Chidambaram's target of making the rupee convertible on trade account in three to five years was achieved within two years!

Six Lessons from 1991

There are six important lessons from the events of 1991 which are relevant today. First and most important, Chidambaram's readiness to give up discretionary power in support of a system with much less discretion was absolutely critical. A similar willingness to give up discretionary power in favour of more transparent market-driven processes is needed in many areas, not only in the Centre but even more so in the states.

Second, both Chidambaram and Manmohan Singh were willing to take a risk: one can never be sure how a policy change will work out in practice, especially in the short run, and the trade policy of 1991 was a major change. The finance ministry officials, who opposed the liberalisation, were not willing to take the risk: they suffered from the fear of flying syndrome.

Third, when radical policy changes are contemplated, bureaucrats may have different views, as indeed the senior bureaucrats in the finance ministry did on trade liberalisation, but this need not become an obstacle to reform when the political decision-makers are clear about what they want.

Fourth, it is easier to make major changes when they are based on ideas that have been discussed and on which some consensus on policy has emerged. The need for trade policy liberalisation had been extensively discussed among economists. The specific idea of Exim scrips was first mooted by Prakash Hebalkar in an article in *Business India* some years earlier, and both Dr C. Rangarajan and I had written papers supporting and

3. The exchange proceeds surrendered at the official exchange rate were used for oil imports and government debt service payments, and all items previously on the restricted list were made freely importable using foreign exchange obtained from the market.

elaborating this approach. There are many ideas on the table today which have been similarly extensively discussed on which there is considerable professional agreement, though not a complete consensus.

Fifth, it is extremely important to adopt a holistic approach in designing policy to make the maximum impact. The trade policy reforms were explicitly articulated as part of a broader intention to reduce tariffs over time, to open the economy to capital flows, and to move to a flexible exchange rate regime. Had the devaluation and the abolition of CCS been announced as a Finance Ministry initiative on July 3, and the trade policy changes been made a few weeks later, we would not have had the *Times of India* commending the government for thinking big.

Finally, the episode demonstrates that our much maligned system can deliver results very fast when necessary. I cannot recall any other occasion when such a major restructuring of established policy, involving more than one Ministry, and actually requiring the approval of the Prime Minister, was taken in the short space of about 10 hours!

These lessons should be kept in mind as we shape policy to address the challenges facing us in the years ahead.

Conceptualising Faster and More Inclusive Growth

The Twelfth Plan points out that although planners are often criticised for focusing too much on growth, this is not the basis on which Indian plans have ever been made. The Twelfth Plan objective is to ensure a broad-based improvement in living standards which is captured in the formulation 'strong inclusive growth'. Inclusiveness means that growth must not only be rapid, it must also be more inclusive in all the different senses in which the term is used: it must reduce poverty faster, be regionally well-dispersed, reduce urban-rural differentials, improve access to basic service for all and narrow the gaps between historically disadvantaged groups such as SCs, STs, OBCs and minorities and work to eliminate gender differentials.

There is growing evidence that suggests that growth has been more inclusive in recent years than it was earlier. Poverty has fallen much faster after 2004, agriculture has accelerated and real per capita consumption in rural areas has increased at 6.6 per cent per year after 2004-05, whereas it increased by only 1.1 per cent per year in the preceding 10 years. However, expectations have also mounted and much more is expected in this area. Government policy will be judged by how far we can meet heightened expectations. The Twelfth Plan responds to these expectations by identifying 25 monitorable targets which would measure progress towards inclusiveness of which rapid growth of GDP is only one.

There are two ways in which the inclusiveness objective can be achieved and both are important. One is through government financed programmes which deliver various benefits to the poor. The second is through faster growth itself creating faster expansion of employment and income-earning opportunities. Many who are genuinely concerned about inclusiveness tend to underplay the direct impact of growth viewing it as a 'trickle down approach', and prefer to focus instead on government programmes which appear to address inclusiveness concerns more directly.[4] These programmes are indeed important, and indeed even essential, but the direct impact of growth on inclusiveness should not be under-estimated because the 'trickle' can become a 'flood' depending on the pattern of growth. Some types of growth are inherently more inclusive than others, and policies that succeed in making growth as inclusive as possible can achieve a great deal.

The two channels are also not independent of each other. Faster growth helps the first part of the strategy by generating the revenues needed to fund inclusive programmes. Symmetrically, inclusiveness programmes, especially those focussing on health and education improve the growth especially of the economy. In the rest of this paper the focus is on challenges to accelerating growth and the challenge of making growth more inclusive.

The Feasibility of Eight per cent Growth

Accelerating from less than 6 per cent growth in 2012-13 to something more than 9 per cent within three years is obviously difficult. The acceleration is less formidable if we take a longer term perspective

4. The preference for programes is understandable because they provide direct benefits and the effectiveness of the programme is more easily identifiable and attributable to the programme. CSOs have a special affinity to this approach because CSOs are ideally suited to working with such programmes in a supervisory or advisory role.

since growth averaged 7.7 per cent over the past 10 years.[5] Even so, it is reasonable to ask whether it is really possible to accelerate to over 9 per cent in a period when the performance of industrialised countries is expected to be very weak.

If we were counting on an export-led growth strategy to achieve this outcome we could rule it out straight away, since exports are bound to be affected by depressed conditions in industrialised countries. However, India's strategy is based not on an 'export-led' growth, but rather on efforts to increase the capability of the economy on the supply side. This approach implicitly assumes that if the supply side constraints on growth can be overcome, the aggregate demand needed to support the growth will come from domestic sources, i.e., expanding domestic consumption and higher levels of investment. The strategy builds on the fact that performance over the past several years demonstrates that strong foundations have been laid. It calls for action on several fronts, e.g., (a) achieving high levels of investment to ensure a sufficient growth in capital stock, (b) promoting skill development to ensure the availability of skilled labour needed to support higher growth, and (c) complementing growth in capital and labour inputs by a faster growth of total factor productivity resulting from the pursuit of efficiency-enhancing reforms.

Macroeconomic Balancing: Investment, Savings and the CAD

A higher rate of investment is critical to remove supply side constraints on growth because it expands the capital stock and therefore the production potential in the medium term. It also provides a demand stimulus in the short term to substitute for weak export demand. The Plan projects that the rate of fixed investment, which reached a peak of 33.7 per cent of GDP in 2007-08 and was at the same level in 2011-12, will have to rise to 35 per cent in 2016-17. The expansion in investment is expected to be led by private investment which declined sharply after 2007-08 and is likely to revive once growth picks up.

5. Using the 10 year average GDP growth as the base possibly overstates India's underlying growth capacity because the global economy was performing above trend for many years. Bhandari (2012) reports that if an H.P. Filter is used to clean the GDP series the average over the last 10 years is 7.2 per cent. What the Plan target therefore implies is raising this to a sustainable 9 per cent by the last two years of the Plan.

Macroeconomic balancing requires that the increase in investment must be supported by a corresponding increase in domestic savings so that the investment—savings gap, which determines the current account deficit (CAD)—is contained at acceptable levels. The savings implications are summarised in Table 3.1. All three components of savings—household, private corporate and public sector—are projected to increase over time as a percentage of GDP, but the largest improvement is expected from public sector savings, which had experienced the sharpest decline after 2007-08.

Table 3.1

Macroeconomic Parameters of the Twelfth Plan

(As percentages of GDP)

	2007-08	2011-12[1]	2016-17
Ratios in Constant Prices			
1. Gross Domestic Capital Formation	39.0	37.9	40.0
2. Fixed Investment, *of which*	33.7	33.7	35.0
Public	8.2	7.8	8.4
Private Corporate	15.0	11.6	14.8
Household	10.5	14.3	11.8
Ratios in Current Prices			
3. Gross Domestic Savings, *of which*	36.8	30.8	36.0
Household Savings	22.4	22.3	23.6
Private Corporate Savings	9.4	7.2	8.5
Public Sector Savings	5.0	1.3	3.9
4. Gross Domestic Capital Formation or Investment[2]	38.1	35.0	38.5
5. Current Account Deficit	1.3	4.2	2.5
6. Fiscal Balance (Centre plus States)	-4.0	-8.0	-5.0

Note: Data are taken from Tables 2.2, 2.3 and 2.5 in Chapter 2 of the Twelfth Five Year Plan Vol.1.

1 Data for 2011-12 are estimates and for 2016-17 are projections made by the Planning Commission in connection with the Twelfth Plan Exercise.

2 Adjusted for errors and omissions.

If these savings projections are realised, they will reduce the investment savings gap over the Plan period and therefore the current account deficit to 2.2 per cent by the end of the Plan. Even so, the current account deficit is likely to remain high at about 3 per cent for the next two years, which is well above the traditional comfort level. Financing a current account deficit of this size will pose problems and these are discussed below but the improvement in government savings needed to achieve this outcome is itself a major challenge posing difficult policy choices.

Increasing government savings as projected in Table 3.1 implies a reduction in the fiscal deficit.[6] A lower fiscal deficit will help to achieve higher investment levels by reversing the squeeze on resources for the commercial sector caused by the expansion of the deficit in recent years. In 2007-08 the net financial saving of the household sector was 11.6 per cent of GDP and the combined fiscal deficit was only 4 per cent, which meant that about 7.6 per cent of GDP was channelled through the financial system to the commercial sector. By 2011-12, the net financial savings of the household sector had declined to 8 per cent of GDP and the combined fiscal deficit had increased to 8.1 per cent. The volume of savings available from the household sector for other sectors after accounting for the amount absorbed by the government sector was zero. In effect the corporate sector could rely only on its own savings plus sources from abroad. This massive squeeze undoubtedly accounts for the high interest rates and scarcity of finance which has been a constant complaint of investors.

The finance ministry has targeted reducing the fiscal deficit of the Central government from 5.3 per cent of GDP in 2012-13 to 3 per cent by 2016-17. This implies a combined fiscal deficit of around 5 per cent of GDP for the Centre and the states in 2016-17. If the net financial savings of households increase as projected, to say 11 per cent by 2016-17, and the combined fiscal deficit is reduced to 5 per cent, the resources available for the commercial sector would expand to at least 6 per cent of GDP compared with zero in 2011-12.[7]

Reducing the Fiscal Deficit

Reducing the fiscal deficit requires action on two fronts: improved revenue collection and reduction of subsidies. Action to mobilise revenues

6. An increase in public savings need not lead to a fall in the fiscal deficit if capital expenditure in the public sector is also increased. However, the Twelfth Plan does not envisage a large increase in public sector capital expenditure.

7. Some of this increase in domestic intermediation would be offset by the reduction in the current account deficit, but the net availability of finance would expand substantially.

in the short run should ideally focus on better tax administration rather than raising tax rates, since the existing tax rates had produced higher tax ratios earlier. The most important revenue related initiative is the introduction of a goods and services tax (GST) which is expected to improve revenue mobilisation of both the Centre and the states, and also to stimulate economic efficiency. Introducing the GST requires a constitutional amendment and requires the consent of a sufficient number of state governments. Fortunately, there are indications that differences are being narrowed, which means the GST could become a reality fairly soon. Credible progress towards this end is an important positive signal for markets.

The second element in fiscal consolidation is the control of subsidies. The main Central government subsidies are on food, fertiliser and petroleum products (mainly diesel, LPG and kerosene) and these have increased from 1.42 per cent of GDP in 2007-08 to 2.44 per cent in 2011-12.[8] The resource projections of the Twelfth Plan assume that subsidies can be reduced to 1.5 per cent of GDP by 2016-17. Unless this is done, it will not be possible to finance the various Plan programmes outlined in the Twelfth Plan. Reducing subsidies is never easy. There is little appreciation, either by the public or in the political arena, that if subsidies are not reduced, then either the fiscal deficit will have to be higher than planned, or some items of Plan expenditure may have to be reduced, or additional taxes may have to be levied, and each of these alternatives has adverse consequences.[9]

Some subsidies are socially justifiable, but the existing subsidies involve large leakages and are not targeted to the really needy. An innovation that will help in improving targeting and controlling leakage is the decision of the Central government, beginning January 1, 2013 to shift progressively to making payments for various schemes e.g., scholarships, old age pensions, widows' pensions, and also wages under MGNREGA,

8. This estimate probably underestimates the full burden of subsidies because of traditional under provisioning for this item in the Budget.
9. The public debate typically assumes that it is easy to raise resources by taxing the rich and 'bringing back black money stashed abroad' but there are limits to what can be achieved through these means. It should be noted that substantial efforts to improve the tax ratio are already factored into the Plan projections. They need to be supported by action on subsidies in addition.

directly to bank accounts of beneficiaries using an electronic payment system based on the unique ID numbers generated by Aadhaar. In due course, the Aadhaar platform, with its assurance of removing duplication, could be used to provide subsidies directly to beneficiaries in the form of an electronic credit which could be used in PDS shops which would assure physical delivery of commodities at a non-subsidised price allowing beneficiaries to use electronic credit to purchase these commodities by paying only the subsidised price. This would eliminate the incentive on the part of those who manage the supply chain to divert subsidised items for sale in the market.

Financing the Current Account Deficit (CAD)

Even if we succeed in reducing the fiscal deficit as projected, we will still be faced with the challenge of financing a CAD of around three per cent of GDP in the next two years. This requires a net inflow of about $ 6000 to 6500 crore a year, which should ideally consist of FDI and FII flows, with external borrowing being kept within prudent levels. Failure to finance the deficit would destabilise the strategy, putting pressure on the rupee, increasing inflationary pressure on domestic prices, which in turn would trigger pressure for policies of demand contraction, which would hit investment and lead to lower growth.

India was able to attract large volumes of capital flows before the 2008 crisis, but that was in a very different global environment. Although fears of worst case scenarios in the global economy, such as the collapse of the Euro or the US being pushed over a fiscal cliff, have now receded, the availability of capital for emerging market countries remains uncertain. Despite these uncertainties, it can be argued that India can attract external capital on the scale required if the economy is once again seen as reverting to a higher growth path, with macroeconomic balances under control, and a government policy that is seen as welcoming foreign investment.

The prospects for a return to high growth depend on the implementation of the various policy initiatives discussed in this paper. As far as policy towards FDI is concerned, the government has taken several steps which signal its keenness to attract FDI and FII flows. FDI in single brand and multi-brand retail has been liberalised, and FDI limits in airlines, broadcasting, pension fund management and insurance have been increased. Some of these initiatives, especially raising the FDI cap on insurance from 26 per cent to 49 per cent are subject to Parliamentary approval and investors will wait to see if the legislative process is completed, but government's desire to attract FDI should not be in doubt. While those pushing for further liberalisation naturally focus attention on those areas where some restrictions remain in place, the areas of the economy that are already open are very large. On the FII front, some actions taken at the time of the 2012-13 Budget had created uncertainty in the minds of investors. Recognising these concerns, two expert committees were appointed—one under Dr Parthasarthy Shome and the other under S. Rangachary—to look at these issues. Some of the recommendations of these committees have already been accepted and a positive decision on others would greatly help to reassure foreign investors.[10]

Reviving Investor Sentiment

The increase in domestic savings discussed above is necessary to support higher levels of investment, but they do not ensure that investors will make the investment decisions that would actually lead to higher investment. As noted above, the investment revival projected in the Twelfth Plan is based on a strong increase in private investment, and this depends critically upon the state of animal spirits. These in turn are driven by a combination of psychology, perceptions of global conditions and various domestic factors. Global conditions are outside our control, but there are a number of domestic factors that have had a negative effect on investor sentiment that need to be addressed.

In the short run, the most urgent task is to resolve the problems faced by a large number of infrastructure projects that are held up for a variety of reasons. Several power projects are stuck because of non-availability of domestic coal and gas. Both coal and gas can be imported, but import prices of these fuels are much above domestic prices, creating a reluctance to import. Tariff rationalisation is a pre-requisite for absorbing the higher costs of imported fuel. While some tariff revisions have taken place in the recent past, an arrangement that passes on higher fuel prices to consumers is not yet in place. If open access to consumers is introduced, the marginal

10. At the time this paper was written the application of the General Anti Avoidance Rules (GAAR) had been postponed by 2 years.

costs of imported fuel can be passed on to consumers through the market mechanism. Expeditious resolution of this problem would help. Many infrastructure projects are also held up because of lack of environmental and forest clearances. Environmental concerns are certainly important and it is probably true that in the past they were not given the attention they deserve. However, there is also a perception that clearance procedures are unduly dilatory and also non-transparent. Delays are partly a consequence of the fact that Ministries exercising regulatory functions are often under pressure from environment activists, who tend to take extreme positions, and also seek the intervention of the courts.[11] For all these reasons, the system does not function in a manner which encourages adoption of a holistic, problem-solving approach.

The draft Twelfth Plan document had drawn specific attention to this problem, and called for a new mechanism to resolve the problem. When the draft was discussed in the full Planning Commission, it was Finance Minister Chidambaram who suggested that the problem could be resolved by setting up a National Investment Board chaired by the Prime Minister, and empowered to resolve these issues. This idea has since been implemented in the form of a new Cabinet Committee on Investment, chaired by the Prime Minister, which will seek to resolve problems where decisions on large projects are unduly delayed. The establishment of the Committee is an innovation which could help speed up decision-making while also balancing different concerns.

The most effective way of stimulating a strong revival of private investment would be to address India's infrastructure deficit, which is a major factor lowering productivity and competitiveness. The Eleventh Plan emphasised infrastructure development and met with some success in this area as investment in infrastructure increased from 5 per cent of GDP

11. It is worth noting that the courts do not always support environmental activism when it intervenes against projects. In the case of the Vishugad-Pipal Koti Hydro-electric project, an environmental activist challenged the validity of the environmental clearance and the petition was rejected by the Green Tribunal. This was appealed to the Supreme Court. The Bench, consisting of justices H.L. Dattu and Ranjan Gogoi, dismissed the petition and observed that, "The moment a power project is to start, litigation is filed in courts. If initially the project cost is ₹ 1000 crore, it escalates to ₹ 10,000 crore over the years and tax payer money is wasted. We really wonder what people in this country say. They say they don't want a hydro-electric plant or a nuclear plant but every body wants *bijli* (electricity)."

during the Tenth Plan to 7.2 per cent in the Eleventh Plan. Recognising the scarcity of public resources, the Eleventh Plan adopted a strategy of increased reliance on private investment in infrastructure. This strategy proved successful and the share of the private sector in infrastructure investment increased from 20 per cent in the Tenth Plan to 37 per cent in the Eleventh Plan. A recent World Bank report states that India has been the top recipient of PPP activity in infrastructure since 2006.

The challenge ahead is to build on the achievement in the Eleventh Plan and raise the total investment in infrastructure to 9 per cent of GDP by the end of the Plan period. This implies investment in infrastructure in the Twelfth Plan period of around $ 1,00,000 crore. Since there will be heavy demand on public resources from sectors such as health and education, the share of the private sector in infrastructure investment will have to increase to 48 per cent. Much of the increase in corporate investment projected in the Twelfth Plan should be directed to infrastructure. Success in this ambitious endeavour depends critically on our ability to address various problems currently hampering PPP projects.

Problems with PPP-based Investments

While the expansion of PPP projects in recent years is a major achievement, many implementation problems have arisen which need to be addressed quickly if the objective of attracting private investment to build infrastructure is not to be jeopardised. Five elements are particularly important for a successful PPP strategy.

First, PPPs must be governed by well defined concession agreements which specify the expected standards of service delivery, the price that can be charged to customers and the division of risks between the concessionaire and the government.[12] This should be followed by a robust competitive bidding process for award of the project. Subjecting the concession agreements to public scrutiny and debate makes it possible to reassure the public that the process is fair and protects public interest.

12. Logically, risks must be assigned to the party best able to manage them. Thus in a road concession, the risk of non-performance in terms of timely shifting of utilities, or completion of some land acquisition must be borne by the government while the risks associated with mobilising financial and physical resources, and all the construction risks must be borne by the concessionaire.

Competitive bidding is clearly critical to avoid the usual suspicions about cronyism.

Second, concession agreements should include penalties for non-performance on the part of the concessionaire and also the government. Penalties for the concessionaire help to reassure the public that the concessionaire cannot blithely ignore service standard obligations. Penalties on the government for non-performance are also important since they incentivise government officials to deliver as promised in order to avoid accountability for invocation of the penalty. Experience shows that many PPP projects are inordinately delayed because of the lack of clearances of various sorts including relatively simple matters such as shifting of utilities. Compensatory clearances triggered by such delays improve the balance of risks in the project and encourage concessionaires to bid higher amounts for award of the concession.

Third, PPPs once awarded must be closely monitored to ensure that the standards of service prescribed in the concession are actually achieved and that customer grievances are attended to. The Central government has recently introduced a standardised monitoring system for all PPP projects which will ensure effective monitoring and oversight of service delivery.

Fourth, PPPs need effective dispute resolution mechanisms to deal with disputes which are bound to arise in the course of implementation including disputes during the operation of the concession. This is an extremely important requirement as our existing system is visibly deficient on this score. Disputes relating to payment demands are often not settled expeditiously because of the tendency on the part of government agencies to appeal all decisions against the government, often going all the way to the Supreme Court. This only creates an environment in which good quality private investors will shy away from participation. A possible solution is for the government to set up a common dispute settlement mechanism for all disputes relating to PPPs in infrastructure.

Finally, infrastructure projects need to be financed by long-term debt, preferably in domestic currency. Reduction of the fiscal deficit, as discussed above, will help to increase the availability of financial resources. This must be accompanied by progress towards developing a healthy corporate bond market. India has developed a fairly sophisticated capital market for listed equities, but the corporate bond market is much smaller than it should be. Long term debt should be raised through the bond market and not through banks, which are subject to limits on asset liability mismatches. The insurance industry is the most logical source of funds for corporate bonds and the proposal to increase the FDI limit in insurance from 26 per cent at present to 49 per cent, which is pending parliamentary approval, assumes special importance in this context. It is also necessary to consider whether the regulatory restrictions imposed on insurers can be modified to allow such financing. Recent regulatory changes which allowed the establishment of Infrastructure Debt Funds should help and the creation of these funds should be actively promoted.

State governments have a major role in infrastructure development since they are responsible for much of the infrastructure relevant for investors. This includes availability of reliable power, quality of urban infrastructure, especially water and sewerage, the existence of industrial estates facilitating easy location of industry, the quality of state and district roads linking up with the national highway system, etc. Since state governments also have resource constraints, they would be well advised to rely on PPP as much as possible and many states are actually doing so. They should consider creating specialised units within the government that would help implementation of infrastructure projects in PPP mode, taking account of the major problem areas listed above.

Ease of Doing Business

The 'ease of doing business' has a major positive impact on investor sentiment and improvements in this area are urgently needed. India currently ranks 132nd out of 185 countries in a World Bank report on ease of doing business, based on performance on 10 separate components listed in Table 3.2 (IBRD, 2009). Interestingly, India's ranking varies considerably across indicators, from a very respectable 23rd in 'getting credit' to an abysmally low 182nd in 'getting construction permits' and 184th in 'enforcing contracts'.

Table 3.2

India's Rank: Ease of Doing Business 2012

	Indicators	*India's Rank in 185 Countries*	*State or Central Responsibilities*
1.	Starting a Business	173	Mainly state government
2.	Dealing with Construction Permit	182	State government
3.	Getting Electricity	105	State government
4.	Registering Property	94	State Government
5.	Getting Credit	23	Banks/Central government owned
6.	Protecting Investors	49	Centre and States
7.	Paying Taxes	152	Centre and States
8.	Trading Across Borders	127	Central government
9.	Enforcing Contracts	184	Both Centre and States
10.	Resolving Insolvency	116	Centre
	Overall Rank in Ease of Doing Business out of 185 countries	**132**	

Some of indicators listed in Table 3.2 refer to areas in the domain of the states, but others require action by the Central government. Some of the problem areas such as resolving insolvency and enforcing contracts involve deep institutional reform, including changes in the law, and possibly also changes in judicial procedures. The Central government has taken several initiatives in this regard. A new Company Law, with an improved process for resolving bankruptcies, has been introduced in Parliament. The Judicial Accountability Bill provides for the establishment of specialised commercial benches which should accelerate decision-making in commercial cases. Digitalisation of courts and court procedures is underway and should help expedite the legal process. However, the full impact of these initiatives will take time to surface if only because the effectiveness of new laws is known only after they are tested in the courts. Nevertheless, the fact that these issues are being addressed should help create a favourable investment climate.

Some Sectoral Constraints on Growth

The high growth target calls for reforms in many sectors in order to realise the higher rate of total factor productivity growth, which is a key element of the supply side strategy. Discussion of the full reform agenda is beyond the scope of this paper. In this Section, we focus on three factors, energy, water and land that could present serious constraints on growth if necessary reforms are not introduced.

Energy Policies to Support Growth

Rapid growth requires an expanded supply of energy and India is not well endowed with domestic energy resources. We have traditionally been highly import-dependent in petroleum products, but we now face rising import dependence for natural gas and also thermal coal. This would be less of a problem if supplies were freely available in world markets at low prices but in fact imported energy is expensive, and energy prices are not expected to fall. Both balance of payments considerations and energy security considerations therefore suggest that we need to contain energy demand on the one hand and increase domestic production on the other. This calls for action on several fronts. Ten of the most important policy issues are listed below.

First, energy prices have to be adjusted overtime in line with the need to balance energy demand and supply. To constrain demand, prices facing consumers should reflect the true cost of energy, so that energy efficiency is incentivised. To incentivise supply, prices facing producers must reflect the cost of the marginal source of supply, i.e., imports, so that investment in production of energy is sufficiently encouraged. The present configuration of energy prices does not meet these requirements. Domestic prices for diesel, LPG and kerosene are significantly lower than trade parity prices. Prices of Indian coal are also well below the prices for imported coal, even after adjusting for the higher calorific value of the latter. Domestic natural gas prices are around one-third the price at which imported gas is available. Prices cannot be adjusted to cover the full gap at one go, but we should attempt a phased adjustment, over say a two year period for petroleum products including natural gas, and perhaps three to four years for coal.

Second, the need for price adjustment is most urgent in petroleum products where state owned petroleum companies are suffering large under-recoveries on account of diesel, LPG and kerosene, much beyond the capacity of the budget to subsidise. Some steps have been taken. A small adjustment in diesel prices was made in 2011 and a two step approach implemented in January 2013 whereby prices of bulk supply of diesel (about 18% of the total) were fully adjusted, while in the case of retail sales a phased adjustment has been announced involving small monthly increases in prices for retail sales which would eliminate under recovery over 18 months. The supply of subsidised LPG cylinders has been limited to nine per household, with purchases above this number being at the market rate. With these adjustments, the under-recovery on petroleum products in 2013-14 would be reduced from an estimated ₹ 160,000 crore if the changes had not been made, to around ₹ 135,000 crore. This would be further reduced to ₹ 55,000 crore in 2015-16 when the entire diesel under-recovery is eliminated and LPG and kerosene are the only areas of under-recovery. This is a substantial adjustment over a two year period but the subsidy is still very high. It could be reduced further if there is some upward adjustment of the subsidised prices of LPG cylinders and also of kerosene, both of which are much lower than in neighbouring countries.[13]

Third, a phased increase in coal prices is also necessary to align domestic prices with global prices.[14] This should not be viewed as a windfall gain for the domestic coal industry. It is needed to cover higher costs of remedial action to compensate for loss of forest cover, which is likely to become more important in future, and also to encourage a shift to underground mining which is much less damaging to the environment than open cast mining, but is also more expensive. India produces only 10 per cent of its coal through underground mines whereas China relies dominantly on underground mines. It is essential to increase the share of coal produced through underground mines.

Fourth, almost 40 per cent of India's potential coal mines are in forest areas and there is need to streamline the process of granting clearances for mining in a manner which protects the environment. Opening new mines, or even expanding production in existing mines in these areas, requires environmental and forest clearances, including clearances for the construction of railway lines and roads to transport the coal. Environmental protection is critical for sustainability, but the existing process involves a great deal of arbitrariness about the conditions under

13. This calculation assumes no increase in volumes. If we allow for volume increases the subsidy would be higher.

14. It is not easy to define the relevant global price for coal since only a small portion of total coal production is traded, and domestic coal prices in coal producing countries are lower than prices of traded coal. However, some comparator reference price can be worked out.

which clearances will be given. There is need for a comprehensive review of the existing procedure to ensure that decisions are taken on the basis of strictly scientific considerations. Furthermore, if scientifically sound considerations really prevent the exploitation of large volumes of our domestic coal resources, we should recognise this explicitly and plan for a much larger volume of imports, which would make it more urgent to align domestic prices more closely with import prices.

Fifth, there is a strong case for repealing the Coal Nationalisation Act since both petroleum and natural gas are much more valuable than coal, and they are both open to private sector exploration and development. Private sector mining in coal is currently allowed for captive mines, but such mines are not allowed to expand their production to meet other domestic demand even though we are importing much higher priced coal at the margin. There is no logical reason why the coal sector should not be opened up for non captive mining.[15] Until that is done, Coal India should buy surplus coal from domestic captive mines at a suitably incentivised price to avoid having to import at a much higher price.

Sixth, a gradual increase in the prices of primary energy sources, as discussed above, will necessitate a corresponding upward revision in average electricity tariffs which are too low at present to cover current normative costs in many states. Increases in electricity prices are a politically sensitive issue at the state level. Nevertheless, a rise in prices has to be accepted in the interest of ensuring a financially viable power sector. Higher electricity prices will incentivise consumers currently receiving underpriced electricity to economise on electricity use and will also help to encourage a shift to renewable energy which is currently more expensive than conventional energy, and is viable only with a subsidy. The need for a subsidy will be reduced if electricity prices are raised to cover economic costs. The adverse impact of higher electricity tariffs on the poor can be easily met by providing a lifeline supply of electricity to all consumers at a low price for the initial slab and offsetting this by higher prices on the balance amount.

15. This does not mean the privatisation of Coal India; it only means opening coal production to competition from the private sector. Since the government has already decided that coal mining blocks will in future be awarded on the basis of competitive auctions, the private sector could be brought in through a transparent procedure of allocation.

Seventh, reforms are also needed in electricity distribution. This sub-sector in electricity is critical for the viability of the sector as a whole because it is this sub-sector which generates the revenues to cover upstream payments to generating and transmission companies. Distribution remains largely government owned and suffers from losses due to a combination of technical inefficiencies and outright theft. A turnaround in the financial position of discoms is critical for future expansion in the power sector because generation projects will not be able to obtain finance if they are seen as selling power to discoms that are financially unviable. Introducing the private sector into electricity distribution, at least in some areas, could improve efficiency and would facilitate competitive bench marking for the system as a whole. Improved efficiency in distribution will also help moderate the rise in electricity prices that would otherwise be necessary to cover higher fuel costs. This is an area where action lies entirely with state governments.

Eighth is the introduction of 'open access'. This is another important reform which is entirely within the hands of state governments. It would create a competitive market in electricity for bulk consumers, incentivising independent power producers (IPPs) to compete with the local utility to supply reliable power to such customers at a negotiated rate. The distribution companies would be paid a wheeling charge for the use of the network and also a cross subsidy surcharge to cover the cross subsidy which bulk consumers are expected to bear to cover the underpricing for lower income consumers. The competitive pressure introduced by open access would also encourage the utilities to become more efficient in order to retain their paying bulk consumers. The Electricity Act (2003) had mandated that open access should be implemented by January 1, 2009. Unfortunately open access has not been operationalised in any state.

Ninth, it is necessary to review the terms under which contracts are awarded for exploration of oil and natural gas under the New Exploration and Licensing Policy (NELP). Earlier contracts have been criticised because they provided for cost recovery before determining profit petroleum (which is then shared with the government) and this was felt to be prone to misuse. The formula for determining the gas price in the case of gas fields also needs revision to reflect changed market conditions. Recommendations for simplification of the contract terms and a new formula for gas, linking the price of natural gas to be paid to producers to a combination of global gas price indicators are being considered. Early implementation of these recommendations would create an environment which would attract more investors to bid for NELP blocks.

Finally, looking further ahead, it is necessary to plan for a much larger use of renewable energy especially solar and wind energy. Renewable energy is more expensive than conventional energy but costs are falling especially for solar photovoltaic generation. Rationalisation of electricity prices as proposed above will make renewable energy more competitive without the need for a subsidy. The use of renewable energy also needs to be facilitated by allowing easier integration of decentralised electricity production into the grid through use of smart grids, including 'net metering' which allows surplus solar electricity to be fed back into the grid. Time of day tariffs will be particularly supportive of solar energy since it is available precisely at times of peak demand and higher electricity tariffs at times of peak demand would make solar energy more competitive. Once again this is an area where the states have to take a lead, through the state electricity regulatory commissions.

The 10 policy actions listed above define a wide-ranging agenda for reform some for the Centre and other for the states which would go a long way to creating an energy sector which is capable of supporting the country's transition to nine per cent growth. They involve an increase in energy prices which is economically compelling though politically difficult. It is necessary to mould public opinion to a realisation that we need to move in this direction if we want to achieve our objective of balancing energy demand with supply, while also containing import requirements and shifting to renewable energy sources. Most importantly, the public needs to be educated to realise that if we fail to rationalise energy prices we may not be able to achieve the rapid growth targeted which also means other expectations, including those relating to employment opportunities and inclusiveness, will need to be scaled down.

The Problem of Water Scarcity

Water is another area which presents new challenges. Until recently, the overall water availability situation in the country was viewed as reasonably comfortable, although there were areas of acute water scarcity. The latest assessment is less sanguine and it is estimated that on a business as usual basis total demand may exceed supply by as much as 50 per cent by 2020. Since water deficits unlike energy cannot be made up through imports, what this really means is that unless water use efficiency is increased greatly, the growth rate projected simply cannot be achieved.

Water is a state subject and virtually all the steps needed have to be taken by state governments though the Centre can help with financial resources. As in the case of energy, the policy agenda includes many difficult decisions. Public awareness of the issues involved is much lower than in energy, partly because most of the decisions are at the state-level and most state governments have not initiated public discussion on these issues. Fortunately, this is an area where we can move more slowly provided we do so decisively. Ten steps needed to respond to the water problems are listed below.

State governments should give priority to completing ongoing large irrigation projects as quickly as possible, instead of spreading limited resources thinly on multiple projects. Thin spreading of resources is motivated by the desire to stake as wide a claim as possible to available resources, but it has the consequence of greatly delaying benefits from the schemes underway.

Agriculture currently accounts for about 80 per cent of total water use but this could easily be cut by 40 to 50 per cent for many crops by using modern techniques of planting such as the system of rice intensification (SRI) and through greater use of drip irrigation. Unfortunately, farmers have little incentive to use canal water efficiently since it is priced at about 15 per cent of the operating and management costs, with capital costs left out completely. This makes large irrigation systems financially unviable, leading to poor maintenance and deterioration. It also encourages farmers in upper reaches of the system to appropriate disproportionate amounts of water for growing highly water intensive crops, while farmers in the lower reaches of the system don't get water. The problem of equitable access to water cannot be solved by raising prices since the price adjustments needed to ensure equitable distribution over the command area would be too large and politically unacceptable. The problem can only be overcome by establishing water regulatory authorities which are empowered to enforce an appropriate distribution of canal water between drinking needs, industrial use and agricultural use, with further regulation to ensure equitable distribution throughout the command area. This has been done in Maharashtra with some success, and the practice needs to be spread more widely.

Rational use of groundwater is more difficult to achieve because the law at present gives individual farmers the right to extract as much water as they want from bore wells on their own land and underpricing of electricity only encourages over use.[16] The result is gross overdrawal of water in many states, with the water table declining sharply, to the disadvantage of poorer farmers who cannot afford powerful pumps. However, there is hope that once farmers realise the non-sustainability of current practices, they will themselves be willing to accept cooperative solutions which reduce groundwater use. Andhra Pradesh provides an example where farmers have cooperated to adopt cropping patterns which do not involve excessive use of water. Active involvement of NGOs that have built up credibility by working in this area can be a great help.

An important step in encouraging cooperative action by farmers is greater knowledge of the state of the aquifer to determine the sustainable rate of drawal. The Twelfth Plan proposes a detailed exercise for mapping all aquifers over the Plan period which would help establish sustainable rates of drawal. This is a first step for organising farmers to cooperate in finding collective solutions. The Centre has a big role to play in getting this done.

It is necessary to expand the existing programme of watershed management to conserve water as much as possible by constructing water holding structures on the surface and accelerating groundwater recharge. Such projects are much more cost effective than large irrigation schemes, and are also much less disruptive in terms of uprooting people. State governments should give much greater priority to these projects in their own plans and the Central government should incentivise this process by increasing allocations to the Central government watershed management

16. This is sometimes defended by farmers on the grounds that canal water pricing does not even cover maintenance with no coverage of capital costs and it is therefore only fair that electricity is underpriced to put farmers dependent on groundwater on a level playing field since they bear the full capital cost of the pump.

programme, and also by allowing convergence with other central schemes to promote such efforts. Since, the returns from investment in watershed management are much higher than on larger irrigation projects, the entral government would do better to put more resources in this area than supporting large irrigation projects. States could consider imposing a cess on electricity for agriculture in all areas where water tables are falling, and earmark the proceeds of the cess to fund groundwater recharge in those areas.

Given the likelihood of water becoming a scarce natural resource, there is an overwhelming case for the Central government to fund agricultural research directed towards developing crop varieties capable of handling water stress without loss of productivity.

Water efficiency in industrial applications also needs to be increased. Power generation accounts for about 80 per cent of water used in industry and Indian power plants consume 8 to 10 times more water per MW compared to plants in developed countries because of inefficiencies in technology for both cooling and ash handling.[17] There is a strong case for the Central Electricity Authority using regulatory steps to force a switch to water saving technology for future power plants. The additional capital cost involved should be fully reflected in the price allowed to be charged for power.

Pollution of fresh water sources reduces effective availability and regulation should work to prevent it by ensuring that all water drawn from these sources for urban consumption should be treated to an acceptable level before being returned to water bodies or to the ground. Water supplied to urban households and other urban consumers should therefore be priced to cover not only the cost of delivering potable water, but also the associated cost of sewage treatment, so that water is returned in an acceptable condition. Imposition of higher charges for water will be vociferously resisted on the ground that water is a basic necessity, but this concern is best met by ensuring a minimum 'lifeline supply' to each household at an affordable price, while water use above the minimum is priced to cover full cost. Unless user charges are rationalised in this way, the water utility will

17. Most plants in India use the 'once through system' for cooling, in which water used for cooling is discharged without recycling, instead of the 'closed loop system' in which the water is recycled after topping up with fresh water to offset evaporation.

not be financially viable. Since urban governments do not have the fiscal capacity to cover costs, this will mean inadequate investment to expand supplies and continuing water pollution.[18]

Industrial units should be forced to treat all effluent before discharge, and the polluting units should bear the full cost of treatment at the site. Supply of fresh water to such units should also be priced high so as to encourage them to treat and reuse water as much as possible. Where there are a large number of small scale units, it may not be possible for each unit to set up a water treatment facility, but groups of units can do so collectively and bank finance should be provided for this purpose.

Finally, rational management of the nation's water resources requires optimising the use of water in inter-state rivers. Unfortunately, as water is becoming scarcer, it is increasingly difficult to reach agreement among states on sharing of inter-state rivers. Although water is a state subject, the Constitution contains a provision whereby inter-state rivers can be regulated provided Parliament passes a law for this purpose, but this has never been attempted. The only law passed thus far is for the establishment of Water Tribunals to settle inter-state water disputes, and this mechanism is proving less and less effective. A possible way forward is to pass a National Framework Law, with the consent of the states, which would not impinge on their sovereignty but would establish general principles which might govern the sharing of water in inter-state rivers.

Land

Rapid growth of the economy requires land to be available for new industries and industrial expansion, and also for expanding urbanisation. Ideally, land required for such expansion should either be provided by the government from government owned land or be purchased from willing sellers at a market determined price. However, several problems arise. Concern is sometimes expressed that this will divert land from agriculture, compromising food security. This fear is greatly exaggerated since the diversion over the next 20 years will be a miniscule portion of

18. Since inadequate supplies inevitably lead to inequity, with water being denied to poorer areas, the poor get pushed to get water from tankers at much higher cost.

total agricultural land, and can be more than made up by increases in land productivity which is entirely feasible.

A more serious problem is that the existence of multiple owners of small holdings can make it difficult to purchase land in the quantity required of the likelihood that some land owners will refuse to sell. To overcome this problem, land for industry has in the past often been obtained by compulsory acquisition under the Land Acquisition Act. This has led to considerable resistance on the part of land owners for what is seen as coercive acquisition at unfair prices determined on the basis of the very low rates used in official records. The problem is compounded when the acquisition is in tribal areas as in the case of mining leases. In these cases the land is not owned by the tribals, but its acquisition disrupts their traditional lifestyles.

These problems are sought to be addressed by a new Land Acquisition and Rehabilitation Bill which has been introduced in Parliament. The Bill allows compulsory acquisition of land for public purposes, which include the establishment of state owned industrial estates, but with enhanced rates of compensation and provision for rehabilitation of those other than landowners whose livelihood would be disrupted by the acquisition. It can also be used when land is needed for private industry to deal with the hold out problem, when most of the land has been acquired in the market but some pockets cannot be obtained, but with the additional requirement that rehabilitation provisions must apply to the whole project area including the portion acquired through market sales.

The proposed legislation will create a fairer basis for land acquisition from the perspective of landowners. As far as industry is concerned, it will encourage state governments to acquire land that is not fertile and may be remote from urban areas at present, but could be made accessible by building road and rail connectivity. From the environmental perspective, such estates could be pre cleared for certain industries. If state governments were to provide good quality industrial estates, with necessary infrastructure in place, it would automatically put a ceiling on land costs for new industries since those wishing to set up new or expansion units would have the freedom to go to these estates or find their own location elsewhere if they can get it cheaper. States that act quickly to set up such estates would be able to attract more investment.

Growth and Inclusiveness

Thus far we focused on the macroeconomic and sectoral constraints on achieving faster growth. In this section, we focus on the challenge of making growth more inclusive through the two channels discussed earlier, *viz.*, implementing programmes aimed at inclusiveness and adopting policies that will make growth internally more inclusive.

Plan Programmes Aimed at Inclusiveness

Over the years, the Central government has evolved a large number of programmes aimed at promoting inclusiveness. The more important of these are listed in Table 3.3, classified into three broad categories. The first category consists of programmes which aim at increasing the earning power of the poor, either individually or through the development of areas which are backward where development will help hitherto excluded sections of the population. The second category includes programmes for education and skill development and healthcare which not only directly improve welfare but also increase the growth potential of the economy over a longer period by upgrading the quality of the human resources. The third category of programmes can be viewed as transfers to supplement the income of the poor. All these programmes are 'centrally sponsored schemes', for which the Central government provides resources but the schemes are implemented by the state governments.

The total resources devoted to these programmes in 2012-13 amounts to ₹ 2,09,983 crore, or a little over 40 per cent of total provision in the Centre's budget for Plan expenditure, including support to the states. Advocates for greater inclusiveness typically push for more expenditure they are interested in. The level of expenditure is certainly relevant for the inclusiveness of the strategy but, it is necessary to go beyond expenditure to consider actual impact on welfare. Fortunately, there is now an accumulation of evidence on the functioning of most programmes based on monitoring and evaluation studies. As one would expect, performance varies across programmes and in individual programmes across states. However, while monitoring tells us whether the programmes are delivering results, it does not always tell us how performance can be improved. Much depends on how the programmes are designed and how well they are implemented on the ground. The fact that these programmes, though funded by the Centre, are implemented by state government agencies poses its own set of problems.

Table 3.3

Inclusiveness Programmes during Eleventh Plan

S.No.		*2012-13 (BE)*
	Livelihood and Income Support	
1.	Mahatma Gandhi National Rural Employment Guarantee Act (MGNREGA)	33,000
2.	National Urban Livelihood Mission	838
3.	National Rural Livelihood Mission (NRLM)	3,915
4.	Pradhan Mantri Gram Sadak Yojana (PMGSY)	
5.	Schemes under JNNURM for the poor	
6.	Rajiv Gandhi Grameen Vidyutikaran Yojana (RGGVY)	4,900
7.	Backward Region Grant Fund (BRGF)	12,040
	Education and Health and Social Infrastructure	
8.	Sarva Shiksha Abhiyan (SSA)	25,555
9.	Rashtriya Madhyamik Shiksha Abhiyan (RMSA)	3,124
10.	Mid Day Meal (MDM)	11,937
11.	National Health Mission (NHM)	20,542
12.	Integrated Child Development Service	15,850
13.	Rashtriya Swasthya Bima Yojana (RSBY)	1,017
14.	Rajiv Gandhi Drinking Water & Sanitation Mission (RGDWSM)	14,000
	Income Supporting	
15.	National Social Assistance Programme (NSAP)	8,382
16.	Indira Awas Yojana (IAY)	11,075
17.	Welfare of ST including tribal sub-plan and article no. 275(a)	3,861
18.	Welfare of SC & OB	4,753
19.	Scholarship for Minorities	1,260
	Total	**2,09,983**
	As percentage of GDP	**2.07**
	As percentage of total Plan expenditure	**40.32**

The experience in primary education, which has been a priority area, illustrates the potential disconnect between expenditure or outcomes. Substantial resources have been allocated to this area though the Sarva Shiksha Abhiyan and the Mid Day Meal Programme. School facilities have expanded and primary school enrolment is now near universal. School attendance has also improved, thanks to the Mid Day Meal. However, despite the expansion in inputs, the quality of education provided remains poor. The Annual Status of Education Reports (ASER), conducted regularly by Pratham since 2006, show that almost half the children in grade V cannot read what children in grade II should be able to read. The situation is better in some states, and worse in others, but the variation is relatively narrow around a generally low mean. More disturbingly, the surveys show no improvement over time on average, though there are interesting differences across states there is a slow improvement in the Southern and Western States and a slow deterioration in Northern and Eastern states.

Teacher absenteeism and low motivation is a major factor explaining poor learning outcomes, but there is no consensus on how to remedy the situation. Official policy focuses on improving teacher training, but field results show that better trained teachers do not perform better in terms of regularity of attendance or motivation. Some think that the answer lies in better school supervision by the existing system of school administration, with stronger penalties for non-performance such as withholding promotions. Others advocate more radical solutions such as hiring teachers initially on contract, and confirming them only later, and promoting them subsequently only on the basis of performance. However, it is not clear whether existing rules or teacher unions will allow such arrangements. Many believe that the solution lies in empowering *panchayats* to supervise schools through education committees of the *panchayat*. However, states have done little to give these bodies effective control over functionaries and funds and there are also serious capacity constraints which limit the ability of elected representatives in these bodies to exercise effective control.[19]

Similar problems exist in health. Health care centres have not been expanded on anything like the scale that has been achieved for primary education, but the Twelfth Plan has substantially increased the Central government allocation for the health sector, giving it the largest expansion of all sectors. However, while the focus of the health programme is to provide PHCs and sub-centres with qualified staff, the real problem is that even where PHCs and sub-centres exit, and qualified staff have been posted, the service delivery is poor. Field studies show that qualified doctors

19. Evaluation studies have found that whereas Village Health and Education Committees have been set up in many *panchayats*, it is often the case that those listed as Members are not aware of this fact!

do not really perform better than untrained or semi-trained personnel.[20] This suggests that larger financial resources to expand the system without reforming the system itself, may not deliver results.

States often complain that resources provided under various centrally sponsored schemes are encumbered by rigid central guidelines, which are often not suited to the specific conditions of the state. This is a valid concern and the Twelfth Plan therefore, proposes to introduce greater flexibility in the guidelines to tailor them to state specific requirements. It is also proposed to allow states to use 10 per cent of the funds provided by the Centre in specific schemes as a flexi fund for projects in the general area without having to abide even by the state specific guidelines. This will give the states much needed flexibility to innovate, which is highly desirable.

The scope for expanding the set of inclusiveness oriented programmes is obviously constrained by the total availability of resources. Allocations for some programmes—notably health and education—have to be increased substantially over time since the expenditure on these sectors is currently below what may be called a reasonable international norm. There is much that needs to be done to improve the efficiency in use of resources in health and education, but the need for additional resources in these areas cannot be disputed. However, priority to health and education only means that the other inclusiveness programmes will be more constrained.

The scope for expansion in other inclusiveness programmes should depend on the assessment of their effectiveness compared with other claimants for public resources. Two groups of alternative claimants are relevant in this context. The first is the set of programmes which have a direct impact on growth such as expanded investment in infrastructure, investment in science and technology, higher education, and transfers to states to assist in their development. The other competing demand for resources is the subsidies in the system. As noted earlier, central subsidies on food, fertiliser and petroleum products together account for about 2.4 per cent of GDP, which is larger than the total expenditure on all the inclusiveness programmes listed in Table 3.3. The food subsidy can be viewed as sacrosanct, but subsidies for petroleum products and even fertilisers are not, and resources currently absorbed by these subsidies may

20. See Jinshu Das *et al.* (2011).

have a greater inclusive impact if diverted to well targeted inclusiveness programmes or to programmes that promote inclusive growth. Since subsidies are non-Plan expenditure, the scale of subsidies are not part of the resource allocation exercise for the Plan although, as noted above, the resource projections in the Plan are based on a reduction in these subsidies from 2.4 per cent of GDP in 2011-12 to 1.5 per cent in 2016-17.[21]

Making Growth Itself More Inclusive

We now turn to the second track in promoting inclusiveness which relies on adopting policies that will make the pattern of growth itself inherently more inclusive. Two key components of the Twelfth Plan strategy, which are particularly relevant in this context, are the promotion of agriculture and faster employment creation through the manufacturing sector.

Agricultural Growth and Inclusiveness

Agricultural growth is critical for inclusiveness if only because agriculture is the dominant activity for half the population. Fortunately, agriculture has accelerated from 2.4 per cent per year in the Tenth Plan to 3.7 per cent in the Eleventh Plan. The uptrend in productivity that began in the Eleventh Plan is expected to continue and the Twelfth Plan target of 4 per cent growth is therefore eminently achievable.

Since agricultural GDP now accounts for only 14 per cent of total GDP, an increase in agricultural growth from 3.4 per cent to 4 per cent will directly contribute less than a tenth of one percentage point to overall GDP growth. This may appear negligible, but the impact on inclusiveness will be much greater because it accrues to lower income groups in rural areas. Faster agricultural growth will also be associated with greater upstream and downstream economic activity in rural areas which adds to rural income and employment.[22] Higher incomes in rural areas on all these counts

21. A special problem with subsidies is that they are open ended in the sense that the amounts mentioned in the budget are often based on assumptions that prices will be suitably adjusted to live within the total provided, but these decision are not taken.

22. Upstream activity, i.e., traders selling agricultural inputs and the expansion of machine leasing and repair services, does not figure in agricultural GDP, which only measures value added in agriculture, but it adds to non-agricultural GDP and generates rural employment. This is also true of downstream activity related to post harvest management, transport and marketing.

also lead to higher rural consumption, which in turn generates economic activity in the form of shops, food stalls, and even personal services such as beauty parlours. For all these reasons faster agricultural growth can be expected to have a very positive impact on rural poverty.

The policies required to achieve the 4 per cent growth target for agriculture cover a number of areas and action is already underway in many though there is room for improvement. This includes better water management, improved extension services to spread better agricultural technology, strengthened credit delivery, better seeds and improved rural infrastructure generally, especially access to electricity and better road connectivity to markets. Since the mix of crops and non-crop agriculture varies according to agro-climatic conditions, the agricultural strategy varies across agro-climatic zones.

Some aspects that call for focused attention are listed below. As in other areas, some of the actions that have to be taken are in the realm of the Centre but others are in the hands of states.

Indian agriculture has been diversifying away from food grains and towards horticultural crops and non-crop agriculture such as dairying, poultry and inland fisheries. This is a natural process which will accelerate but non-food grain agriculture requires special marketing support, including post-harvest management and logistic infrastructure such as chilling plants, refrigerated trucks, etc. Marketing of perishable produce, unlike the case with food grains, will be dominated by the private sector or cooperatives where these exist and this calls for radical reform of outdated Agriculture Produce Marketing Committee Acts to allow freer private sector entry into markets including the possibility of direct purchase from farmers. This is an area that lies entirely in the domain of state governments, but vested interests have prevented bolder action thus far.

There is need for a strategic shift in agricultural policy away from subsidising inputs, such as fertiliser and power, towards investing larger amounts in other ways of increasing land productivity. The total provision for fertiliser subsidy in the Central Budget in 2012-13 was ₹ 72,000 crore whereas the total Plan provision for agriculture, including agricultural research irrigation and watershed management was only about ₹ 43,000 crore. Not only is the total volume of subsidy too high compared with other support measures, it is also characterised by distortions which have a negative effect on productivity. Nitrogenous fertilisers (N) are excessively subsidised compared to P and K.[23] Excessive subsidisation of N leads to overuse of urea, disturbing the nutrient balance in the soil and reducing soil productivity over time. Furthermore, while chemical fertilisers are subsidised, organic fertilisers, which are environmentally better, are not. Fertiliser subsidy is entirely in the hands of the Central government and corrective steps must be taken by the Centre.

Similar considerations arise in relation to the subsidy on electricity supplied to agriculture, which is borne by state governments. The scale of this subsidy is not easily quantified because most state governments keep electricity tariffs lower than they should be, but it is at least ₹ 30,000 to ₹ 40,000 crore if properly computed.

Rationalisation of tenancy laws is another area which is important for inclusiveness. The agriculture dependent population includes a very large proportion of families with very small holdings which are not viable to cultivate. However agriculturists are typically unwilling to sell their land, and they are also unwilling to lease it out for fear that the tenant may gain tenancy rights. In some states, tenancy is not legally allowed. There is a strong case for amending the laws to allow small and marginal land holders to lease out their land, with the confidence that they could reclaim it if needed; there would be a more efficient allocation of land to farmers able to expand, while facilitating those wanting to move out of farming to do so, at least temporarily.[24] The Twelfth Plan has proposed an innovative idea of creating a 'Village Land Bank' in which farmers could 'deposit' the land, with the right to withdraw the land after a specified number of crop years, and the land bank can then lease out the land for the stated period

23. The imbalance has worsened recently because the subsidy for P and K fertilisers has been shifted to a fixed nutrient based subsidy, with prices to the farmer varying with world market prices while urea prices have not been changed since 2002. As world prices of DAP and MOP have shot up, the prices of these fertilisers have increased sharply

24. NSSO Surveys reveal that 49 per cent of farming families want to move out of farming because they no longer view it as profitable. This is often projected as a failure of policy but a gradual shift out of farming to more productive job opportunities is a natural part of the development process. The key issue is whether such opportunities outside agriculture are being provided. The object of policy should not be to stop the efflux but rather to make sure that it is a smooth shift to higher income earning activity.

paying the lease rental to the original depositor. Interposing a public agency between the lessor and the lessee will increase the security that the land can be reclaimed.

Agricultural research needs to be greatly strengthened both in terms of the resources devoted to it and also by implementing institutional reform along the lines recommended by the Mashelkar Committee and the Swaminathan Committee. While some changes have been made, the bulk of the recommendations have yet to be implemented. With the looming threat of climate change, it is necessary to strengthen the National Agricultural Research System very substantially. Some of the uncertainty that has been introduced into the procedures for clearing new GM varieties also needs to be resolved.

Employment Generation in Manufacturing

Among the best ways of making growth more inclusive is to ensure that it creates a sufficient number of new employment opportunities to satisfy the aspirations of the new entrants into the labour force, and also absorb some of the labour which should move out of agriculture.[25] This can be done in many non-agricultural sectors such as transport, tourism health, education, etc., but the experience of other emerging market countries is that a large part of the new employment must be created in manufacturing. Manufacturing in India has underperformed in this respect because it has not grown as rapidly as it should have, and it has also been much less labour intensive than might have been hoped.

The growth of manufacturing in the Eleventh Plan was only 7 per cent against a target of double-digit growth. The Twelfth Plan assumes a significant acceleration in manufacturing from 2.7 per cent growth in 2011-2012 to 10 per cent by the end of the Twelfth Plan. Some of the reasons why the growth of manufacturing has disappointed have already been discussed. They include weaknesses in infrastructure, especially power supply and transport connectivity, problems related to the ease of doing business and the scarcity of financial resources because of high fiscal deficits. Corrective action in these areas should raise the growth of manufacturing in future.

25. Agriculture should not be seen as an area for increase in total employment. In fact we need to plan to facilitate people moving out of agriculture for better paying jobs outside which will also raise income levels of those who remain.

Faster growth in manufacturing also requires a shift in the size composition of the sector, which at present is characterised by a few large firms at the capital intensive end of the spectrum, which account for a substantial proportion of manufacturing value added but relatively little employment, while at the other end of the spectrum there is an inordinate concentration of small firms with employment below 50 workers per firm. There are not enough firms in the middle category, employing say between 100 to 300 persons. Whereas the very small firms are very labour intensive, they typically do not operate at high level of technology, and do not offer quality jobs and most of them are unlikely to have the dynamism to support rapid growth. It is the missing middle category, which could have provided the foundation for strong manufacturing sector providing a wide range of high quality jobs. The more successful of these firms could be expected to grow to larger scale, exerting competitive pressure on established larger units, while also expanding total employment in the process.

Encouragement of this middle size segment would contribute to both faster growth and greater and better quality employment generation. One of the ways in which middle sized companies can be incentivised to expand is the development of industrial estates which provide ready availability of land and other necessary infrastructure. The development of clusters, which provide economies of agglomeration, is also important. As noted earlier in the context of land availability, state governments need to plan actively for setting up modern industrial estates and also for the development of clusters in order to create an environment in which middle sized technologically capable firms can flourish. The proposal to establish National Manufacturing Zones, which is an integral part of the Twelfth Plan manufacturing strategy, is a step in this direction and success in this area would be critical.

Another area of policy that is relevant for both the growth of the manufacturing sector and its employment generation potential is the reform of labour laws. India's labour laws are generally regarded as more complex than those of most other countries and also less flexible. Employers do not have the flexibility to reduce the size of the permanent work force, or to close down an industrial unit, when faced with a decline in demand, except with the permission of the relevant government, which is almost never granted in practice. This discourages investors from labour intensive areas of production. Those that do venture into this area and are in a position to expand, often forego economies of scale that might come from expansion and set up multiple smaller units in different locations to avoid having to deal with a large labour force. Employers also try to get around the law by hiring a large proportion of their labour force in the form of contract workers, who are kept on the rolls only temporarily, and rotated out before the time period when any worker has to be given permanent status. Restrictive labour laws are often cited as one of the factors that prevented Indian entrepreneurs from reaping the full benefit of the abolition of the Multi Fibre Agreement, which eliminated quota restrictions on imports of textiles and garments into the industrialised world.

Reform of labour laws is a politically sensitive issue and there is widespread suspicion that those advocating it are taking an anti-labour position, based on simplistic 'hire and fire' notions. This suspicion is understandable in a country where unemployment is a problem and especially at a point when the economy is going through a slowdown. Recognising this political sensitivity, the government has taken the position that a change in labour laws will only be made when a consensus has evolved. This has yet to happen, but there is no doubt that the issue is important and will have to be addressed sooner or later.

It needs to be clarified that no reasonable person would advocate a simplistic hire and fire policy in our situation. However, many of the provisions in the existing laws are archaic and could be changed without compromising genuine labour interests. Looking ahead, there is a case for arguing that Indian industry needs a degree of flexibility comparable with that available in the countries with which we are competing both in our domestic markets and globally and this can be done while observing accepted standards of labour rights.

The real problem is that we do not have a system of social security which would provide unemployment benefits to individuals who lose their jobs, with the scale of the benefits related to the period of employment. In the longer run, it is necessary to move towards such a system to be funded by a combination of contributions by employers and workers with the government having a residual role. Setting up such a system may initially involve payments by the government to cover the excess of payments that may have to be made until a reasonable corpus is built up and this deficit would have to be covered by the government, but it would quickly be self financing. Introduction of such a system as part of a package which gave greater flexibility to shed labour if needed might be acceptable to labour interests. It would certainly encourage a much faster growth of employment in the organised sector, which is surely what any trade union leadership would want.

Conclusion

The issues discussed in this paper are only a subset of the full agenda of reforms which needs to be undertaken if India is to realise the scenario of 'strong inclusive growth' presented in the Twelfth Plan. These reforms will contribute to the growth of total factor productivity which, together with growth of primary inputs, mainly capital and human resources, provides the impetus for growth from the supply side. A comprehensive discussion of these reforms is beyond the scope of this paper. The paper has attempted to highlight a number of critical policy challenges which need to be addressed if we are to achieve the objective of strong inclusive growth. A credible response requires actions by the Central government and also by the state governments.

The key message is that business as usual, with incremental change here and there will not do. Harking back to the lessons of 1991, we need to think big and do things differently, often taking a risk with new approaches, and finding ways of over-riding bureaucratic delays. If we fail in this endeavour, we will be reduced to trying what the *Times of India* in 1991 rightly derided as "a scratch here and a fiddle there," which will definitely not achieve the objective of achieving faster, more inclusive and sustainable growth.

References

Das, Jishnu, Alaka Holla, Veena Das, Manoj Mohanan, Diana Tabak and Brian Chan (2012). "In Urban and Rural India: A Standardized Patient Study Showed Low Levels of Provider Training and Huge Quality Gaps", *Health Affairs* 31(12): 2774-84.

World Bank (2012). *Doing Business 2012: Doing Business in a More Transparent World.* International Finance Corporation.

4 Rejigging the Elephant Dance*

Duvvuri Subbarao

India clocked an average annual growth of 9 per cent in the five-year period 2003–2008. For a nation that once believed that the Hindu rate of growth was its destiny, this remarkable growth performance has been cause for celebration. It has also become the trigger for setting off an aspiration for double-digit growth.

If the East Asians are 'the tigers' and China 'the dragon', India is commonly 'the elephant'—a strong animal with enormous potential but given to a lumbering pace. For a world that once believed that an elephant does not have any spirit, India's march up the high growth trajectory has proved that the elephant too can dance. The dance was interrupted by the global financial crisis of 2008 which engulfed virtually every country in the world. India recovered from the crisis sooner than other countries but the growth rate has not reached the pre-crisis level. Can the elephant rejig its dance to achieve double-digit growth and prove that the growth story is still intact? In order to do this, the country needs to address several challenges.

Raising Agricultural Production and Productivity

The first challenge is to step up agriculture production and productivity. India has come a long way from the chronic food shortages of the early years after independence, and even as population increased, it maintained food self-sufficiency thanks to investment in irrigation, improved farming practices and better technologies. But in recent years, there has been an erosion at the margins of food self-sufficiency. The supply–demand gap in the food sector is, in part, a problem of success, a consequence of a shift in

---

* This chapter is based on the Haksar Memorial Lecture delivered at the Centre for Research in Rural & Industrial Development, Chandigarh on November 25, 2011. The Haksar Memorial Lecture is a lecture series in honour of P.N. Haksar, an outstanding civil servant and a visionary.

dietary habits from cereal to protein-based foods, reflecting rising incomes, especially rural incomes. Regardless, the quest for inclusive growth is in jeopardy if the root causes of structural food inflation are not addressed.

Some analysts argue that agriculture cannot be a concern from an overall growth perspective because it accounts for only about 15 per cent of GDP, and that the share will decline further as the economy matures. This argument is flawed. Even if its share in GDP is small and declining, agriculture still accommodates 53 per cent of the labour force. Besides, agriculture has very vital supply–demand linkages with other sectors of the economy. Raising agricultural production and productivity is, therefore, important for containing price pressures, raising rural incomes and making growth more inclusive.

There are several initiatives necessary to launch a second Green Revolution—larger public investment, greater input efficiency, soil conservation, improved farming practices, developing resilience to rainfall variations and climate change effects, to name just a few. To build forward and backward linkages, there is a need to invest in rural infrastructure and the supply chain. We also need to be mindful that land and water costs will only increase over time; inclusive growth will push up wages, thereby putting upward pressure on inflation. In the context of rising costs, improving productivity becomes imperative to balance the needs of higher prices for producers and the demand for low prices by consumers.

Expanding Employment

The second major challenge to making growth inclusive is to expand employment opportunities. Even as increasing numbers than ever before find work, there remains a sense of crisis about jobs. This is not surprising because unemployment is the most significant cause of economic pain in a poor country.

Analysing the problem of unemployment is the biggest challenge because there are no reliable statistics. There is enormous unemployment and underemployment in the rural sector but the size and nature of the problem is unclear. Millions of people are locked in low productivity jobs in the unorganised industry and service sectors. India's high-end IT service sector dazzles the world but, contrary to popular perception, it employs no more than 3 million. So, the problem is that a lot of people are out of work, and where they do have work, they are performing below their potential.

The 66th round (July 2011) of National Sample Survey Organisation (NSSO) data suggest that both unemployment rate and employment growth declined during the period 2004–05 to 2009–10. This is intriguing but has been explained as a result of a large number of young people pursuing education, resulting in fewer job seekers. This means only a temporary respite, as once out of school, they will be added to the labour force. There will be other pressures too. As agricultural productivity goes up, it will release millions of surplus labour who will seek jobs outside the farm sector. Also, more women will join the labour force adding to the demand for jobs. Putting all these trends together, various estimates suggest that India's labour force will increase by 250 to 300 million in the next 20 years.

Finding productive jobs for such huge numbers is a tremendous challenge, and clearly the answer lies in stepping up growth; more importantly, in stepping up the employment intensity of growth. Where are the jobs going to come from? To examine that, it is interesting to look at the relative shares of different sectors of the economy in GDP and in jobs (Table 4.1).

Table 4.1

Sectoral Shares of GDP and Employment, 2009-10

Sector	*% Share of GDP*	*% Share of Employment*
Agriculture	15	53
Industry	20	12
Services	65	35

Source: CSO and NSSO.

These numbers clearly underscore the need to move people out of low productivity jobs in agriculture to industry and services. A portion of the surplus labour in agriculture could be absorbed in non-farm allied activities. There will also be opportunities in the construction sector which is growing but a major expansion of job opportunities in the service sector will not be possible without skill improvement. That will inevitably take time. So, much of the burden of job creation will fall on the manufacturing sector.

For a long time, many believed that India defied the textbook development paradigm by leapfrogging directly from agriculture to services, skipping the manufacturing sector. Experience clearly demonstrates that such a 'frog leap' cannot be sustained. Manufacturing has to expand to provide jobs. The National Manufacturing Policy, unveiled in 2011, aims at raising the share of manufacturing in GDP from 16 per cent to 25 per cent and generating additional employment of 100 million by 2022. To exploit the full job potential of this emphasis on manufacturing, India needs to liberalise labour laws and employment regulations so that perverse incentives to push labour into the unorganised sector are eliminated.

The challenge of job creation is related to the issue of India's 'demographic dividend'. The demographic dividend argument, which has gained increasing currency in recent years, suggests India's demographics are favourable because the working age population is growing faster than the overall population. This expanding working age population will earn and save, thereby contributing to higher savings and higher investment, which will lead to higher growth. However, we need to recognise that there is nothing inevitable about the demographic dividend. Demographic dividend will flow if, and only if, we are able to find jobs for the growing labour force.

Raising Productivity

Job expansion is one side of the challenge to inclusive growth. The other side is enhancing productivity. Historical evidence clearly demonstrates a quantum jump in productivity as labour moves from the agriculture to the secondary and tertiary sectors. Back-of-the-envelope calculations show that at the current stage of India's economic development, as a worker moves from agriculture to other sectors, his/her productivity increases by nearly a factor of five.

Productivity improvement entails managing factors of production as well as factor productivity better. In terms of factors of production, managing surplus labour in the farm sector, raising the rate of domestic savings, attracting stable foreign savings, sustainable use of natural resources and managing the demand for land from key growth sectors are important.

Improving factor productivity hinges critically on raising the skill endowment of the labour force. The skills gap is no longer just a handicap; it is turning out to be a crisis. To scale up steel production to 120 million tonnes requires millions of skilled people. Yet, finding a crane operator is oftentimes a challenge. Even as demand for skills increases, the supply side response lags far behind. India churns out 350,000 engineers every year but barely a quarter of them are employable. There are 7,000 Industrial Training Institutes but their curriculums are woefully outdated.

There is an incentive issue in skill training. Skill development is a quintessentially merit good where the societal cost–benefit calculus is higher than the individual cost–benefit calculation. The private sector will be reluctant to invest in skills since workers can migrate with their skills. This was the understanding that prompted the government to launch the ambitious National Skill Development Programme as a public–private partnership (PPP) initiative to train 500 million people by 2022. Several states are also allowing vocational training institutions to be set up as PPP initiatives as well as not-for-profit societies.

Managing Urbanisation

Historically, there has been a strong correlation between urbanisation and economic growth across countries and across time, with the causation possibly running both ways. Empirical studies show that middle income countries reach about 50 per cent urbanisation and high income countries typically have 70 to 80 per cent urbanisation. China's rapid growth over the last two decades, for example, ran concurrently with an increase in urbanisation rate from 32 per cent in 1997 to 50 per cent in 2010, consistent with its low-middle income status. India lags in urbanisation. In the 20 years since the start of reforms in 1991, the proportion of urban population has increased from 26 per cent in 1991 to just about 31 per cent in 2011.

Accelerating growth presents two tasks from the urbanisation perspective. First, the rate of urbanisation has to pick up so as to move people up the productivity ladder and, second, the pressures of urbanisation have to be managed proactively. The costs of unplanned urbanisation are very visible in terms of huge strains on infrastructure and sanitation, pressure on utilities and inadequate and low quality social service provision. Indian cities are clearly unprepared for the influx of migrants on the scale that it is occurring and the result is slums and squatter settlements. Unplanned urbanisation also entails other problems ranging from crime, law and order to pollution, congestion and environmental degradation.

Expanding urban infrastructure demands huge resources. Isher Judge Ahluwalia and others[1] have estimated that investment requirements for urban infrastructure over the 20 year period—2012–2031—would be about ₹ 40 trillion, which translates to an annual average investment of about $100 per capita. Mobilising resources of this order is obviously a big challenge and will call for more effective taxation, efficient project planning and implementation, innovative urban governance and much greater sensitivity to embracing migrants into the urban ecology.

Bridging the Infrastructure Deficit

It is widely acknowledged that infrastructure deficit is by far one of the most binding constraints to accelerating growth. Even so, India's efforts to bridge the deficit have fallen way short of the mark. The Eleventh Five Year Plan (2007–2012) projected investment in infrastructure of $500 billion but the final expenditure is likely to fall well short of that. The Twelfth Plan (2012–2017) doubles the projected investment over the five-year period to $1 trillion, which means that annual investment in infrastructure has to increase from the current level of 6 per cent of GDP to over 10 per cent. Given its fiscal compulsions, the government will clearly not be able to mobilise resources of this order. The Twelfth Plan projections call for 50 per cent of the projected investment to come from the private sector and much of the project implementation to happen in the PPP mode.

Infrastructure investment poses three sub-challenges: (a) mobilising necessary resources, (b) reforming regulations and contractual arrangements, and (c) efficient project planning and execution.

Infrastructure requires long-term finance, and it should ideally be funded by long-term sources like insurance and pension funds. Since these markets in India are not deep enough, the burden of financing

1. High Powered Expert Committee for Estimating the Investment Requirements for Urban Infrastructure Services, 2011 (Chairperson: Dr Isher Judge Ahluwalia).

infrastructure is falling on banks. Banks cannot expand lending for infrastructure beyond a point because of exposure risks. In financing infrastructure, banks also face an asset–liability mismatch (ALM) problem since their liabilities are largely short-term whereas infrastructure funding is typically long-term. The role of the Reserve Bank of India (RBI) in financing infrastructure in such an environment then becomes crucial. In order to support infrastructure financing by banks, the RBI has relaxed regulatory norms to the extent prudent limits permit. These include higher exposure norms in respect of single borrowers and borrower groups, permitting banks to invest in infrastructure debt funds (IDFs) and enter into take-out financing arrangements, relaxing regulations governing bank guarantees for infrastructure financing and financing promoters' equity, and creating a separate category of non-banking finance companies (NBFCs) specialising in infrastructure finance (infrastructure finance companies).

Development of the corporate bond market by both the government and the RBI will go a long way in augmenting infrastructure financing. Even as measures to ease the supply side of the corporate bond market are important, it is also the case that the corporate bond market remains demand constrained.

Improving Social Sector Outcomes

Historical evidence shows that economic development and social development are strongly correlated, with the causation possibly running both ways. In spite of higher-than-expected economic growth, India's human development indicators are distressing. As per the UNDP's Human Development Index (HDI) 2011,[2] it ranks 134 out of 187 countries, clearly in the bottom third of the league of nations. Government expenditure on education, health and nutrition has increased, social sector programmes have been revamped and delivery systems have been improved. Education and health outcomes have seen marginal gains, yet on many indicators such as life expectancy at birth, educational attainment and nutrition levels, the country is well below international standards.

Among the many lacunae of India's social sector programmes is that there is continued emphasis on outputs and not outcomes. The combined

2. *http://hdr.undp.org/en/statistics/*

public expenditure on education by the Centre and the states in India was little less than 4 per cent of GDP at the beginning of the Eleventh Five Year Plan (2007-08 to 2011-12), which was envisaged to be raised to 6 per cent of GDP. That is necessary but not sufficient. Neighbouring countries like China and Sri Lanka spend less than 4 per cent of their respective GDPs on education. Yet they have literacy levels in the range of 90+ per cent as compared to India's 74 per cent. The same goes for the health sector. Spending more on the twin merit goods of primary education and basic health is necessary. But the spending needs to be more efficient because better education and health are a function not just of the quantum of expenditure but also of the quality of that expenditure.

Promoting Financial Inclusion

Financial inclusion is important because it is a necessary condition for sustaining equitable growth. There are few, if any, instances of an economy transiting from an agrarian system to a post-industrial modern society without broad-based financial inclusion. Economic opportunity is strongly intertwined with financial access. Such access is especially powerful for the poor as it provides them opportunities to build savings, make investments and avail credit. Importantly, access to financial services also helps the poor insure themselves against income shocks and equips them to meet emergencies such as illness, death or loss of employment. Needless to add, financial inclusion protects the poor from the clutches of usurious money lenders.

Apart from helping the poor at the micro level, financial inclusion delivers benefits at the macro level too. By transferring money directly to the bank accounts of beneficiaries, the government can minimise leakage in its affirmative action programmes. Financial inclusion gives banks access to a large pool of low cost and stable funds which will aid their ALM. Financial inclusion is, therefore, a win-win proposition for the poor, for banks, for governments and the national economy.

The extent of financial exclusion in India is staggering. The proportion of people having any kind of life insurance cover is as low as 10 per cent and the proportion having non-life insurance is an abysmally low 0.6 per cent. Out of the 600,000 habitations in India, less than 30,000 have a commercial bank branch. Just about 40 per cent of the population across the country have bank accounts, and this ratio is much lower in north-east India.[3] Even where bank accounts are claimed to have been opened, verification has often shown that these accounts are dormant. Few among the poor conduct any banking transactions and even fewer receive credit. Millions of people across the country are thereby denied the opportunity to harness their earning capacity and entrepreneurial talent, and are condemned to marginalisation and poverty. By far the biggest factor inhibiting financial inclusion is that banks continue to see it as an obligation and not an opportunity.

Managing Globalisation

Globalisation as an economic force is here to stay. It is too potent a force to be comprehensively reversed, although there may be some short-term blips. Globalisation was, is, and will always be inevitable. No revolution in human history has been totally benign. So is it the case with globalisation. It comes with benefits and costs.[4]

Globalisation, as measured by the movement of ideas, people, goods, services and capital across borders, has undoubtedly been one of the defining features of the last 25 years. For countries that believed that geography is destiny, globalisation has opened up incredible opportunities but has also exposed them to ruthless challenges.

India's integration with the world has occurred faster and is more extensive and deep than we tend to acknowledge. India's remarkable growth acceleration in the period 2003–2008 is a demonstration of the positive side of globalisation. But on the flip side, the impact of the global financial crisis is an illustration of the negative side of globalisation. The reason for the greater impact of the 2008 crisis is that between the Asian crisis of the late 1990s and the global financial crisis of 2008, India's integration with the world had deepened (Table 4.2).

---

3. *Source*: IRDA and RBI, 2009.

4. Chanda, Nayan (2007). *Bound Together: How Traders, Preachers, Adventurers and Warriors Shaped Globalization.* New Delhi: Penguin Books India.

Table 4.2

India's Deepening Global Integration

Percentage of GDP	*1998–99*	*2008–09*
(Export+Import)/GDP	20	41
Two-way capital+current flows/GDP	44	112

Source: RBI.

India's two-way trade flows doubled in the 10-year period 1998 to 2008, but the two-way current and capital flows increased by more than two and a half times. This means that while India's trade integration deepened, its financial integration was far greater.

The challenge ahead is to minimise the costs and maximise the benefits of globalisation. From the macro perspective, the country needs to manage the 'impossible trinity'. A country cannot simultaneously have a fixed exchange rate, an open capital account and an independent monetary policy. Most advanced economies give up the fixed exchange rate to gain policy leverage on the other two parameters. Emerging economies typically eschew corner solutions in favour of middle solutions. In India, the capital account is partly open, the exchange rate floats (the government intervenes only for the purpose of managing excess volatility and disruptions to macroeconomic stability) and the monetary policy operates taking into account the impact of external developments on the domestic situation.

Another dimension of the globalisation challenge is 'innovation'. Innovation has always been, and will always be, the well-spring of growth but its importance increases in a knowledge economy. History has shown that as an economy grows, incomes and wages rise. It then loses competitiveness in labour-intensive industries, forcing it to seek new sources of growth through innovation; otherwise it gets locked into what is called the 'middle income trap'. India enjoyed a comparative advantage in the IT industry because of superior technical manpower and knowledge of English. But that advantage is now threatened as other countries catch up fast. The only way to continue to benefit from this sector is to move up the value chain through innovation.

Providing a Stable and Predictable Macroeconomic Environment

A stable and predictable macroeconomic environment is a necessary condition for growth. It is only in such an environment that both savers and investors can make informed decisions so that savings translate efficiently into productive investment. Every country that has reached a crisis in the last quarter century is a story of excess; excess carried to an unsustainable level leading to implosion. Fast growth gained through excess can be alluring because the signs of instability brewing in the underbelly are oftentimes not visible in real time. But when the implosion inevitably happens, the losses by way of lost growth and welfare are monumental.

The importance of a stable macroeconomic environment for India rests on two big factors. First is reducing fiscal deficits at both the Centre and in the states to stabilise the debt–GDP ratios at sustainable levels. In charting a road map for fiscal consolidation, India also needs to be mindful of the quality of fiscal adjustment by weeding out unproductive expenditure and protecting, if not enhancing, growth-promoting expenditure.

The second is to bring inflation down well below five per cent, consistent with India's broader integration into the global economy. High inflation makes both savers and investors uncertain. Inflation experienced as a consequence of both supply shocks and demand pressures has to be controlled by restraining demand and anchoring inflation expectations. This has to be supplemented by supply-side responses to raise the potential output of the economy.

Good Governance

Identifying challenges and drawing up plans to address them is the relatively easy part of the growth game. What is infinitely more difficult is the translation of policies into action. That is the challenge of providing good governance. Good governance is at the very heart of economic growth and poverty reduction, and even political legitimacy. In the ultimate analysis, it is the quality of governance that separates success and failure in economic development. Across countries, application of the same policies in roughly similar contexts has produced dramatically different results. India has seen vast differences across states in development outcomes resulting from the same mix of development policies. These differences, even as similar policy packages are adopted, arise because of differences in governance. Research has shown that per capita incomes and the quality of governance is strongly correlated, indicating a virtuous circle in which good governance results in economic development.

The elephant's amble is rarely applauded when compared to the tiger's sprint. Yet few animals have an elephant's stamina. Thus, when the elephant finds its rhythm, it can dance for a very long time. India needs to find its tempo and rejig the dance in order to trigger and sustain inclusive robust growth.

5 Financial Inclusion

An Insider's View

Ashok Jha

It is a great privilege to be invited to contribute to a festschrift to facilitate such a distinguished policymaker as P. Chidambaram. I first worked with him in the Ministry of Commerce in 1991 when he was appointed Commerce Minister. In a very short time, he left his imprint there as he rewrote the export-import policy, making it focussed and user-friendly. Subsequently, I had the good fortune to work with him between 2005-2007 when he was the Finance Minister.

His razor-sharp intellect, insightful analysis and speed of decision-making were attributes that astounded all who came into contact with him. If between 2004 and 2008, the Indian economy surpassed all expectations by growing at an average annual rate of nearly 9 per cent, if all the three deficits—current account, revenue and fiscal—were reined in, if inflation was on a tight leash, credit must go to Chidambaram for managing the economy efficiently. He is back in the finance ministry (after more than three years of successfully battling the fires of internal security) at a juncture when the Indian economy is exhibiting all signs of early *rigor mortis*. There are great expectations that under his watch, the slide will be arrested and the country will once again capture the trajectory of high growth.

It is widely recognised that India is a country of great paradoxes. Amartya Sen, the Nobel laureate, famously remarked that he had once been told by one of his teachers, the Cambridge economist, Joan Robinson, that "the frustrating thing about India is that whatever you can rightly say about India, the opposite is also true." This is reinforced by the following:

(i) India is second only to the US in the number of affluent households. Yet millions are without homes.

(ii) Italian luxury brand Salvatore Ferragamo is growing at 40 per cent in India while it stagnates in Europe.

(iii) During the last financial year, sales of passenger cars were flat, but expensive brands such as BMW, Audi and Mercedes Benz grew handsomely. All this in a country which boasts a low car density of less than 11 per 1000 people.

(iv) The number of private jets in India is 50 per cent more than that in China and nearly double that of Japan, making it number one in Asia with the largest fleet of private jets. Sadly, more than 85 per cent of the population are yet to experience air travel.

How do we explain this? There are two Indias—an urban rich India and a rural poor Bharat. Some studies suggest that the Gini co-efficient increased in the rural areas since the start of the economic reforms, i.e., rural inequality increased. This was accompanied by an increase in rural-urban inequality as well as regional inequality. Logically, since rapid growth leads to wealth creation in urban areas, it is not unreasonable to expect urban-rural inequality to increase, at least initially. On the other hand, others argue that inter-state inequality or inequality between urban and rural areas is much lower than the inequality across households within their aggregates. However, sustained high levels of growth are possible only if large segments of the population are included in the growth dynamics. The government of India recognised this and for the last few years has been stressing on inclusive growth. The Twelfth Five Year Plan (2012-17) aims at "faster, sustainable and more inclusive growth."

The document "Approach to the Twelfth Five Year Plan" acknowledged the importance of agricultural growth as "an important component for inclusiveness in India." It suggested, on the basis of past experience, that high GDP growth sans commensurate improvement in agriculture would push up inflation and "jeopardise the larger growth process." It clarified that even if agricultural growth is satisfactory, the responsibility for absorbing the growing labour force, "will rest on manufacturing and construction and on the services sectors." This is so as despite the contribution of agriculture to GDP being whittled down to 14 per cent, the share of agriculture in employment is still over 50 per cent. One of the main ingredients for realising inclusive growth is financial inclusion.

What is financial inclusion? The Committee on Financial Inclusion, set up in 2006 under the chairmanship of C. Rangarajan, defined it as "the process of ensuring access to financial services and timely and adequate credit where needed by vulnerable groups such as weaker sections and low income groups at an affordable cost." Another way of looking at the issue is to view it from the following parameters:

(i) Exclusion from the payments' system, i.e., not having a bank account.

(ii) Exclusion from formal credit markets forcing the excluded to seek informal and exorbitant channels of credit.

On both these yardsticks, we fare poorly. According to the 2011 Census, out of a total of 246.9 million households, only 58.7 per cent had access to banking facilities, with about 100 million of the households being excluded. Generally, a discussion on financial inclusion begins and ends with the supply of credit to farmer households. This is partly because of the historical importance of the agricultural sector and partly because there are no reliable estimates of financial inclusion of urban India. There is, therefore, a need to focus on the role of stock exchanges in financial inclusion and employment, and not just limiting it to the involvement of banks and microfinance institutions (MFIs).

There are 27 public sector banks, 22 private banks, 31 foreign banks apart from 86 rural regional banks (RRBs) and 4 local area banks other than cooperative banks in India. While between them, there are thousands of branches, they are not adequate to service the needs of a growing economy. On an average, India has only 6 bank branches per 1,000 sq km, while Brazil has 15 and the US 31.

In 2009, the Reserve Bank of India (RBI) had estimated that 480 million people in India living mostly in its 6,30,000 villages did not have the facility of banking services. It laid down a two-phase programme:

a. All 74,000 villages with a population of more than 2,000 to have access to banks by March 2012, and

b. All 3,48,000 villages with a population of over 1,000, to have banking access by 2013.

The idea was that by March 2013 about 70 per cent of Indian villages would be covered by banking facilities. According to the RBI data, by March 2012, about 98 per cent of villages with a population of over 2,000, have been provided with banking facilities through the opening of about 2,500 branches, about 2,300 ATMs, etc., and the establishment of over 69,000 Business Correspondents (BCs). Consequently, a large number of bank accounts have been opened.

However studies by independent researchers point to a very high percentage—as high as 80 per cent—of these accounts to be inactive. Even if the RBI statistics are taken at face value, a mere opening of accounts cannot be tantamount to financial inclusion. Financial inclusion can be assumed only if the holders of such accounts are able to access all banking services, including loans. On this reckoning, the programme fails the test of financial inclusion. At best, it may have succeeded only in statistical inclusion.

The recent attempts at financial inclusion in terms of 'no-frills accounts' and 'banking correspondents' have had a very modest impact. Most no-frills accounts are dormant. According to the RBI data, there were about 103 million such accounts by March 2012, with an average balance of less than ₹ 1,000. Even though the RBI had advised banks to provide small overdrafts in such accounts, only about 1.5 million accounts or less than 1.5 per cent had been provided this facility. Since a stigma was attached to no-frills accounts, they have been recently rechristened as 'Basic Savings Deposit Accounts' with no minimum balance requirement. Banking correspondents were struggling because of high operational costs, forcing the RBI to enhance their eligibility criteria to include companies with large and widespread retail outlets.

Even though the RBI in its push for financial inclusion mandated in April 2011, that 25 per cent of new branches to be opened by banks will have to be in unbanked rural areas, the statistics show that the share of rural branches has fallen over the years from a high of 59 per cent in 1985 to 36 per cent currently. Since brick-and-mortar branches are increasingly not found viable, 69 banks have been permitted by the RBI to provide mobile banking services. Even though this service is increasing rapidly, its impact is still negligible.

Since about 70 per cent of the banking space is occupied by public sector banks, there is obviously a tremendous room for new private sector banks to enter. In this connection, the move by the RBI in floating a concept paper before finalising guidelines for new private sector banks is commendable. However, this initiative which originated in the Finance Minister's Budget Speech in February 2010, seems to have been dissipated. There is a strong case for laying down clear guidelines for licensing new banks. There is an equally strong case for inducting not 5 or 10 new banks but a much larger number (200 as reportedly suggested by a Deputy Governor of the RBI) to take care of the financing needs of the economy. In this connection what is required is not a blind replication of the existing paradigm—which has had a limited success in fostering financial inclusion—but a bold new approach.

The issue of financial inclusion is tied up closely with employment. It is estimated that there are around 480 million workers in India and their number is increasing by about 10 million per year. Since the agricultural sector is already burdened with a very large population dependent on it, the major chunk of the addition to the labour force will have to be employed in industry or in the services sector. For a variety of reasons, including perhaps labour laws which preempt employment, the organised sector's contribution to job creation has been minimal. Their preference has been to adopt capital intensive methods of production in a labour abundant country. So there will have to be a greater dependence on small and medium enterprises (SMEs) in the manufacturing and services sector to absorb fresh entrants to the job market. The micro, small and medium enterprises (MSMEs) sector in India contributes 45 per cent to the manufacturing output, about 40 per cent of exports and is the second largest employee after agriculture, but is perennially starved for funds. According to the Fourth Census of MSMEs, only about 5 per cent of them obtained finance from institutional sources, 2 per cent were financed by non-institutional sources, leaving in the lurch 93 per cent of the balance that got no finance at all! The global experience (e.g., the US) has been that small banks are more effective in providing credit to small businesses. The policy guidelines should encourage the establishment of such banks.

One of the agencies involved in financial inclusion are MFIs. They lend money to both the rural and the urban poor without collateral. Micro-finance has shot into the limelight of late, due to entirely wrong reasons. In a country where the bulk of the population does not have meaningful access to banks, MFIs over the last decade and a half, have provided a lifeline to about 30 million households who are otherwise outside the banking system. If the Self-Help-Group-bank linkage programme is included and adjustment made for overlap, the number of households covered by micro-credit was estimated to be more than 50 million in 2010. This is huge considering that according to the 2011 Census, more than 40 per cent of households did not avail themselves of any banking services. Commercial banks as they are structured today are unable to service the requirements of micro-credit to those who have no collateral.

MFIs have brought banking to the doorstep of the borrower whereas commercial banks typically expect the borrower to come to their doorstep. A global survey of microfinance by the Economist Intelligence Unit (EIU) of 54 countries, ranked India at the fourth position in 2009. Because of the activities of some MFIs, there is an attempt to strangle the entire sector, as a result of which India slipped to eighth position in 2010 and slumped to a rank of 27 in 2011. Onerous conditions are sought to be placed on their functioning. An impression is being created that rates of interest at which they lend should be capped as they are earning usurious profits.

The fact of the matter is that out of about 250 MFIs that reported information in 2010, about one-third were making losses. A global comparison showed that on average, return on assets of Indian MFIs was 0.7 per cent—considerably less than Brazil: 6.4 per cent, Mexico: 3 per cent and Indonesia: 3.1 per cent. So while some larger, older MFIs in India may have been enjoying substantial profits, most of the others were not. It is axiomatic that extraordinary profits garnered from poor customers cannot be accepted. At the same time, formulating public policies on the basis of a few outliers is fraught with a number of unintended consequences.

The most extreme consequence will be that MFIs will vacate the credit space which will gratefully be re-occupied by the local moneylenders with all their associated ills. Another possibility is that MFIs will perforce have to borrow at a higher rate of interest from unconventional sources and therefore their lending rates would go up rather than come down. A third consequence will be that only the very large MFIs will survive. The fourth and extreme possibility is that the entire industry may be wiped out.

There is no doubt that there is need for regulation. The RBI's response was to appoint a committee. The Malegam Committee came up with a generally comprehensive report containing useful recommendations. However, some of its conclusions/recommendations seemed to defy accepted norms and are counter-intuitive. For instance, it concluded that smaller MFIs are able to access funds at a cheaper rate than the larger ones. It recommended a ceiling at which MFIs could lend—24 per cent. The committee then went on to stipulate a maximum margin—the difference between the cost of funds of the MFI and its lending rate. It recommended a margin of 12 per cent for small MFIs and 10 per cent for large MFIs.

These recommendations were entirely unrealistic as the rate of interest charged by MFIs will depend upon its cost of funds. Given the tight monetary policy stance of the RBI, the interest rates are generally moving up. Considering that many small MFIs were borrowing in 2010 at about 16 per cent, with the addition of a margin of 12 per cent the cap of 24 per cent would be breached. While the RBI raised the cap to 26 per cent when it notified the Malegam Committee recommendations in May 2011, it did not address the fundamental flaw that fixing both the overall cap as well as the margin was hopelessly contradictory. Fortunately, the RBI in early August 2012 realised the folly and removed the overall cap and stipulated a maximum margin of 12 per cent for small MFIs and 10 per cent for larger ones. By then considerable damage was done as a number of MFIs went out of business, the sector's growth was severely curtailed and many reports indicate that moneylenders are back in business with a bang.

Capital market reforms have the potential to create at least 10 million jobs (direct and indirect) over the next five years. Competition in capital markets will play a vital role as it did in the telecom sector. Thanks to the liberal policy adopted in the telecom sector, today there are many service providers catering to a whopping 900 million subscribers at rates which are probably the lowest in the world. Similarly, capital markets could target at least 100 million customers instead of 15 million today (number of depository accounts currently) within a pre-defined timeframe. This will happen if there are multiple exchanges competing to provide services to the investing public in India.

For penetration, it is essential to develop an 'India Model' for equities, bonds, currencies and commodities. Today, only about 1.5 per cent of the population holds demat accounts, of which about six lakh are active on a given day, representing less than 0.06 per cent of the population. The 'India Model' will ensure a penetration of the services of capital markets on a scale similar to that of the telecom sector. This can easily be achieved as we now have world-class regulators, technology, clearing, settlement and depository systems. What is missing is product innovation because of inadequate competition in the exchange space resulting in complacency in the ecosystem.

In the 1930s, economist J.M. Keynes likened stock exchanges to casinos and was of the view that these exchanges, like casinos "should in the public interest, be inaccessible and expensive." Since then reforms such as the shift from 'The Open Outcry Trading to Screen Based Trading' and de-mutualisation have helped to sharpen the role of exchanges in economic development. Economic growth hinges on an efficient financial sector that aggregates savings and harnesses these savings for productive investment. This function becomes all the more relevant for a country like India which has a high savings rate and is seeking to develop its economy on a sustainable basis.

The potential of financial markets for economic development has been under-rated in India. For example, stock exchanges can play a very important role in not only bringing capital to new ventures but also in providing investment choices for savers and in mitigating risks. Stock exchanges can substitute as well as complement banks in the mobilisation and use of savings. But how effective have they been in India?

Some peculiarities of the Indian capital market are:

(i) Equity derivatives comprise 5 to 7 per cent of total turnover in the US and EU. In India, it is two-thirds of the market turnover.

(ii) Interest rate derivatives constitute 80 to 90 per cent of turnover in the US and EU. In India it is negligible.

(iii) The corporate bond market is in its infancy despite attempts by the government to kick start it.

The regulations of 2006, under the Securities Contracts Regulation Act (SCRA), were well-intentioned. According to the regulations, no single person or entity can own more than 5 per cent shares in a stock exchange (except some financial institutions that were permitted to hold up to 15 per cent). Theoretically this was a sound requirement, as it sought to prevent concentration of ownership. However, its implementation by the regulator was designed to protect existing players by creating an insurmountable entry barrier.

It become an entry barrier as the regulator was not giving adequate time or the full range of products for new entrants to become viable. Unlike in the banking or insurance sector, where the concerned regulators permitted up to 10 years to bring down the shareholding to 10 per cent/26 per cent, respectively, and allowed all products to be covered in the interim period, the manner of implementation by the regulator of stock exchanges had given rise to a *de facto* monopoly which was a totally unintended, undesirable result of the policy of corporatisation and demutualisation of exchanges. The extent of the monopoly can be gauged from the fact that although there were, for the record, two country-wide exchanges till July 2012, one of them had a market share of 97 per cent in products other than currency derivatives.

Today, more than 90 per cent of the trade in exchanges is confined to only 10 cities and 100 companies and over 70 per cent of total volume is in the cash settled F&O segment. For true financial inclusion, products for masses across multi-asset classes should be made available across the country, and this could increase penetration of the capital markets to many more cities, towns and even *tehsils*.

Our aim should be to channelise at least 10 per cent of estimated annual domestic savings of $ 50,000 crore to multiple investment options by expanding the reach of the of the fixed income secondary markets for government and corporate bonds and creating an SME exchange segment based on a hub and spoke model for high national penetration. Ten per cent of the total savings, which is $ 5,000 crore per annum, is substantial when compared with $ 4,500 crore of FDI last year.

The regulations of 2012 (Stock Exchanges and Clearing Corporation Regulations) have tried to codify some of the grey areas. For instance, in order to promote competition, it provides three years to new entrants to dilute their stock holdings to the stipulated maximum. These regulations, which have repealed the earlier 2006 regulations, have however imposed certain conditions which go beyond the Indian Companies Act, 1956. Some of these conditions e.g., transfer of 25 per cent of net profits of stock exchanges every year to the clearing corporations, certain restrictions on key management personnel etc., would ultimately result in reducing the attractiveness of investments in stock exchanges and thereby limit competition as prospective entrants may not find it commercially attractive.

Generally, a discussion on financial inclusion gets limited to the banking sector—the percentage of population that has access to banks, the number of accounts opened, etc. Banks are, however, only one instrument for attaining financial inclusion. In any case, an undue focus on the number of bank accounts is not a valid test for financial inclusion. In fact, an over-emphasis on this parameter can at best lead to complacency and statistical inclusion. It is not generally recognised that MFIs can play a pivotal role in taking care of the credit requirements of both rural and urban households which have no collateral to offer. Stock exchanges also can function as effective supplements to banks in channelising savings for productive investment.

6 Urbanisation and India's Economic Development

Isher Judge Ahluwalia

I must begin by thanking the editor for giving me the honour to contribute to the festschrift volume for P. Chidambaram, one of our most talented and brilliant political leaders, who was not only part of the Dream Team of the 1990s but is spearheading economic reforms, once again, as Finance Minister. I have known Chidambaram for over 25 years and have admired his ability to take on the challenges of policy making when in government, and equally, his facility to analyse and criticise constructively when in opposition. Those who hope to influence policies through the power of ideas and evidence by engaging in policy-oriented research, find it very rewarding to interact with political leaders like Chidambaram.

The challenges of urbanisation in India have not been adequately discussed in the context of the debate on the overall strategy of development. As of 2011, 31 per cent of India's population is urban. This is admittedly much lower than in many countries such as Indonesia (45%), China (48%), Korea (83%), Mexico (78%) and Brazil (87%), but is projected to increase to 40 per cent by 2031. Having increased from 28.6 crore in 2001 to 37.6 crore in 2011, urban population in India is projected to reach 60.0 crore by 2031, and the absolute numbers are staggering.

There is an urgent need to improve the quality of life of those living in Indian cities within an inclusive framework of planning. Besides, India needs to make its cities attractive destinations for large-scale investments from industry and service sectors. Only then can Indian cities act as engines of growth.

It is also important to develop a global outlook which recognises the importance of cities in exerting global influences as well as attracting and retaining global flow of ideas, investments and people to any country. World over, cities are becoming more and more globally competitive not only by providing an appropriate climate for investments but also by being highly functional and retaining their specific cultural roots in a global context. Indian cities, on the other hand, are slipping on global competitiveness scale, as discussed later in this paper.

I have chosen to write on urbanisation because I wish to emphasise that India's growth momentum cannot be sustained if urbanisation is not actively facilitated. As Finance Minister of India, Chidambaram can provide effective leadership in facilitating urbanisation for sustained growth.

Rapid Growth and Urbanisation

India has been among the fastest growing economies for some time now. Even with a distinct slowing down in 2011-12, average growth of GDP from 2001 to 2012 was 7.7 per cent per annum. This growth was dominantly led by the services sector, but industrial sector also played a major part. The economy is currently experiencing a downturn which is because of a combination of the adverse international economic environment and some home-grown problems. The Twelfth Five Year Plan has highlighted the importance of regaining the momentum of growth for inclusive development, setting the target for the period 2012-2017 at 8 per cent per annum. The plan has also emphasised the role to be played by an investor-friendly policy regime in bringing this about. Whether this targeted growth is achieved or not, even a conservative projection would suggest that India can record a growth rate of GDP of around 7 per cent per annum over the next 10 years. Once again, this growth will come from industry and services sectors, as agriculture will grow at most at 4 to 4.5 per cent per annum.

The urban share of GDP is projected to increase from its current estimated 66 per cent to 75 per cent by 2031.[1] Investors look for economies of agglomeration in cities and in turn contribute to these economies. Both market forces and the government play an important role in generating these economies. In the absence of urban planning and city management,

1. *The Mid-Term Appraisal of the Eleventh Five Year Plan* puts this share at 62 per cent in 2009-10. Given the importance of this share, it is high time CSO provides official authenticity to this figure.

investors will find diseconomies of congestion and environmental degradation instead of economies of agglomeration and they will contribute further to the deterioration in the standards of urban living.

The state of public service delivery in Indian cities is abysmal. This is as true for the availability and quality of drinking water as it is for solid waste management, or for the state of urban roads or street lights. The service level benchmarks were first prescribed by the Ministry of Urban Development, Government of India, only in 2008, but even now they tend to be observed more in the breach.

A few cities like Bangalore, Hyderabad, Chennai, Mumbai and Ahmedabad have acted as engines of growth in the past decade. But these cities are showing the stress of inadequate infrastructure of urban roads, public transport, affordable housing and water and sanitation. Combined with weaknesses in delivery mechanisms, this has resulted in a significant deterioration in the state of public services and proliferation of slums. While about a quarter of the urban population of India is estimated to be living in slums, the proportion is much higher in metropolitan cities (with population of 0.1 crore and above), the worst case being that of Mumbai where more than 50 per cent of the population lives in slums. Not all who live in slums are poor, however. Some not-so-poor also find shelter in slums because the market for affordable housing is heavily distorted by multiple regulations including those pertaining to rent control. Urban poverty is emerging as a major challenge with 25 per cent of the urban population estimated to be poor.

India needs rejuvenation of existing cities as well as creation of new cities as engines of growth if she is to keep her tryst with inclusive and rapid growth on a sustainable basis. Since the private sector will play an important role in exploiting opportunities for economic growth in the years to come, it is very important to build synergy between the processes of socioeconomic development and spatial planning.

As drivers of national economy, cities should be able to enjoy fruits of economic and technological success without having to disregard their environmental, human and cultural capital. Even the best of Indian cities rank pretty low in a number of indices that have been prepared on global competitiveness of cities worldwide. Only 4 cities from India made it to the Global City Index (GCI) 2012 which combines attributes of business activitiy, information exchange, political engagement, human capital and cultural experience in ranking a total of 66 cities. Indian cities with their respective ranks were: Mumbai (45), New Delhi (48), Bangalore (58) and Kolkata (66), and among these, only Mumbai improved its ranking from 47 in 2010. The Global City Competitiveness Index prepared by the Economist Intelligence Unit (EIU) in 2012 uses somewhat different attributes in ranking 120 of the world's major cities, i.e., economic strength, physical capital, financial maturity, institutional effectiveness, social and cultural capital, human capital, environmental factors, vulnerability to natural hazards, and global appeal. Besides the four cities selected by GCI, Chennai, Ahmedabad and Pune are included in the EIU group. An interesting finding of this study is that mid-sized cities are set to drive the world economy due to their growing appeal to residents. This offers tremendous promise for India. Urban planning has to be directed towards making at least some Indian cities globally more visible and competitive and locally much more functional and inclusive. The size of city has little to do with its global appeal or competitiveness; it has more to do with ingenuity and innovation in running the city or enhancing certain special assets of a city that may be cultural, natural, built or environmental.

Expansion of city boundaries and large villages growing into towns *in situ*, are forces which call for urban planning to accommodate rapid growth and inclusive development. It requires conservation and protection of natural resources and heritage as well as an integrated approach in planning for transport and land use with special focus on public transport and affordable housing. It is important to create conditions in which the development of new slums is ruled out and also redevelop the existing slums with better linkages between the formal and the informal sections of the city. It is equally important to build greater synergies with the rural sector. Urban planning provides an overall framework within which larger investments in urban infrastructure and better governance can ensure that good quality public services are delivered to all.

Similarly, new cities have to be planned along the transport and growth corridors in an inclusive manner. Work on the Western Dedicated Freight Corridor from Delhi to Mumbai is in progress and is expected to be completed by end-2017. This is where Delhi-Mumbai Industrial Corridor

(DMIC) is being planned for manufacturing-led urbanisation through developing seven greenfield cities. These cities must be planned such that they avoid the problems faced by the existing metropolitan cities. Better connectivity must link numerous existing cities to new cities, attracting investments in manufacturing and logistics.

There is a growing realisation that urbanisation is inevitable for India in its current stage of high growth and structural transformation, and it has to be facilitated. But there is inadequate understanding of an equally important phenomenon, i.e., that fortunes of the rural sector are crucially linked to the quality of industrialisation and urbanisation. For example, the Eastern Dedicated Freight Corridor will link Kolkata to Ludhiana, and will pass through Dadri in Greater Noida near Delhi where it meets the Western Corridor. As cities come up along the corridor, the fast track transport network would make it possible for the northern states to transport their agricultural produce to Mumbai as well as Kolkata thereby fostering multiple rural-urban links in the economy. Similarly, modernisation of the retail sector including FDI in retail can be orchestrated to encourage investments in logistics and back-end infrastructure which strengthens rural-urban integration.

Punjab is a good example of adverse consequences of inaction in building rural-urban synergy. The agricultural prosperity resulting from the Green Revolution of the 1970s was not harnessed through an industrial strategy which would build upon the rich agricultural base, provide fillip to agricultural modernisation and support the resulting structural evolution, while reaping the benefits of a good road network established by the legendary Chief Minister S. Partap Singh Kairon in the 1950s and early 1960s. The state did not put in place investments in urban infrastructure for the delivery of urban services in subsequent years, such that industry and services sectors would thrive. As a result, not only was industrial growth slow but agricultural growth also stagnated, while water table and soil quality deteriorated at a rapid rate, lowering Punjab's per capita income ranking among the larger states of India from number 1 in 1980-81 to number 6 in 2010-11.

A major challenge that has emerged in the context of the accelerating growth rate of the Indian economy is that of scarcity of skills. It took only 10 years of economic growth at close to 8 per cent per annum during 2001-

2011 to show how unprepared India is with respect to the demand for skilled manpower. India's current phase of demographic transition is such that the population of working age as a proportion of the total population will continue to rise pretty much until 2040 and even then begin to decline only modestly. This is in contrast to China which is already experiencing a decline in the share of this population since 2010 and Brazil where the decline begins in 2020. The challenge is to convert India's demographic opportunity into a demographic dividend. For this, the young population needs to be empowered with higher education and skills which are in demand, taking note of the sectors and areas in which demand is growing.

At the same time, it is necessary that employment opportunities expand rapidly as growth becomes more labour intensive (because of a more open economy environment and assuming that labour laws will provide greater flexibility in hiring and firing). Also, opportunities to invest must also increase through an improvement in the investment climate. Only then can the growing proportion of the working age population be gainfully engaged in high-productivity jobs and/or setting up their own businesses. Since 80 per cent of the population is currently engaged in economic activity in the informal sector, skill development and promotion of self-employment has to take cognisance of this feature of India's manufacturing sector and also of social security provision for workers in the informal sector. If the challenge of livelihoods and social protection is not addressed effectively, the demographic 'dividend' has the potential of turning into a demographic disaster with maximum impact in urban areas.

Investment Requirements of Urban Infrastructure

A High Powered Expert Committee (HPEC) on Urban Infrastructure and Services was set up by the Government of India in 2008 to estimate the investments needed to bridge the urban infrastructure deficit over a 20-year period going forward. The committee submitted its report in March 2011. I had the privilege to chair the committee.

Taking as the point of departure the service delivery norms which had been prepared by the Ministry of Urban Development in 2008 (Table 6.1) and assuming that these norms will be universally applicable, the committee prepared the estimate with the further assumption that the coverage of services will be extended to currently un-served and underserved population and to the additional urban population that will come on board over the 20-year period. The resulting estimate for the investment requirement for urban infrastructure to be incurred during 2011-2031 is ₹ 34 lakh crore at 2009-10 prices (equivalent to $ 717 billion at the then prevailing exchange rate), not including the cost of land. This estimate does not cover education, electricity and health care. The detailed estimates for the major sectors are given in Figure 6.1.

Table 6.1

Service Standards

Water Supply	100 per cent piped water, 24x7 flow, and 135 lpcd consumption per capita	
Sewerage	Underground sewerage with 100 per cent collection and treatment of waste water	
Solid Waste	100 per cent collection, transportation and treatment	
Urban Roads	Area under roads (per cent)	11 for cities
		7 for towns
	Road density (km per sq km)	12.25 for cities
		7 for towns
Storm Water Drains	Network covering 100 per cent road length on both sides of the road	
Urban Transport	• Rail-based and road-based Mass Rapid Transit System for cities with population of 1 mn and above • City bus service for smaller cities and towns	
Street Lighting	• Illuminance: 35 Lux for all cities and towns • 40 m spacing for major roads • 45 m for collector roads • 50 m for access road spaces	
Traffic Support Infrastructure	Type of Infrastructure	For cities with population (over)
	Intelligent transport systems and area traffic control	50,00,000
	Vehicular and pedestrian underpasses	100,000
	Parking systems	100,000
	Bus Terminals	50,000
	Bus Depots	20,000

Source: Ministry of Urban Development, 2008

Figure 6.1

Urban Infrastructure Investment Requirement: 2012 to 2031
(₹ Lakh Crore)

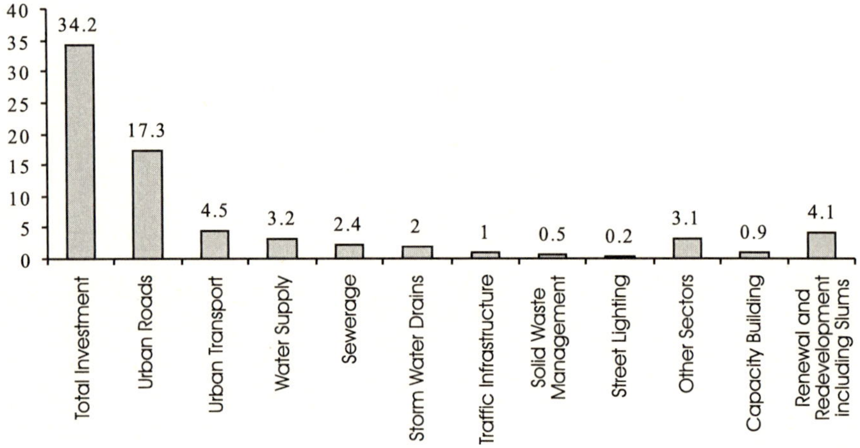

Source: HPEC (Ahluwalia) Report, 2011

The largest requirement of investment (51 per cent of the total) is for urban roads (Figure 6.2). This is because the backlog of urban roads in Indian cities is very high, ranging between 42 per cent for cities with population of over 50 lakh to 84 per cent for cities with population of less than 1 lakh.[2] Urban transport and traffic support infrastructure account for another 16 per cent of the total. Thus, urban roads, transport and traffic support infrastructure together account for two-thirds of the total urban infrastructure investment requirement. By contrast, the investment requirement of water supply, sewerage, storm water drains, and solid waste management, altogether accounts for only 24 per cent of the total, i.e., ₹ 8.1 lakh crore. If allowance is made for renewal and redevelopment (including slums) and for capacity building, the total cumulative investment over the 20-year period amounts to ₹ 39.2 lakh crore ($ 827 billion) at 2009-10 prices. In addition, the cost of operation and maintenance of the existing and new assets is estimated at ₹ 20 lakh crore ($ 422 billion).

2. If the assumption with respect to population density is higher, road density lower, and/or FSI larger, this will lower the investment requirement for roads.

Figure 6.2

Share of Major Sectors in Urban Infrastructure Investment Requirement (Per cent)

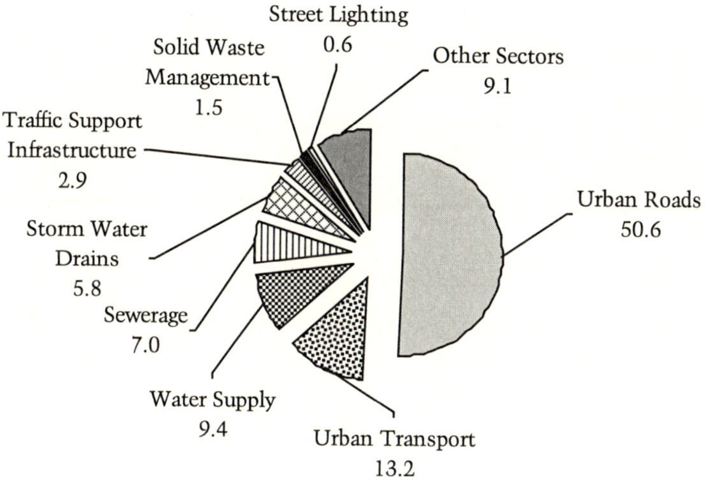

Source: HPEC (Ahluwalia) Report, 2011

Considering the current low level of investment in urban infrastructure, this amounts to a projected increase of 15 per cent per annum in the Twelfth Five Year Plan (2012-13 to 2016-17), 12 per cent per annum during the Thirteenth Five Year Plan (2017-19 to 2021-22) and 8 per cent per annum in the two subsequent Plan periods (2022-23 to 2031-32). If this investment scenario were to materialise, capital expenditure in the urban sector will increase from its very low level of 0.7 per cent of GDP in 2011-2012 to 1.14 per cent of GDP in 2021-22 and will be sustained at that ratio up to 2031-32.The total urban expenditure is estimated to increase from 1.6 per cent of GDP in 2011-12 to 2.1 per cent of GDP in 2021-22 and then stay at that ratio up to 2031-32 (increasing at the same rate as GDP).

A better perspective on urban infrastructure investment requirement is provided by comparing the 0.7 per cent of GDP in 2011-12 with the 2 per cent of GDP which the Government of India spent on subsidies on fertilisers and petroleum products in the same year. Similarly, in 2011-12, state governments' budgets absorbed losses of close to 1 per cent of GDP arising from only the distribution segment of the power sector. Against this background, the investment increase on urban infrastructure from 0.7 per cent of GDP in 2011-12 to 1.14 per cent of GDP in 2021-22 is very small indeed. However, it is important to emphasise that the investments alone will not ensure public service delivery to the requisite standards unless better planning, financing and governance mechanisms are put in place, which involve systemic reforms.

Implications for Planning, Financing and Governance

The large investments needed to bridge the urban infrastructure investment deficit have to be planned and financed within the existing distribution of power and financial resources that exists in the current federal structure. This poses several problems since the principal player for city infrastructure has to be the city government, while there is need for close cooperation of the state government and active engagement of the Government of India.

The state government is currently responsible for many parts of the urban infrastructure including water and sanitation but especially roads which connect cities with the rural hinterland and other cities, and also for electricity. This is because the Constitution of India originally placed the responsibility for urban development on state governments. The Government of India provides rail connectivity and linkage with national highways. While the state governments have tended to neglect urban development, the Government of India has also looked the other way. The political economy of development in India has remained dominantly focussed on rural development. In the minds of many politicians, India continues to live in its villages even though more and more Indians are shifting to cities and towns. For the first time in 2005, the Government of India proactively engaged in the process of urban development through the Jawaharlal Nehru National Urban Renewal Mission (JNNURM).

In 1992, the 74th Constitutional Amendment formally recognised Urban Local Bodies (ULBs) as the third tier of government. It recommended that state governments transfer to local governments a set of specified functions, assigning to them the responsibility for the provision of water, solid waste management, waste water treatment, storm water drains, etc. On funding, the Constitutional Amendment recommended that State

Finance Commissions (SFCs) be set up by the state governments to spell out the principles for sharing/devolving a part of the revenue of the state government to local governments.

Effective devolution requires transfer of functions, functionaries and funds. In the event, there has been some progress on transferring the functions but little if any on transferring funds. As for transferring functionaries, again, there has been very little action in making municipal functionaries employees of the cities and recruited by the cities as opposed to being employees of the state government posted to cities.

The expectation was that SFCs will follow the exemplary tradition of the Central Finance Commission (CFC) in the quality of their membership and recommendations. This has not happened. As a result, the mandates of ULBs have remained unfunded. The third tier of government remains hamstrung by the lack of finances.

The limited financial strength of the ULBs is clearly a major problem which can only be solved by: (i) greater devolution from the state governments which unfortunately has not happened, and (ii) greater use of their own power to raise resources, especially through property tax collection and user charges. Effort in both areas has been weak in spite of the fact that JNNURM has put property tax and user charges among 'mandatory' reforms.

It is sometimes argued that capital market and public-private partnership (PPP) can provide external sources of financing for urban infrastructure and this is indeed true. But the ability to mobilise these sources of financing is itself contingent on the ability of the local government to evolve a revenue model which enables repayment of the loans raised from the capital market and/or generate returns on investment. The latter could be done, for example, by levying appropriate user charges for services rendered or by realisation of some of the increase in land value through betterment charges or allowing private concessionaire to develop land commercially as part of the PPP project.

A municipal finance list should specify taxes that are exclusively the domain of local governments. ULBs must be empowered with exclusive taxes to increase their revenue base. Property tax reform has been on the agenda for quite some time, but despite the use of GIS maps for better coverage and recognition of the need for better valuation methods such as area based method for assessment, progress on updating of property registers and on transition to more effective valuation methods has been slow, and state government control on the fixation and revision of rates and exemptions has tended to considerably reduce the autonomy of ULBs. It is also important to levy water and sewerage charges separately from property tax.

An important source of generation of internal revenue of ULBs could be devolution of pre-specified percentage of states' revenues from all taxes on goods and services. A good opportunity is provided by the GST (goods and services tax) when the Constitutional Amendment is undertaken, where a small proportion of GST can be earmarked for transfer to local governments.

The ULBs must also have effective power to levy user charges to cover their O&M cost. A Municipal Service Regulator at the state level can be assigned the responsibility for recommending revision in user charges regularly. Other conventional sources of non-tax revenue such as trade licensing fee, parking fee and advertising revenue, etc., must be combined with land-based financing sources such as land use conversion charge, betterment charges, impact fees, pricing for Floor Space Index beyond a standard entitlement, etc., to strengthen the financial base of ULBs.

The state government also needs to provide institutional support, e.g., by training municipal personnel in accrual based double entry financial book keeping, encouraging regular audits, setting up a Local Funds Audit Commission and establishing financial intermediaries, e.g., the Tamil Nadu Urban Development Fund (TNUDF) or Karnataka Urban Infrastructure Development and Finance Corporation (KUIDFC), which can facilitate planning, financing and implementation of projects. In the case of smaller ULBs, the TNUDF was able to encourage pooled financing through the capital market.

The practice of municipal bond financing for urban infrastructure began in India in the late 1990s with a municipal bond issue of ₹ 125 crore by the Bangalore Municipal Corporation in 1997 and a landmark bond issue (not backed by a state government guarantee) of ₹ 100 crore by the Ahmedabad Municipal Corporation in 1998. Between February, 2001 when municipal bonds were allowed 'tax free' status and December, 2005 when JNNURM was launched, over ₹ 600 crore was raised through municipal bonds by a number of cities including Ahmedabad, Hyderabad, Visakhapatnam and Chennai. The fact that tax-free municipal bonds were subject to a fixed interest rate cap of 8 per cent per annum, however, meant that as the market dynamics changed in an environment of rising interest rates in 2007-08, the appetite for these bonds diminished significantly.

Pooled finance bond market for small and medium towns and cities had emerged in the first half of the 2000s. The first such bond was issued for ₹ 304 crore in Tamil Nadu in 2002, facilitated by the TNUDF, pooling projects from 13 ULBs (backed by the escrow of property tax and other collections). Encouraged by the success of this issue and a similar one facilitated by the KUIDFC in Karnataka, a Pooled Finance Development Fund (PFDF) was set up by the Government of India in 2006, aimed at supporting small and medium towns for raising funds in the capital market. But this fund suffered the same fate because of the fixed interest rate cap. Some have argued that the availability of JNNURM funds, especially under its sub-Mission UIDSSMT for small and medium towns on very soft terms acted as a disincentive for ULBs to mobilise finances through pooled finance bonds on their own.

Another policy/planning area which needs to be brought in focus is that of integrated planning of transport and land use. By modernising the multiple laws including those pertaining to town planning and land acquisition, state governments can encourage integrated planning of land use and transportation. Departments of Urban Development, Urban Transport, and Housing and Poverty Alleviation will need to be combined into one, or work with much greater coordination than is the case at present. Public transport and low income housing will have to be explicitly planned for. Given the expanding scale and scope of investments, there will also be need for regional planning, for which the District Planning Committees and the Metropolitan Planning Committees will have to be rejuvenated.

JNNURM: An Assessment

In December 2005, the Government of India launched the Jawaharlal Nehru National Urban Renewal Mission (JNNURM) for a period of 7 years (subsequently extended by 2 years) to address the growing challenges of urbanisation to help the state governments and ULBs in fulfilling the mandate of the Constitutional Amendment of 1992. JNNURM channels resources to ULBs for improving urban governance and by locating financial resources at the city level, seeks to enable the city to make a programme of urban renewal and inclusive urban development. By combining this with incentives to the state governments to carry out the necessary reforms in legislation and regulations pertaining to municipal planning and functioning, the mission has tried to get the state governments on board.

The objective of JNNURM is to ensure provision of urban infrastructure for service delivery on a sustainable basis by partially funding the projects and linking such support with specific reforms at the state and the ULB level. This is to be done within an inclusive framework with due attention to providing basic services for the poor. JNNURM has four sub-missions, of which (i) Urban Infrastructure and Governance (UIG) and (ii) Basic Services for the Urban Poor (BSUP) each covers the 65 cities known as Mission cities; while the other two, i.e., (iii) Urban Infrastructure Development in Small and Medium Towns (UIDSSMT) and (iv) Integrated Housing and Slum Development Programme (IHSDP) are meant for other cities.

The Government of India committed ₹ 66,000 crore under JNNURM as its share in the total investment of over ₹ 100,000 crore for a pool of selected projects to be proposed by the ULBs and state governments and to be approved by the Government of India. The state government and the ULB were expected to make their specified parallel financial contributions for each project.

Mandatory reforms at the level of the state government included implementing the decentralisation measures as envisaged in the 74th Constitutional Amendment Act, repealing the Urban Land Ceiling & Regulation Act (ULCRA), reforming Rent Control laws by balancing the interests of landlords and tenants, rationalising Stamp Duty to bring it down to no more than 5 per cent within 7 years, earmarking budgets of the

ULBs for basic services to the urban poor, enacting Public Disclosure Law and Community Participation Law, and associating elected ULBs with city planning functions.

For ULBs, mandatory reforms included adoption of accrual based double entry system of accounting, e-governance using GIS, MIS or IT applications, property tax reform using GIS, and recovery of O&M through user charge, etc. In addition, there were a number of optional reforms such as earmarking 20-25 per cent of developed land in all housing projects for economically weaker sections and low income groups of society, encouraging PPP and introducing computerised processes of registration of land and property. The mission used project-oriented fund transfers as a driver of change for reforms in the second and third tiers of government to improve the state of Indian cities.

With the ambition to make India slum-free, the Government of India launched a pilot phase of Rajiv Awas Yojana (RAY) in June 2011. The scheme mandates providing property rights to slum dwellers and assistance to state governments for taking up projects for *in-situ* slum rehabilitation. In the event, RAY has received tepid response from the banking sector, which suggests that residential vulnerabilities of the urban poor will have to be addressed within an integrated framework of urban planning.

Table 6.2 summarises the status of physical progress as well as financial approvals, commitments and releases under the two sub-Missions of UIG and UIDSSMT under JNNURM as of end-January, 2013. Of the 1358 projects approved, 484 have been completed. The total cost of these projects was ₹ 75,722 crore, of which ₹ 39,905 crore was the share of the Government of India, but only ₹ 28,411 crore was released because of the slower than expected pace of implementation.

Water and sanitation projects received high priority, getting ₹ 23,144 crore, i.e., 81 per cent of the total funds disbursed. Once all the projects are completed, total spending on water and sanitation would be almost ₹ 59,000 crore. Although it forms a large share of the total spending under JNNURM, this is only about 7 per cent of the total requirement for bridging the infrastructure investment deficit, as estimated by the HPEC (Ahluwalia) Committee over the 20-year period.

Table 6.2

*JNNURM: An Overview of UIG and UIDSSMT**

Sector	Total Projects	Completed Projects	Total Cost (₹ crore)	Government of India		
				Funds Committed (₹ crore)	Funds Released (₹ crore)	Funds Released (% share)
Water Supply	610	231	29,390	17,274	13,245	47
Sewerage	201	31	17,798	9,348	6,010	21
Drainage/Storm Water Drains	141	44	9,162	4,152	2,991	11
Solid Waste Management	100	25	2,315	1,305	891	3
Roads/Flyovers/RoB	220	124	9,304	4,275	2,847	10
Other Urban Transport including MRTS	39	14	5,992	2,739	2,069	7
Others**	47	15	1,761	813	351	1
Total	1358	484	75,722	39,905	28,411	100

Note: * As of end-January, 2013.

** Besides urban renewal and parking lots, "other sectors" include heritage area development and preservation of water bodies for UIG Sub-Mission and preservation of soil erosion for UIDSSMT sub-Mission.

Source: Ministry of Urban Development, Government of India.

The priority given to water and sanitation under JNNURM is not surprising and is entirely desirable. This is because water and sanitation is an urgent need on public health grounds and also because building infrastructure for water and sanitation involves digging of roads to lay the pipelines and has to precede the task of building roads. The committee has highlighted the shortage of urban roads and estimated that 50 per cent of the deficit in urban infrastructure investment is in urban roads. But preparing road projects and the process of bidding and award of contracts tends to be more time-consuming because of issues of land encroachment, delay in land acquisition, and obtaining permission and clearances. While it is extremely important to cut short the delays in getting roads in place, work on water and sanitation must take precedence.

A number of projects were initiated in the water and sanitation sector under JNNURM, but not all have progressed at the same rate or yielded similar results. The integrated water development project to deliver water 24x7 under PPP in Nagpur was an ambitious project under JNNURM.

It has suffered roadblocks in raising user charges to cover O&M costs to ensure economic viability. But the project is making progress albeit at a slower rate than originally envisaged. The waste water treatment plants in Navi Mumbai, integrated solid waste management programmes in Coimbatore, Rajkot and Kanpur, and BRTS (Bus Rapid Transit System) projects in Ahmedabad and Bhopal, showcase some of the successes of JNNURM. The Mission has certainly raised the ambition of Indian cities. The most important contribution of JNNURM has been to inject a new dynamism in the much neglected urban sector and establish credibility that the state of service delivery in Indian cities can be transformed.

Among the many challenges that emerged in implementing the JNNURM, the principal one related to enforcing the conditionality of reforms in a project-based financing approach. It was difficult enough to measure the reform being asked for, but it was even more difficult to enforce the conditionality. For example, failure on the part of the state government to implement a reform could technically hold back funding for a project in a city or town when the planning and implementation of the project was all in keeping with the commitments made at the project level. When a state failed to meet its commitment on reforms, the Government of India had a difficult choice. Not releasing the next instalment would mean letting an infrastructure project languish for no fault of the project managers at the ULB level, while releasing the funds would create moral hazard for other state governments who were complying with reforms in other similar projects. This inevitably led to delays in releases and time and cost over-runs. It also meant that the pace of reform did not match the promise, and was uneven across ULBs and state governments.

There was very little progress on the reform of the Rent Control Act. While over 25 states had already repealed ULCRA (Urban Land Ceiling & Regulation Act) at the time JNNURM was launched, this 'reform' was deceptive, as the repeal was prospective and all cases already in court continued to be governed by the earlier Act. First steps to reform property tax regimes were taken in many states, but there is large variation in the state of reform beyond getting GIS maps. Progress on decentralisation measures in the spirit of the 74th Amendment was very poor. In particular, the slow progress on the setting up of District Planning Committees and Metropolitan Planning Committees has taken its toll on planning for transport connectivity. There was also slow progress on the reservation of land for housing for economically weaker sections of society.

A second major challenge was the lack of capacity to prepare and implement projects in urban infrastructure within the framework of a development plan. City Development Plans (CDPs) were hastily put together by officials with little training in urban planning, and specific projects were prepared with inadequate technical background or appreciation of financial issues. The challenge of urban development not only requires skills in planning, engineering, finance and management but a stable manpower which can learn from experience and training and put it to effective use. A state-level municipal cadre is extremely important in driving the process of planning, project preparation and implementation, and city management. The cadres are important for building, retaining and utilising human resource capacity for urban management.

A third challenge was the need for a legislative framework which would facilitate land acquisition for urban development. The Land Acquisition Act of 1894 has been massively misused and a new Bill has been presented in Parliament which has generated heated debate on this contentious issue. Legislations relating to urban planning (town planning, regional and metropolitan planning) are also in desperate need of modernisation. Gujarat and Maharashtra have amended the Bombay Town Planning Act of 1915 and Gujarat has successfully used Town Planning Schemes to bypass the impediments presented by the Land Acquisition Act of 1894 in planning for urban expansion. Since PPP was expected to play an important role in building and maintaining urban infrastructure and delivering public services, a few states have enacted legislations to facilitate PPP.

Finally, the fact that a CDP could not be backed by a financial plan from the ULBs because of their weak and vulnerable finances, proved to be a major challenge.

The Government of India and state governments can help in responding to the financing challenge by working towards an effective devolution of funds to ULBs. As and when an agreement is reached between the Government of India and the state governments on GST and the necessary Constitutional Amendment is brought about, a very small part of the revenue from GST must devolve to the third tier of government including ULBs. This will provide a basic foundation on which the ULBs can work to bring their financial turn-around through instruments such as their own taxes, user charges, unlocking land value, and better efficiency in their operations. This will require institutional reforms for better governance.

JNNURM has been an experience in learning by doing for the Government of India. It has also encouraged some state governments to become pro-active in facilitating the process of urbanisation. For example, Maharashtra has launched a state-wide programme on water and sanitation for cities other than Mumbai—Maharashtra Sujal Nirmal Abhiyan Programme. This is a reform-centric programme in three phases across the state, incentivising the ULBs to focus on efficiency improvement and capacity building on the way to delivering water 24x7. Karnataka has set up a Municipal Reform Cell to monitor and compare the performance of different ULBs on service delivery in order to encourage performance orientation in its ULBs. This offers the potential for ranking the ULBs by their creditworthiness and guaranteeing their market debt selectively. Gujarat has forged ahead with Town Planning Schemes to facilitate planned urbanisation as cities expand. Tamil Nadu has provided an enabling environment for smaller ULBs to come together and access the capital market for urban infrastructure development.

The Mission has also stimulated a number of innovations in using IT for better planning and improving service delivery. GIS, GPS, and user-friendly software packages for on-line delivery of public services have emerged as powerful instruments for e-Governance. Software such as Auto DCR (Automatic Development Control Regulation) are being used for on-line approval of building plans in a number of cities. ICT has imparted transparency in government operations. It has been accompanied by re-engineering the underlying administrative processes such as shifting from manual record-keeping by different departments of a ULB to a single online database. This not only allows for integrated financial accounting and monitoring of projects, thereby improving the efficiency of these operations but also helps in strengthening their finances by improving collections through identifying citizens who have not paid their utility bills.

Karnataka is using ICT for gathering comparative information on performance indicators of service delivery through the use of common software for e-delivery of services across all its ULBs with a central server. Maharashtra is also working towards state-wide integration of e-Governance processes. Andhra Pradesh, Gujarat, Madhya Pradesh, and Tamil Nadu have used e-Governance to improve city planning. As these innovations inspire similar practices in other states, e-Governance has tremendous potential for improving efficiency and reducing cost of service delivery.

The experience of JNNURM has shown that states which provided an enabling environment for ULB level reform and innovation, where there was capacity to plan, implement and manage projects, and where the ULBs were financially relatively strong, were able to benefit from the mission.

One area in which JNNURM has not been successful is in motivating ULBs to tap external sources of funding through municipal bonds and/or PPP. The expectation was that the ULBs would improve their financial position by engaging in reforms in finance and governance. They would thereby access the capital market through municipal bonds or attract private partners with finance for PPP. But this expectation of leveraging government funds with private finance remained largely unfulfilled.

Since most ULBs did not cross the threshold of reforms which would generate a credible revenue model, it is not surprising that PPPs were also few and far between, and they have mostly taken the form of outsourcing services to the private sector. Besides financial sustainability, there is need to ensure (in the design, management and execution of urban infrastructure projects) that the projects are environmentally sustainable.

It is clear that capacities need to be created for urban planning, finance and management at all levels of government. The mission has been extended until 2014 and the expectation is that larger part of the allocation of funds will flow to medium and small cities. The time up to the launch of the new JNNURM in 2014 should be used to build capacities across the board.

In designing the new JNNURM, reform-orientation of the programme must be preserved with a clearer and measurable definition of the reform. Incentives will have to be provided for large cities and financially strong cities to leverage government funds for attracting private finance. For smaller cities and towns and financially weaker ULBs, the mission will have to focus on improving their capacity and financial position through reforms in administrative and financial governance. It is also very important to shift the focus from bridging the deficit in infrastructure investment to ensure service delivery on a sustainable basis. This will compel urban planners and city managers to build economic viability and sustainability into the process of planning and managing infrastructure projects. Only then can we ensure the quality of life for India's urban population, while also realising our potential for economic and social development by pushing cities as engines of growth.

7 Goods and Services Tax

Challenges of Ensuring an Acceptable Structure

M. Govinda Rao

Introduction

It is an honour to write an article in a volume honouring P. Chidambaram, who is one of the foremost tax reformers in India. There are very few leaders with a fiscal foresight and vision, and Chidambaram belongs to that rare species. A political leader who implements reforms in a systematic manner in India has to be more than a mere politician—he should be a statesman and Chidambaram has shown statesmanship in adopting a modern approach to tax reforms in the country.

The world over, economists recognise that the best practise approach to tax reforms is to adopt the 'broad base low rate' (BBLR) approach. While the paradigm shift in tax policy from a regime of high tax rates to the BBLR was initiated in the Tax Reform Committee reports chaired by Raja Chelliah in 1991-92, it was operationalised effectively by P. Chidambaram in his 'Dream Budget' of 1997 when the marginal personal income tax rate was reduced to 30 per cent which has resulted in significant improvement in tax compliance.

The two major tax reform initiatives on the agenda which Chidambaram, as Finance Minister, will have to address in the short and medium term are the direct taxes code (DTC) and the introduction of goods and services tax (GST). In both cases, the attempt is to broaden the base, reduce the rates, minimise rate differences and ensure a simple and transparent tax system.

In this short paper, an attempt is made to list the challenges faced in reforming the consumption tax system in the country by introducing the GST.

Consumption Tax Reform: Bullockcart Stuck in the Mud

In 1994, the expert group appointed to introduce the value added tax (VAT) stated that the domestic consumption tax system in India is in urgent need of reform. The statement continues to be valid even after significant reforms were undertaken by transforming the cascading type sales taxes with several tax rates into a much simpler VAT with two main rates in 2005. Despite this, the consumption tax base continues to be narrow with consumption of services excluded from the state VAT and the central VAT confined to the manufacturing stage with high threshold (₹ 1.5 crore), and the continuation of the tax on interstate sale of goods converting the taxes into a largely 'origin' rather than 'destination' based and creating severe impediments to trade in goods across the federation. The introduction of GST, therefore is important next stage of consumption tax reform.

In Indian context, the consumption tax system reform is currently jammed like a bullock cart stuck in the mud. There is no doubt that replacing the prevailing narrow based, complex system of multiple indirect taxes with a comprehensive GST holds the key to ensuring fiscal stability in the country and it is important for both central and state governments to meet the emerging challenges of globalisation. Indeed, the report of the Thirteenth Finance Commission with its 'flawless' GST advocacy, essentially that IMF type 'one size fits all' reform should be implemented. This is clearly unrealistic as there are 28 states, two UTs with legislatures and the union government involved in negotiation and bargaining, and the interests of all the parties do not coincide. Therefore, the ultimate outcome will be anything but flawless. It is also important that GST reform in India should accord greater recognition to the sensitivity to the views of the states. At the same time, while it is legitimate for the states to bargain to retain their fiscal autonomy, they should not use this autonomy to export the tax burden to non-residents. The predominantly origin based sales tax system has caused inequitable and inefficient inter-regional transfers. It is important that fiscal autonomy must be exercised within the constraint of evolving a destination-based consumption tax system.

The international experience is that for long, GST has been essentially a central tax and the levy by two different levels of government was considered infeasible or undesirable due to high collection costs, compliance costs and possible distortions arising from tax disharmony and the possible limitations on the central government's powers to undertake effective macroeconomic and redistribution policies (Bird and Gendron, 2007). Technical objections for the levy of subnational GST were also raised on account of cross-border trade. Therefore, most federal countries have the VAT at the federal level though some of them share the revenues with subnational governments.

The earliest subnational VAT was introduced in Brazil on origin basis. European Union (EU) implemented the VAT on the basis of the destination principle, but the issue of cross-border trade continues to be a subject of discussion (Keen, 2009; Cnossen, 2010). Canadian experience with dual VAT by harmonising the tax bases, and to some extent rates, has shown that the system is eminently workable. Indeed, Canada has four different systems with five provinces having fully harmonised GST with the federal government (Newfoundland and Labrador, Nova Scotia, New Brunswick, Ontario and British Columbia), three provinces having their own retail sales taxes with tax bases harmonised (Prince Edward Island, Manitoba and Saskatchewan), one province (Quebec) having the GST administered by the province and one province (Alberta) not levying the provincial GST at all. Sijbren Cnossen summarises the experiences of Canada, European Union and Brazil respectively as the good, the bad and the ugly. Though the cross-border trade issue has not yet been resolved, our own experience with the levy of state VAT since 2005 shows that it is eminently feasible to move into the next stage of reform of introducing the destination-based consumption type GST. Thus, although the debate on how best to design and implement GST at subnational levels is far from settled, there are no doubts on its feasibility and this is definitely on the policy table in large multilevel fiscal systems with strong regional governments. After reviewing international experiences of subnational VATs, Bird and Gendron (2007: 159) conclude, "In striking contrast to the way the fiscal world saw matters until very recently, the question of subnational VATs is now definitely on the policy table around the globe."

A Fiscal Contagion Called GST

Indeed, few fiscal innovations in the 20th century have had such a pervasive influence on the countries as VAT on goods and services. The promise of greater revenue productivity and neutrality in resource allocation has led over 140 countries in the world to adopt one form of VAT or another and the discussion of reform is gaining ground even in the United States, the last bastion which has resisted its imposition thus far. Over the last 60 years since VAT was first introduced, there have been several lessons learnt, innovations made and different variants of the levy implemented depending upon not merely best practices but also political acceptability. Needless to add, except for five countries which repealed the tax after its imposition, all others found it worthwhile to continue with the tax (Bird and Gendron, 2007). The reasons for the popularity of the tax has to be found in the fact that it has been a revenue spinner; a well-designed GST has much lower distortions than both the tariffs and any other broad-based consumption tax, and as the tax is supposed to be self-assessed, it minimises the compliance cost as well. Without exception, the developing countries need both more revenue and better revenue systems. A broad-based consumption tax is almost always a critical element in such systems and GST is considered to be the best form of general consumption tax.

Need to Customise GST

The two most important factors for the popularity of GST are, first, its perceived success in several countries, particularly its early success in the EU and second, the key role played by the IMF in spreading this in developing countries. As Keen (2009) states, "...there is a strong and significant positive correlation between participation in a Fund program and the probability of adopting a VAT." Surely IMF has been a major 'change agent'. However, unlike other Washington Consensus reforms, this is perhaps the least controversial. Much of the writings on GST are by IMF economists and not surprisingly, there is considerable craziness in the policy design and implementation, which has been candidly discussed in a recent comprehensive survey by Bird and Gendron (2007: 2) who nevertheless, argue that "...on the whole we conclude that much of the conventional wisdom about VAT design is sound" and the main difference between the Fund view and Bird-Gendron view is that the latter does not consider GST to be a Gorrilla or a Chimpanzee but a species of primates which allows them to choose the design which suits every country rather than having a 'one size fits all' design, and in their view different designs may be best for different countries though some features are desirable. The country has to make the difficult choices and sometimes, even "...some bad initial features may be an essential element of getting the tax accepted in the first place" (p.4).

From the viewpoint of implementation, even if many elements of the model GST are desirable, it may not be possible to secure immediate agreement from all the states. Therefore, it is necessary to look at the reform as a process rather than as an event. As argued by Bird and Gendron (2007), "some bad initial features may even be an essential element of getting the tax accepted in the first place. Indeed, some of the features recommended may not even be desirable in a developing country. The political and social values may necessitate two tax rates, rather than one, for distributional considerations—a lower tax rate on essential items besides a general rate. Finally, there are questions of fiscal autonomy to the states. Curiously, it is not clear why the Commission took upon itself the responsibility of making recommendations on the structure and implementation details of GST when the term of reference wanted it to merely take into account the impact of the proposed GST in April 2010, including its impact on external trade."

It is important to note that the consumption tax reform involving central and state governments will have to be a compromise between tax uniformity and fiscal autonomy (Rao, 2007). While the aim should be to get the fundamentals of the reform right, compromise is unavoidable and the solution may have to settle at less than the best. To state that the "GST grant compensates for the seeming limitation in fiscal autonomy by enhancing expenditure autonomy through compensation payments and additional formulaic transfers" (p.71), is to totally misunderstand the concept of fiscal autonomy altogether. First, compensation is given against the loss of revenues and not a bribe for implementing GST reform. If it is a bribe, the compensation could be much higher than the actual revenue loss! Second, fiscal autonomy under fiscal decentralisation means manoeuvrability to change standards of public services by changing tax rates and not simply softening the budget constraint to spend more money though transfers. The simple issue is that there is no single ideal system of GST that every country must adopt. Countries have implemented what is workable in their contexts.

The important questions raised by the states in regard to the structure of GST relate to fiscal autonomy and redistribution. Surely, forced uniformity in the rate structure will impinge on fiscal autonomy. Similarly, many states consider levying GST at one rate which does not ensure the required progressivity. In addition to these, there are difficult questions of which items should be exempted and should domestic consumption be zero-rated? What should be the threshold? Is there a case for taxing 'luxury' items of consumption like luxury cars, at higher rates? What should be the threshold? How do we deal with the issue of tax incentives? These are apart from the issues of dealing with interstate transactions and transactions relating to consumption of services with interstate spillovers, and the issue of technology to track the transactions.

On some of the non-contentious issues, international experience can provide useful guidance in designing the tax. It is clear that the tax should not be applied to the stage of transaction but should be based on the threshold. Classification according to manufacturers, wholesalers and retailers does not carry much meaning in the modern world. It would be useful to keep the exemptions to the minimum in order to make the tax comprehensive for crediting input taxation. Furthermore, the international experience shows that the threshold should be relatively high. The threshold should be chosen to balance the collection cost with marginal revenue gains as Keen and Mintz (2004) show and typically, the number of taxpayers in low thresholds is large but their revenue contribution is not very significant. It is desirable to keep the threshold high enough, for even if some revenue is lost by dropping small taxpayers, the administration can be freed to make greater effort on those who can contribute more. The international experience shows that high thresholds also are important for equity because the consumption of the poor largely comprises purchases from small traders. Of course, international experience shows wide variation in the thresholds. In the case of developed countries it varies from zero in Sweden to $ 600,000 in Singapore. In the case of developing countries, the thresholds vary from $ 18,000 in Morocco and Pakistan to € 100,000 in Lebanon. After reviewing the experiences of several countries,

Bird and Gendron (2007) suggest a thumb rule that a threshold of $ 100,000 should be generally acceptable.

The international experience with GST suggests that it is necessary to keep the exemptions to the minimum, but resisting the pressures from various political groups to accord exemptions in one pretext or other is not going to be easy. However, it is possible to prune the list collectively by all the states concerned in a reform exercise like this. Keeping the exemption list long will not enhance states' fiscal autonomy, makes the tax base narrower and in any case will not ensure comprehensive crediting of input taxes. International experience also suggests that zero rating domestic consumption is a bad idea. It is also not a good idea to have tax incentives and concessions in the GST regime, and any incentive that is proposed should be given in other forms and not by way of tax preferences.

In India, there is considerable discussion on what should be taxed and what should not be. The present list of exemption is expansive. The central government taxes on manufactured goods and, even here, those produced by units with less than ₹ 1.5 crore turnover are exempt and only selected services are subject to tax. Similarly, at the state level, a large number of goods are exempt and except for entertainment tax and passengers and goods tax (which in most states is merged with motor vehicles tax), states are not allowed to levy the tax on any of the services. In addition to these, there are a plethora of exemptions for the so-called small enterprises—area-based exemptions and exemptions for entities located in special economic zones. Although, the states have desisted from giving sales tax exemptions and deferments in recent years, the burden of past policies continues even as studies have shown that they only create fiscal holes and create additional distortions with little benefits to the economy. It is important to have minimum exemptions not only to broaden the base of the tax but also to ensure comprehensiveness in the input-credit mechanism. Exempting unprocessed food items is necessary for both equity and administrative reasons. It is also important to keep the threshold relatively high again, both for equity and administrative reasons. It may also not be feasible or even desirable to tax government services and meritorious services like education and health care, stationary and books, and life-saving medicines. There are hard-to-tax services like financial services, housing and real estate. Most countries exempt real estate transactions, and subject land

and real property to taxes other than the GST. Levying taxes on financial services even in developed countries has been difficult, and the feasible option for countries like India is to include all fees and commissions and subject all margin services to GST. Among different countries, New Zealand has the least number of exemptions and the most comprehensive coverage of GST but it may not be possible to follow that in a country like India. At the same time, it is important to resist the political pressures to accord exemptions to fulfil ostensible objectives of equity, administrative ease, regional development, employment creation through small-scale industry development and many more.

What should the rate structure be? Expert advice on the issue is simple: there should be only a single and uniform rate. This is also the usual IMF recommendation for the developing countries. This is based on the assumption that the gains from lower administrative and compliance costs outweigh the loss from efficiency and equity arguments. Although the optimal tax theory argues for multiple tax rates depending upon the price elasticity of demand, it does not provide practical help in formulating tax policy. Besides the problem of inadequate information to design such a tax, there are administrative and equity considerations in addition to political economy dimensions, preventing application of the approach for practical policy formulation in developing countries. It is argued that multiple rates in the given political economy environment actually leads to distortions in choice and welfare losses. Most tax advisers, therefore, are comfortable advocating a single rate of tax. It is also argued that in the presence of a lower rate of tax, the general rate of tax will have to be much higher to raise the same amount of revenue and as the distortions from the tax are equivalent to the square of the tax rate, it leads to much higher inefficiency in resource allocation. Redistribution in tax policy is supposed to be taken care of—as exempting essential food items and keeping the threshold high enough. Having a lower rate of tax on items of common consumption, predominantly by the poor, benefits the non-poor as well and although for the poor, the items claim a larger proportion of total consumption in absolute terms, the benefits could be higher for the non-poor. Further, it is argued that redistribution should be pursued through tax policy as a whole and not through individual taxes, and a progressive income tax is supposed to be a better tool to ensure the required progressivity.

There is much to be said in favour of having a single tax rate from the viewpoint of minimising administration and compliance cost. This is particularly advocated for the developing countries which have low administrative capacity. However, most countries do not seem to be listening and, not for the first time, the world does not seem to care for the expert advice. The real 'standard' seems to be to have at least two (non-zero) rates though more recent adopters seem to have opted for a single rate. In the EU where adherence to the Sixth Directive is a precondition for joining the Union, with the exception of Denmark, there is no country with a single rate and most countries have two reduced rates. Even as the economists overwhelmingly argued for having a single rate in Sweden recently, the government found it impossible to embrace it. Given the highly unequal distribution of incomes in developing countries, distributional policy objective mandates a more explicitly progressive GST.

For the same reason, sometimes, it is argued that items of conspicuous consumption should be subject to a much higher rate of tax. Indeed there are arguments that people who enjoy conspicuous consumption, like travel in luxury cars, should pay higher rate of taxes. However, too much of rate differentiation would add to administrative complexity and compliance cost. Furthermore, it is important to consider the total effects on employment and poverty rather than simple consideration of whether the item is consumed predominantly by the poor or rich. The best way to deal with the issue is to levy a separate excise on such items just like the excises levied on sumptuary items like alcohol and cigarettes and levy GST at the general rate on the excise paid value. The case of levying taxes on diesel and motor spirit is similar. The present draft of the Constitutional amendment seeks to exclude motor spirit and diesel from the coverage of GST which is clearly inappropriate. Indeed, revenue is important but this should not be done by truncating the GST coverage. A separate excise in addition to the GST is the answer for sin taxes, green taxes or even additional levy on a few items of conspicuous consumption. Furthermore, to exclude it in the Constitutional amendment will make it difficult to include it when it is desired and therefore, it should be a part of the Act rather than the Constitutional amendment. Hopefully wiser consul will prevail.

The related question we need to deal with in the proposed GST is whether it is necessary for having uniform rates. The issue is particularly relevant in the context of fiscal autonomy of states wherein, if uniform rates are mandated, they lose manoeuvrability to vary tax and expenditure levels. Thus, the trade-off is between fiscal autonomy on the one hand and higher administrative and compliance costs on the other. These issues were discussed in detail at the time of levying the VAT by the states in 2005 and at the time, they decided in favour of adopting uniform rates. Nevertheless, the issue has been raised by many states once again and, therefore, merits reconsideration. If indeed, the states feel strongly that they need to retain their power to vary the rates, the compromise could be the adoption of floor rates rather than fixed rates. Surely, absolute autonomy in the choice of rates could create a chaotic tax regime similar to the one that existed before the introduction of VAT with many states (and prominently union territories) adopting the 'race to the bottom' strategy.

Although both administrative and compliance costs will be lower when the tax rates across states are uniform, international experience does not show that uniform rates are imperative. In both Brazil and Canada, the tax rates vary among the provinces. In the EU, despite the need to adhere to the Sixth Directive, the tax rates vary widely among different members. The standard rate of VAT in the EU varied from 15 to 25 per cent with a mean of 19.4 per cent and except for Denmark, every other European country has one or more rates in addition to the standard rates. It is not to argue that multiple rates are desirable and surely, every effort should be made to minimise rate differentiation from the viewpoint of reducing the collection cost, compliance cost and distortions in the economy. Uniform rates applied to the state VAT in 2005-06 have been fairly successful. However, if the states insist on having uniform floor rates rather than fixed rates, it should be admitted. With this the question of autonomy would be settled for; even when the nominal tax rates are broadly uniform, the effective rates have varied significantly depending on the efficiency of administration. Furthermore, with the states empowered to levy selective excises on items of conspicuous consumption, sumptuary items and petroleum products, they would have some leeway, albeit limited, in varying their taxes.

The most important issue in a subnational VAT is dealing with cross-border transactions. The states have agreed on the model in their first discussion paper but the issue keeps cropping up again and again with some states seeking to continue the central sales tax, which goes against the very spirit of destination-based tax and ensuring a common market. The idea of having Integrated GST (IGST) and a clearing house mechanism to deal with the interstate transactions is eminently workable and is the way forward. As the Centre and states, collectively, have agreed to incubate the technology by choosing a partner in National Security Depository Limited (NSDL) and create a separate special purpose vehicle (SPV) with both central and state governments contributing majority stake when it is developed, holds promise. At the same time, there is need for considerable capacity building of both taxpayers and tax collectors. It may be recalled that the tax information network instituted for administering the income tax with NSDL as a technology partner has been a great success but at the same time, the teething trouble continues. It is important that both importers and exporters in interstate transactions are provided with the necessary training to avoid the problems.

The Way Forward

It was George Santayana who wrote: "Those who do not remember the past are condemned to repeat it." We may recall that it took the states several years to come together to reform their cascading-type sales taxes with irrational multiple rates to an intrastate VAT with just two rates. Although the discussion on the reforms started in 1994 and implementation was planned early in the new millennium, it got finally implemented in April 2005 even as Tamil Nadu and Uttar Pradesh jumped on the reform bandwagon later. However, unlike in the case of VAT reform, GST reform requires that all the states should join together in implementing it.

Restarting the reform requires a thrust and perhaps the central government should provide it. In fact, Constitutional amendment is important but the reform process need not wait for it. Perhaps, the Union finance minister should reboot the process by pruning the list of exemptions to the minimum, unify the rates of excise duty by converting the specific duties into *ad valorem* and unifying them with the general rate, and extend the tax to all services by converting the prevailing selective tax into a general tax. It is necessary to have a common threshold and rate for both goods and services. The threshold could be kept at ₹ 50 lakh manufacturing turnover in the case of goods and sales turnover in the case of services, and the tax may be levied at a uniform rate of 10 per cent. A separate sumptuary tax can be levied on cigarettes. With the computerised information system linked to Permanent Account Number (PAN) put in place, and with exchange of information between excise and income tax departments, there could be significant revenue gains. This reform will secure a place for the finance minister in history as the statesman who introduced GST in spite of formidable difficulties.

It is important that the states should collectively finalise the design and operational details and set a clear timetable for implementation. It appears that there is a broad agreement to have two rates rather than one and it may be appropriate even to begin with floor rates than fixed rates. Once the exemption list and the list of commodities for lower tax rate category are finalised (services will in any case be taxed at general rate), the progress in the collection of central GST at the manufacturing stage should give a clearer idea about the revenue neutral rates. In any case, on the basis of prevailing information, my colleagues at NIPFP have estimated that on an average, it is possible to recover the VAT revenue at about 10 per cent if it is a single rate and 5 and 12.5 per cent if the tax is levied at two rates. On sumptuary items, tobacco products, motor spirit, high speed diesel and a few selected items of conspicuous consumption, in addition to the general rate, the states may be allowed to levy a special excise at the floor rates decided collectively. The Centre should agree to compensate any shortfall in revenue collections estimated at 10 per cent general rate including the revenue from central sales tax for the first three years. The progress in revenue collections should be monitored continuously and at the end of three years, the rate structure should be reviewed and if necessary, realigned to ensure that the states do not lose out after the compensation period is over.

There are other institutional details that need to be settled as well. This includes setting up a GST council and a dispute resolution mechanism. Indeed, unlike in the case of state VATs where the Centre does not have much role and, therefore, its participation in the decisions was not crucial, Central government is a party to GST and it must be represented in the Council. There is nothing wrong with the Union Finance Minister chairing the council so long as the decision relating to the states are decided by the states themselves and the centre's participation is confined to Centre-state harmonisation issues. This implies that the chairman of the Empowered Committee who will be the vice chairman of the Council will conduct the regular businesses of the Council, and the chairman of the Council will chair the meetings relating to only the Centre and states. The decisions relating to the states, like at present, will be taken unanimously. There will be a dispute resolution mechanism in the form of a tribunal headed by a retired High Court Judge and the decisions of the tribunal should be binding on the parties concerned.

If these basic issues are settled, it should be possible to move ahead on the Constitutional amendment. It has been agreed that the enabling provision for GST will become a part of the Constitution itself and not a part of union, state or concurrent lists. The important point is that the Constitutional amendment should only be an enabling provision and the details should become the part of the GST Acts. There is no need to exclude any item such as petroleum products from the purview of GST as is proposed in the present draft of Constitutional amendment. GST should cover all commodities and services, and additional excises can be levied for revenue, environmental or sumptuary reasons. Effectiveness of GST reform critically depends on the reforms in tax administration because, in developing countries as Casanegra (1990) stated "...in developing countries, tax administration is tax policy." Unfortunately, in all our tax reform exercises, reforming tax administration has never been a priority. International experience also shows that self-assessment is a critical element of successful GST implementation but that would require adequate checks and balances to be put in place. Organising the tax administration on functional rather than regional lines, selection of the sample for detailed audit based on assessed risk, ensuring timely refunds and timely resolution of disputes are some of the elements of a good tax administration. Equally important is the need for systematic collection of data and information for both analysis and administration.

Another important issue in the levy of GST is the technology to deal with cross-border transactions. The Empowered Committee has done well to select the technology partner in NSDL to incubate the technology. As NSDL is already the technology partner for the tax information network (TIN) for income tax, it is possible to match the information gathered from GST with the information on income tax and this could become an effective deterrent for tax evasion and could improve compliance significantly. Hopefully, there will be progress on this front. At the same time, it is important to initiate capacity building to ensure efficient use of the technology, both for taxpayers and tax collectors.

The reform of the consumption tax system to levy GST is not just an option but imperative. The reform is necessary not only for minimising the collection, compliance and resource allocation costs but also to raise significant additional revenue over the medium term. The much-needed resources for universalising health care, augmenting expenditures on education and, above all, to contain the fiscal deficit at the level recommended by the Finance Commission which has been accepted by the Centre would require an additional resources amounting to almost six per cent of GDP and a significant volume of that will have to come from raising additional taxes. Introduction of GST will be a win-win strategy for both the Centre and states and there is every reason to embrace it. However, reform of this nature involving both the Centre and states is an experiment in cooperative federalism and requires stewardship by the statesmen. In fact, that is the difference between leaders and statesmen and who better than Chidambaram is suited to the task?

References

Bird, Richard and Pierre-Pascal Gendron (2007). *Value Added Taxes in Developing and Transitional Countries.* Cambridge and New York: Cambridge University Press.

Cassnegra de Jantscher, M. (1990). "Admnistering the VAT", in M. Gillis, C. Shoup and G.P. Sicat (eds.), *Value Added Taxation in Developing Countries*", Washington D.C.: World Bank. pp.171-90.

Cnossen, Sijbren (2010). "VAT Coordination in Common Markets and Federations: Lessons from the European Experience", *Tax Law Review* 63: 584-622.

Keen, Michael (2009). "What Do (and Don't) We Know about the Value Added Tax?", *Journal of Economic Literature* 47(1): 159-70.

Keen, Michael and Jack Mintz (2004). "The Optimal Threshold for a Value Added Tax", *Journal of Public Economics* 88(3-4): 559-76.

Oates, W.E. (2005). "Toward a Second Generation Theory of Fiscal Federalism", *International Tax and Public Finance* 12: 349-73.

Rao, M. Govinda (2007). "Resolving Fiscal Imbalances: Issues in Tax Sharing", in Robin Boadway and Anwar Shah (eds.), *Intergovernmental Fiscal Transfers: Principles and Practice*. World Bank. pp.319-37.

8 Banking for the Last Mile

Sameer Kochhar

Finance Minister P. Chidambaram has a metaphor to describe his unshakeable belief in the role of economic growth to spread inclusive growth: "a rising tide lifts all boats."[1] As far metaphors go, this is even more powerful than Deng Xiaoping's dictum, "crossing a river by feeling the stones," which basically meant to indicate a slow, pragmatic approach to China's economic reforms. Indeed, like Deng, Chidambaram is among the rare breed of politicians who identified, before others could do so, economic reforms and institutional changes as the two essential elements for the country's transformation from a poor to a developed one. This, he believed, will engender higher GDP growth rates which, in turn, will leave sufficient financial resources at the disposal of the government for rapid poverty alleviation. He once wrote that no country has clung to the plough and yoke, or the handloom, or tiny industries, or the bicycle and bullock-cart, or to single-teacher village schools, "and yet has been able to abolish poverty."[2]

Chidambaram has been one of the principal architects of India's first wave of economic reforms started in 1991, which put the country's GDP growth rate in a steady upward march. The tide had obviously turned. As the reform story has entered its third decade, it's worthwhile to ask, has the tide indeed lifted all boats in the past two decades of so? In other words, has the pace of poverty reduction accelerated in this period? Though there still remain pockets of abject poverty in India, the twin engines of poverty alleviation and inclusive growth have gathered an unprecedented pace in the last 20 years. As Chidambaram would say, the tide has wielded its mighty power.

1. "Chidambaram on Chidambaram", *Inclusion* 3(2), April-June. New Delhi. 2012. p.63.
2. *Indian Express*, October 6, 2002.

Noted economist Surjit S. Bhalla had examined various definitions of poverty line and the National Sample Surveys (NSS) for years from 1983 to 2010. He observed that "the steady decline in official poverty estimate is from close to 60 per cent in 1983, to less than 30 per cent in 2009-10. The official poverty ratio is very close to being half the 1993-94 level in 2009-2010, i.e., the Millennium Development Goal of halving poverty by 2015 has been met in India."[3] He concluded that "the major result emerging from the analysis is that the story of poverty reduction (and therefore inclusive growth) in India is very impressive."[4]

This view is supported by Columbia University's Prof Arvind Panagariya. In his chapter in the book *India on the Growth Turnpike*, he noted: "On poverty front, all states have seen the rate of poverty decline between 1993-94 and 2004-05 largely representing the post-reform period.... An important aspect of this impressive growth story is the phenomenal growth some of the poorest states have experienced in recent years."[5]

Development economists have seen growth not as an objective in itself but as a tool of poverty alleviation. It's clear that rising incomes have been translating into reduced poverty, and to that extent, India's reform story has worked very well so far.

Chidambaram has been vindicated: economic revival has changed India and the country was ready for it. Since 1991, he had three stints at the North Block as Finance Minister, and each has been marked by one epochal moment in the reform story or the other. In his first stint, the 'Dream Budget' of 1997-98 changed the ground rules of India's taxation policy. In the second stint of 2004-09, he revitalised the idea of 'financial inclusion' and it was on this plank a whole new series of social welfare programmes, like the Mahatma Gandhi National Rural Employment Guarantee Scheme (MGNREGS), was rolled out. In his third stint, from 2012, he strengthened the sinews of an insipid reform process as soon as he assumed charge, and steered it to a new direction. The decision, taken no sooner than he took oath as finance minister, to raise the FDI bar in organised retail was one of

3. Bhalla (2012).

4. Ibid: 141.

5. Panagariya (2010).

the noteworthy, yet controversial, policy initiatives taken in many years. The direct benefit transfer (DBT) of subsidies and welfare schemes, which was introduced from January 1, 2013, is a milestone decision in terms of financial inclusion.

Chidambaram has taken these bold steps despite having his government working under coalition compulsions. This means that the Finance Minister and the Congress party leadership are on the same page as far as reinvigorating economic reforms and achieving inclusive growth are concerned. Perhaps, within the Congress, Rahul Gandhi is emerging as the chief proponent of good economics, which often means good governance, too. This is indeed a welcome break from the old mould of Indian politicians, who, while professing they are pro-poor, actually pursued policies that were pro-poverty.

The DBT is, of course, being branded as a visionary programme in ensuring financial inclusion. Chidambaram himself has called it a "gamechanger" in India's road to accomplish inclusive growth. *"Aapka paisa, aapke haath"* (your money in your hands) is the slogan the government has adopted to promote the DBT scheme, which would be rolled out in phases to cover the entire country by the end of 2013. In the words of Prime Minister Manmohan Singh, the twin pillars for the success of the system of DBT "are the Aadhaar platform and financial inclusion. If either of these pillars is weak, it would endanger the success of the initiative."

The government hopes that the DBT would enable it to better targeting of subsidies and welfare schemes, like scholarships and pensions. At the heart of the scheme is the design of a new brand-new delivery method based on biometric identification and other technological tools to replace the existing rotten system that is both unscientific and leak-prone.

I met Chidambaram for the first time to record a video interview with him that was to be edited as a message for a conference organised by Skoch on financial inclusion in Mumbai. My first question itself elicited a lucid expression of his view on financial inclusion, which goes as follows.

> The phrase financial inclusion means that the banking sector must reach out to more people who need credit, who deserve credit, and who cannot access credit. It is not enough to have technology. Banks have core-banking solutions, that doesn't mean that they reach out to everyone. Banks are computerised, that doesn't mean that they

> reach out to everyone. What is needed is technology plus design; technology plus the willingness to associate different intermediaries and different players. For example, we think that the banking system and the post-office system can be married to each other, to reach out to more people. Self-help groups (SHGs) certainly have opened the door to more people to access credit. But SHGs do not form themselves, somebody has to promote them. We have examples of very successful SHGs in different states. What is important is to have intermediaries; catalysts, may be State governments and the NGOs, may be others who can form these groups, train them and then bring them to the banking system. Banks themselves have undertaken the responsibility in a limited way of promoting SHGs. But, then that's just one way to enlarge the reach of the banking system, but we must find other ways also.[6]

Needless to say, there was no need to ask more questions and retakes. The clarity of Chidambaram's thoughts, in single burst of thoughts full of passion, was stunning to me, as I have been closely studying the subject since 1997. A more nuanced view on the scale and sweep of financial inclusion was hard to articulate. I came away from my meeting with Chidambaram with the feeling that India should be fortunate to have such an eloquent votary in the government for financial inclusion.

I remember my meeting with Chidambaram took place nearly one-and-half years before the Rangarajan Committee on Financial Inclusion submitted its report to the government in January 2008. The report has since then entered the annals of India's economic vision as the roadmap for financial inclusion. The report sketched out the process as a three-way process:

> Financial inclusion denotes delivery of financial services at an affordable cost to the vast sections of the disadvantaged and low-income groups. The various financial services include credit, savings, insurance and payments and remittance facilities. The objective of financial inclusion is to extend the scope of activities of the organised financial system to include within its ambit people with low incomes. Through graduated credit, the attempt must be to lift the poor from one level to another so that they come out of poverty....While financial inclusion can be substantially enhanced by improving the supply side or the delivery systems, it is also important to note that many regions, segments of the population and sub-sectors of the economy have a limited or weak demand for financial services. In order to improve their level of inclusion, demand side efforts need to be undertaken including improving human and physical resource endowments, enhancing productivity, mitigating risk and strengthening market linkages.[7]

In light of the Rangarajan panel's recommendations, Chidambaram swung into action pretty quickly. In his Union Budget 2008-09 speech,

6. P. Chidambaram's Address at *Skoch Financial Technologies Summit 2006*, Mumbai, June 2006.
7. "Preface", *Report of the Rangarajan Committee on Financial Inclusion*, January 2008.

he announced the immediate formation of two funds proposed by the Rangarajan panel to get the ball rolling on the Mission Financial Inclusion front. He announced the constitution of the Financial Inclusion Fund (FIF) for meeting the cost of promotional and developmental interventions and the Financial Inclusion Technology Fund (FITF) to meet the cost of technology adoption to take the banking services to the unbanked, with an overall corpus of ₹ 500 crore each.

However, the only kicker is that nothing productive has come out of these two funds till now. Bureaucratic lethargy of National Bank for Agriculture and Rural Development (NABARD), the administrating authority of FIF and FITF, has aborted both of them. Moreover, Chidambaram was moved to the Home Ministry in December 2008 in the wake of Mumbai terror attacks with the task of strengthening the country's security, and hence was not apparently able to follow through on the progress on FIF and FITF.

Since Chidambaram's departure from the Finance Ministry from December 2008 to July 2012, the Mission Financial Inclusion had been kind of botched up by bureaucratic apathy and incoherent regulation. While his vision of financial inclusion was very clear, somehow, during the time that he was not at the helm of Finance Ministry, the implementation got diluted and remained limited to opening of no-frill accounts. However, Sonia Gandhi attempted to bring it back on track to achieve target of complete financial inclusion when she launched Swabhimaan during February 2011. She had said,

> One of the most important objectives of the campaign will be to enable small and marginal farmers to obtain credit at lower rates from banks and other financial institutions, insulating them from exploitation by moneylenders. Village artisans will be able to procure their working capital rapidly and effectively. I believe that this will lead to the emergence of the rural entrepreneur.... At the same time, we need to recognise a weakness in some of our most revolutionary flagship programmes, in that, the intended beneficiaries are not sufficiently informed about them, about their rights and how best to derive advantage of what they have to offer. I hope that beyond the provision of financial services, the Swabhimaan campaign will also seek to impart financial education and financial literacy, through communication and training, to the people it is seeking to benefit. This will enable them to make better and more responsible financial decisions.[8]

8. Gandhi (2011).

Despite such clear direction towards financial inclusion, the focus has continued to remain on the BC model. The initial regulatory guidelines were perhaps a case of over-regulation that all but scuttled good ideas like the business facilitator/business correspondent (BF/BC) models and mobile phone banking as effective instruments of financial inclusion.

The BF/BC models were introduced in 2006 by the Reserve Bank of India (RBI) to ensure greater financial inclusion. Banks were instructed to employ the services of business facilitators and correspondents to increase the outreach of the banking sector. The business facilitators were responsible for identification of potential borrowers, data collection and creating awareness about savings. Business correspondents helped customers in rural areas access banking services such as small-value cash deposits and withdrawals, disbursal of small-value credits, remittances and balance enquiries on the lines of ATM facilities available to in urban areas.

The BF model has virtually collapsed by now. Banks argued that the facilitators were not able to provide business commensurate to their commission, thereby impacting their margins. Instead, in many cases banks suggested facilitators to follow the business correspondent model in setting up customer service points (CSPs) and conducting banking operations through point-of-sale terminals, mobile phones or other such modern devices.

The BC model was tied in regulatory knots from the very beginning. Since its introduction the BC model struggled to create a viable business model. Generating volumes had proved to be a big challenge because of high operating costs. Most BCs were confined to no-frill accounts and limited remittance services, thus circumscribing their product and service range. In states where the BC model has been up and running, the experience shows that it has run out of steam owing to the flawed cost structure, lack of commitment on the part of banks, absence of financial literacy, lack of knowledge between CSPs and clients, and the near-absence of a platform to resolve grievances.

According to the RBI data, the number of CSPs shot up to around 1,16,000 in March 2012 from 13,000 in 2009. Anecdotal evidence and Skoch's field research, however, reveal that many of the CSPs only exist on paper in rural areas. Curiously enough, the average growth of urban

CSPs has been around 400 per cent in 2011-12, whereas rural CSPs grew sluggishly, by 81 per cent. What does this prove? Doesn't it appear like that the whole logic behind BCs—that is, taking banking to the rural hinterland—stands on its head?

Focus on opening no-frill accounts has led to neglecting other banking products like fixed deposits or recurring deposits. Nevertheless, in 2009 when Skoch had come up with the first state of the sector report, the usage of no-frills accounts was a minuscule 11 per cent. This meant that the vast majority of them are dud accounts. If the whole objective of opening these accounts was to give some semblance of credit, only 2 per cent of these accounts actually have an overdraft account facility. The Indian Banks Association had spent a fortune on advertising that banks were having no-frills accounts out of which ₹ 1.08 billion crore overdrafts had been given. Yet, 98 per cent of these accounts don't have overdraft facility is the unvarnished truth one gets for all these money spent on advertising the 'success'.

What needs to be done to fix this situation? First, allow BCs to charge a transaction fee so that they can scale up. Alternatively, the government could provide for a 3 per cent transaction fee in all direct benefit transfers, and the fee may go up as the volume of transaction increases. The transaction fee can be either a percentage of the amount transacted or a fixed amount, and this won't dissuade people from operating no-frills accounts. Second, attach an overdraft incentive to the maximum number of no-frill accounts possible. It's also necessary to channel micro-insurance products through these no-frill accounts so that they remain active. Third, link more and more Kisan Credit Cards and General Credit Cards to no-frill accounts.

The problem with the existing BC model is that it fails to appreciate that there's a cost associated with its working. Banks would find employing correspondents unsustainable if a transaction fee is absent, as they have to foot the bill for setting up the infrastructure and then for meeting regular expenses of maintaining back-end systems and paying BCs. As one bank official said, "You cannot have a model under which the financial inclusion rollout is subsidised. It needs to be sustainable." Paying a small amount like ₹ 3 for a ₹ 100 transaction would be preferable to the customer than travelling 20 km to reach the nearest bank branch, the official noted. Of course, reason suggests that.

The government had announced the nation-wide financial inclusion plan called Swabhimaan in February 2011. The plan was chalked out to allow millions of small and marginal farmers and rural artisans obtain credit at lower rates from banks and other financial institutions. This campaign, according to the government, has met its targets benchmarked to March 2012—banking facilities have been provided to 74,194 hitherto unbanked villages with over 2,000 population and about 3.16 crore new financial accounts have been opened. Flush with this success, the government decided to extend the campaign to habitations with population of more than 1,000 in north-eastern and hilly states.

Yet, by the government's own admission, "ensuring accessible and affordable financial services in all of the 600,000 villages in India is a herculean task and given the enormity of the task, a lot of ground still needs to be covered."[9] However, in view of the crippled state of BF/BC models—the main plank of Swabhimaan—it seems that one has to take the official claims on the success of the programme with a pinch of salt.

The heart of the matter is, according to economist Nitin Desai, that transaction cost or cost of delivering small amounts of credit is very high. "Several measures have been tried—group lending, lending through micro-credit institutions, business correspondents—all with an effort to reduce cost of delivering credit. Still, financial inclusion remains a far cry," he adds.[10]

No-frill accounts were pressed into service for the MGNREGS and consequently, there has been a mass migration of benefit transfer from post offices to banks. But the absence of a transaction fee had left in its wake a great proportion of inactive accounts, as indicated earlier.

It's good that for DBT pilot project, the government is mulling a transaction fee. It's said that the government is sitting on ₹ 5000 crore kitty to support BCs.

---

9. Singh (2012).
10. Nitin Desai is a noted economist. He was speaking at Skoch Financial Inclusion Day, 5th January 2013, New Delhi.

Warren Buffett's famous mantra for achieving success is that, for genius to flourish, attitude is as important as talent. "It's not about your potential horse power. Whatever you have, learn it to utilise fully," so goes the Oracle of Omaha's refrain.

I am not sure if Chidambaram is aware of Buffett's this particular pearl of wisdom. In any case, I would certainly venture to say that Chidambaram is a visionary politician in India who combines innate talent with right attitude. He has proved time and again that he has what it takes to be a transformational figure in India's economic scene.

If all goes according to his plan, the DBT scheme can become yet another masterstroke, because it is the first time the government is attempting to converge all of social benefit scheme to the financial inclusion platform. The government, for the first time, has spelt out a comprehensive plan to streamline cash transfers through the biometric identification platform, Aadhaar. "It is now going to be 100 per cent possible for cash transfers to be delivered into the bank account of the person for whom it is meant," says Montek Singh Ahluwalia.[11] "The costs of the system are trivial compared to the efficiency gains when you consider the total payment the government makes in benefit schemes."[12]

One of the teething problems with DBT has been that very few beneficiary accounts were linked with Aadhaar cards. Fortunately with a very significant political focus on this scheme it is quite likely that all these issues would be sorted out more sooner than later and given the resolve of the government to get it going, banks, institutions and domain ministries will fall in line. This hopefully will address the major issue of providing bank accounts to the unbanked before the 2014 elections in a big way.

Yet, the innovative biometric technology-based welfare targeting cannot be a substitute for good governance and systemic reform at the grass roots level. Nor is it a magic wand to achieve financial inclusion. For financial inclusion to happen in letter and spirit, the developmental banking parameters need a paradigm shift. As Nitin Desai argued in the Skoch summit marking the Financial Inclusion Day 2013, 75 per cent of India's economy lies outside the corporate world. "So, we have to worry

11. *The Hindu*, 8 February 2012.

12. Ibid.

about what we need to do in order to get the 75 per cent of the economy that lies outside the corporate sector moving. This is where the issues of financial inclusion and microenterprises come in," as he succinctly put it.

To begin with, India's banking push requires a new pivot. Despite the government's Financial Inclusion Plan and Swabhimaan, much of rural India still remains 'unbanked', plain and simple. There has to be a uniform know your customer (KYC) system so that people can open bank accounts early. The RBI's own data finds that between 2004 and 2012, the change in percentage (46%) of total bank branches reflects the yawning gap between urban/semi-urban and rural India in terms of penetration of banking services. In the same period, the percentage of growth of new bank branches in metro cities went up by 93.63 per cent, urban areas by 72.12 per cent and 69.61 per cent in semi-urban areas. In contrast, new bank branches in rural areas—India's underdeveloped and credit-starved heartlands—registered a measly 12 per cent growth. On the other hand, the BC model, which was conceived as the axis on which rural outreach turned, has almost collapsed from the strain it has been subjected it to. There ought to be meaningful action to revive the BF/BC models and a higher degree of involvement of elected women *panchayati raj* members, ASHA workers and community-based organisations in them. Mobile phone banking should be unshackled from unnecessary regulatory curbs on transactions.

Second, we need realistic, need-based microcredit delivery. The effects of all the poverty alleviation programmes in India that Bhalla and Panagariya conclusively proved would have had multiplier effects if banks had taken a more pragmatic approach on microcredit delivery. Readily-available credit is a key enabling factor in poverty alleviation. All indicators provide cause for concern: the declining growth rate of self-help groups, negative growth in the loans issued by cooperatives and a drastic fall in the growth of agriculture credit from nearly 23 per cent in 2009-10 to 10.6 per cent in 2010-11.

The Rangarajan panel report of 2008 has stressed the Self-Help Groups (SHGs)-Bank Linkage Programme as "the most potent initiative since Independence for delivering financial services to the poor in a sustainable manner." Skoch's research on SHGs has painted a gloomy picture on SHGs. They are rapidly shrinking in size and scale. The stunted growth rate of SHG linkages over the last four years was striking. The negative growth rate went from -1.4 per cent in 2009-10 to -2.5 per cent in 2010-11 and then -4.2 in 2011-12. The declining trend in priority sector lending is also a cause for concern. The lending decelerated to 12.9 per cent during 2011-12 from 13.5 per cent in the previous year. Non-food credit growth was down to 17 per cent in 2011-12 from 20.6 per cent in 2010-11.

These are the areas that call for the government's refocus. Besides, we still have to cover financial literacy as a huge challenge. All financial inclusion initiatives in the country have been undertaken from the supply side. Therefore, livelihood promotion and credit needs of the people at the grass roots have largely remained unmet. Even the growth of self-help groups has suffered in the last couple of years. Skoch recently started a programme called Samavesh—an idea that was born to bridge this lack of financial and digital literacy, which is one of the key precipitating factors for exclusion. Skoch propounded its model of inclusive growth way back in 2009 based on its learning from over a decade through several field visits, studies, impact assessments, round table discussion and think tank activities.

The Samavesh was started in the pilot district of Dehradun with the objective to create one financially literate resource person per Gram Panchayat. The first leg of Samavesh covering Kalsi and Chakrata—two most unbanked blocks of Dehradun district—was implemented through community participation with focus on elected women *panchayati raj* members and community-based organisations. Nearly 200 women Gram Panchayat representatives and 100 Ward members, small and medium enterprises, individual entrepreneurs and other interested individuals participated in two-day intensive financial literacy workshop wherein they were informed about the need for savings, fixed deposits, insurance (life and general) and also benefits under social sector schemes that are going to be disbursed through Aadhaar-linked accounts. Under the programme, a team of 15-Master Trainers was prepared who, in turn, created the financial literacy curriculum customised to local conditions and comprehension levels of the participants that included play-way methods, games like snakes and ladders, skits, audio-visuals, and group discussions.

Samavesh puts a high degree of emphasis on functional literacy with the objective of reaching direct financial services (without intermediaries) to the people who need them the most. It makes a case for micro products to address the financial needs of people at the bottom of the pyramid. Samavesh will also try to dovetail electronic delivery of citizen services with delivery of financial services. It aims at promoting both supply-side and demand-side measures to achieve the objective of credit availability, livelihood promotion and poverty alleviation. The initial results have been very encouraging.[13]

In 2013, Skoch's State of the Sector report has advocated a holistic approach to solve the financial inclusion conundrum, and pinpoints the challenges and possible solutions.[14] In the section "Need to Reorient Financial Inclusion", the challenges are identified as: (i) ensuring adequate and timely credit supply; (ii) supporting livelihood initiatives; (iii) promoting entrepreneurship; (v) creating a sense of empowerment in the people; (vi) enabling poverty alleviation programmes; and (vi) bringing about a conducive environment for access to financial services.

The report moots several initiatives as answers. Setting up of a financial inclusion mission mode project is one essential step, it notes. Financial literacy is critical to make this effort successful and the goal should be to promote one financially literate woman per gram panchayat as a BF at a realistic compensation. It recommends convergence of all DBT benefits with the Financial Inclusion Plan of the government.

On the banking side, the report calls for setting demand-side targets on SHG formation, entrepreneurial credit, and lending to priority sector and marginalised sections of society. The report stresses the importance of a realistic interest rate regime and a technology-driven, but technology platform neutral, push to make available all relevant products to the unbanked. Among other initiatives mentioned are ratcheting up of banking-on-wheels, banking kiosks as well as micro-branch facilities; and sensitisation of bank manpower. On the regulatory side, the report underlines the need for all regulators to work on silo-bursting and create common distribution channels. A liberal policy stance on new bank licences is also proposed.

---

13. Samavesh (2012).
14. *State of The Sector Report, 2013.*

Clearly, the Skoch report can serve as a barometer to measure the progress on the three-way process the Rangarajan panel on financial inclusion had alluded to. It makes credit available to all vulnerable sections; widens financial services to all economic activities, whether it's agriculture, manufacturing or services; and erases regional disparities in the provision of financial services.

And also, as my friend Ashok Jha has indicated in a chapter in this book, financial inclusion should not be limited to just the banking sector. Reforming financial markets and making them a part of the inclusion process are essential steps, too.

Chidambaram characterised the role at the helm of finance ministry in these words in a newspaper article he wrote nearly a decade ago: "The finance minister is not a solo player. He is the conductor of an orchestra. He must take charge and conduct all other players to play the same tune. The buck, so far as the economy is concerned, stops at his desk."[15]

I have always believed that in Chidambaram, we have a very good conductor of a financial orchestra. His career record is ample proof of his no-nonsense, methodical and thoughtful approach to statecraft.

I have mentioned earlier how he could hold me in thrall, back in 2006, with his magnificent grasp on the topic of financial inclusion. His approach reminded me of those famous Robert Frost lines:

> Two roads diverged in a wood, and I/I took the one less traveled by,
> And that has made all the difference.

And I believe Chidambaram can make all the difference in making financial inclusion a reality.

References

Bhalla, Surjit S. (2012). "Poverty in India: Facts and Interpretation", in Sameer Kochhar (ed.), *Policymaking in Indian Planning: Essays in Honour of Montek Singh Ahluwalia*. New Delhi: Academic Foundation. p.140.

Gandhi, Sonia (2011). "Economic Growth for AamAadmi", *Inclusion* 2(1): 52-53, January-March. New Delhi.

Panagariya, Arvind (2010). "India on the Growth Turnpike: No State Left Behind", in Sameer Kochhar (ed.), *India on the Growth Turnpike, Essays in Honour of Vijay Kelkar*. New Delhi: Academic Foundation. p.56.

15. *Financial Express*, 14 September 2003.

Samavesh (2012). "Accelerating Inclusive Growth", *Inclusion* 3(4): 56-65, October-December. New Delhi.

Singh, Ravinder (2012). "Facts for You: Financial Inclusion to Bring Every Household in Banking Ambit", *Press Information Bureau Release*. 27th November.

9 Security

What Chidambaram Changed?

Sameer Kochhar and
Gursharan Dhanjal

"December 2008 was the most horrific time, most depressing. At the time of the (26/11) Mumbai attack, I was in my constituency. It was a Saturday when I got a call asking me to rush back to Delhi by 5 pm. There was an extended (Congress party) working committee meeting at 10 Janpath, which had been deferred till I reached. The working committee expressed its shock and deep regret at what had happened in Mumbai and the general mood was that (the incumbent Home Minister) Shivraj Patil should step down. Nobody explicitly made the demand though. The next morning, on Sunday, he tendered his resignation. I was called by the Prime Minister's Office to meet the Prime Minister at 9 AM where I was told that a decision had been taken by him and the Congress President that I would move to Home. I was very reluctant but I had to move," this is how Mr P. Chidambaram described the circumstances that contrived to him to be appointed the Home Minister in 2008, in an exclusive to *Inclusion*.[1]

By his own admission, Chidambaram was the reluctant Home Minister of India. All along, the finance ministry was that consumed his passion, with achieving higher growth rate for India and redistributive justice central to the scheme of things when he was in charge of the ministry since 2004. This passion translated into ideas, policies and results. India was able to grow at 8 per cent plus rates for three years in a row, and even with what he called the "rude disruption" of the Great Recession in the world in 2007-08, the country managed growth at a pretty decent clip. The economic reforms process was a going concern, despite coalition compulsions the UPA government was labouring under. In four

1. Inclusion (2012).

years, he demonstrated his conviction that higher growth is *sine qua non* for inclusive growth.[2]

Just as India's economy was being put on an even keel by Chidambaram's able hands during the perfect storm of global financial crisis, another perfect storm suddenly brewed in November 2008 within India's borders. That was the horrendous terrorist attacks in Mumbai, which came to be known as 26/11. It left 166 people dead. From 26 November onwards, for four days, 10 terrorists trained in Pakistan held the India's financial capital hostage to a vicious campaign of terror.

In many ways, it was the perfect storm on India's security front that was waiting to happen. The savagery had put the maladies afflicting the whole Indian security establishment—from response and organisation of law-enforcement agencies to the quality of intelligence the agencies come up with—in stark relief. Even more troubling was the political indecision and dither that marked the initial response to 26/11. The credibility of not only the internal security establishment but also the political leadership was at stake.[3]

Amongst other things, it exposed chinks in internal security; more so, ill-equipped police forces, which were also short of manpower. The sanctioned and actual police personnel per 100,000 people (police-population ratio) at the all-India level was 145.25 and 117.09 respectively, on 1 January 2007 as per the Bureau of Police Research and Development (BPR&D). The number of policemen per 100,000 people in India is 130. The minimum United Nations norm is 220. At 220, we are approximately 600,000 policemen short.[4] However, as per a UN report, such ratio in some countries like Italy (559), Mexico (491.8), Saudi Arabia (386.5) and Belgium (357.5) is much higher than India's.[5]

2. In October 2007, Chidambaram delivered the keynote address at the Norwegian Nobel Institute, Oslo, on "India's Socio-Economic Agenda: Development with Democracy". In the speech, he had underscored his profound belief on this score. The text of his speech is available at: *http://pib.nic.in/newsite/erelease.aspx?relid=32151*

3. During and after the 26/11 terrorist attacks, media reports were legion that brought out the frailties of India's internal security preparedness. For instance, an article published in *The Indian Express* underlined the chinks in India's internal security armour. *http://www.indianexpress.com/news/muddled-in-mumbai/405308/0*

4. Business Standard (2010).

5. Cited in UN Division for Policy Analysis and Public Affairs, United Nations, 31 March 2005.

Against this backdrop, Prime Minister Manmohan Singh appointed Chidambaram as the Home Minister within days of the 26/11 attack. His brief was unambiguous: overhaul India's security preparedness and suffuse paradigm shift into it.

After economic liberalisation put India on a faster growth trajectory and brought the country greater international heft, internal security's importance in economy had multiplied several times over. Post-1990 economic growth has served as a catalyst for foreign investment, and the country now can ill-afford to lose that advantage on account of terrorist strikes and internal strife.

Chidambaram's reluctance to move to the home ministry was understandable,[6] because he had his eyes firmly set on the economic horizon to realise the goals he had set for the country at a time the Great Recession still was a potent hazard. "I was mentally prepared for a six-month tenure in the home ministry. For one reason or another, six months have now extended to little over three years." But he hastened to add: "It's a job, someone has to do it."[7]

Doubtlessly, it was a formidable job that Chidambaram was up to at the Ministry of Home Affairs (MHA). There was no clear established link between counter-terrorism capability with operational capability in India's internal security paradigm until that point in time. The internal security apparatus was in a state of despair, with outdated counter-terrorism philosophies and even more outdated weapons and other essential equipment in the hands of the forces on the ground. Funding was insufficient to make them a modern, technologically advanced force to begin with, but even the earmarked budgets for internal security were unused year after year. There were turf wars raging among a multitude of law-enforcement and intelligence agencies, and coordination among them meant traversing through a potential minefield. Over and above, the political vision to fix things was sorely lacking. Internal security management, in effect, meant the country lurching from one crisis to another without acquiring the strategic thought framework or the

6. Even though Home Ministry was a kind of back-to-home assignment for Chidambaram, as he had earlier served as Minister of State for Internal Security in the Rajiv Gandhi government.

7. Cited in Inclusion (2012).

operational capacity to mount real-time anti-terrorism or anti-insurgency campaigns, let alone coordinated collection and collation of actionable intelligence to forestall attacks.

When 9/11 happened, the US too had not delineated clearly the link between the two; but the bipartisan 9/11 Commission had completely transformed the thinking in the US about counter-terrorism and homeland security.[8] India, being a victim of terror aided and abetted from abroad many times since 1990s, should have drawn the right lessons early, but 26/11 was indeed a rude wake-up call.

In the same interview, Chidambaram remarked, "We have put in place in the last three years a good analytical group at the central level, a reasonably good one at the state level, but we don't have counter-terrorism capability. Yes, if there is a terrorist attack, a force will immediately arrive and pick up the forensic evidence and chase the culprit. That is not the same as counter-terrorism. Counter-terrorism is about anticipating sources of threat and places of threat, going after them proactively and apprehending them before they are able to launch a terrorist attack. That is the capability, we don't have yet."[9]

That capacity might have eluded India in the three years when he was at the helm of the ministry, but what Chidambaram achieved constituted no less than a complete rebooting of the internal security system. And this he achieved in style, with forging a wider political consensus to summon the will to act.

The Initial Steps: Business-Like Approach

To paraphrase John F. Kennedy, one of the thing that surprised Chidambaram when he took office in December 2008 would have been that the most things were as bad as sensible people had been saying they were.[10]

8. The 9/11 Commission Report, formally named Final Report of the National Commission on Terrorist Attacks Upon the United States, is the official report of the events leading up to the September 11, 2001 attacks. The text of the report is available for download at: *http://www.9-11commission.gov/report/index.htm*

9. Cited in Inclusion (2012).

10. President Kennedy's original remarks, made in 1961, the year he took office, were: "When we got into office, the thing that surprised me the most was that things were as bad as we'd been saying they were."

The first thing he noticed was the rot started from the office of the Home Minister itself. The *'chalta-hai'* (everything goes, even though this translation can't do full justice to the colourful Hindi expression) attitude was writ large everywhere. As officials who worked with him can aver, Chidambaram is a tough taskmaster. He has a will to monitor, is hands-on and has his own timelines. "He is the first person to know about projects and knows how to push things. Under him the work culture in the MHA totally changed. Now there is nobody for a status quo," a few high-ranking officials who worked with him at that time recall.

The issue of punctuality in the MHA has brought Chidambaram's disciplinarian approach to the fore. In September 2009, he asked the entire staff to report at 0900 hrs, the official timing, and became the first to register his biometric print on the attendance machine. Since then, over 20 machines have been installed in MHA. The ministry time and again warned to punish employees who do not record attendance or clock mandatory 40 hours in a week. It has quoted the rule that any person who is late by 10 minutes thrice a month loses a casual leave.

His second move involved a welcome break from the past. In a bold step, Chidambaram encouraged the officials to think out-of-the-box. One of the first executive actions Chidambaram took after taking office was to send a questionnaire to all 28 Joint Secretaries in the ministry asking them as to how quickly they could improve functioning of the departments under them. He also told them to spell out any lacunae which could warrant his intervention and be removed for better results. Though it was not known what the bureaucrats wrote to Chidambaram in response but it made one thing clear that the new minister meant business.

The third move was the reintroduction of daily briefings of the Home Minister by Intelligence Bureau (IB) chief. In fact, to remove multiplicity and bring in some integration among the intelligence units, he also started holding joint sessions with National Security Advisor and heads of Research & Analysis Wing (RAW) and Joint Intelligence Committee (JIC).

Fourthly, he set deadlines for every task officers in the ministry were assigned. He not only 'ordered' the bureaucrats to stick to the timeframes but would also announced these to the press in his bi-monthly briefings to create a healthy dose of pressure on them.

Intelligence Coordination and Police Reforms

Agencies tasked with intelligence-gathering, analysis and sharing have historically been going around in circles in India, with little coordination —or even cooperation—among them. The result of the disorderly and often chaotic nature of intelligence operations was that more often than not, they were working at cross-purposes. The lessons we learnt the hard way on intelligence failure have been lost in transmission somewhere.[11]

Sorting out that kind of a mess was not an easy task. Yet, Chidambaram took the first serious steps that heralded a new era in intelligence-gathering and sharing. He strenuously made effort to get the central government issue an executive order to give legal cover to near-defunct Multi Agency Centre (MAC), and then made it operational from January 2009, chairing a meeting of senior officials from different intelligence agencies. The agenda was to chalk out a mechanism for sharing intelligence among the spymasters. He discussed with the chiefs of Intelligence Bureau (IB), RAW (Research and Analysis Wing) and Military Intelligence (MI) and other senior officials the modalities of the MAC related to the functions, powers and duties, which the MAC, established in the IB, has to take up.[12]

Around the same time, a few subsidiaries of the MAC (state MAC or SMAC) too were set up in states with Chidambaram promising to extend them to all states 'in due course.' The MHA also facilitated online and secure connectivity between MAC, SMACs and state special branches. He also approved a computerisation scheme for better surveillance and monitoring by the special branches.

MAC now has more than 15 law-enforcement and intelligence agencies working under its umbrella. Besides revival and legalisation of MAC, Chidambaram's other early feats included amendment in Unlawful

11. The Kargil Review Committee set by the Government of India went into the failure to share intelligence, seen as one of the causes of the Kashmir war, and recommended corrective action, but there had not been a piecemeal implementation of the recommendations.

12. The MAC was created in 2001 following the recommendations of the Group of Ministers that probed comprehensive reforms in India's national security apparatus in the wake of the Kargil conflict. The government had set up the body to coordinate and share intelligence available with different agencies, including the Intelligence Bureau, RAW and Military Intelligence. But it had not been in full operation till Chidambaram, as Home Minister, prescribed its functions, powers and duties.

Activities (Prevention) Act to strengthen arrangements for speedy investigation, prosecution and trial of cases related to terrorism and an ordinance to extend Central Industrial Security Force cover to industrial establishments in the joint and private sectors.

He announced National Security Guard (NSG) hubs at Chennai, Kolkata, Hyderabad and Mumbai and gave legal powers to DG, NSG, for requisitioning aircraft for movement of NSG personnel in the event of an emergency.[13] Within this period, he also got National Investigation Agency (NIA) Act enacted and notified NIA headquarters as a police station.

Unlike his predecessors, who would not go beyond issuing advisories to state governments during violence, Chidambaram not only did some plainspeak with them but also provided with whatever forces they asked for.[14]

When Chidambaram took over, there were 5,30,580 vacancies in the state police forces. The states had added 1,16,903 personnel by November 2011. Chidambaram called it a remarkable achievement but was also mindful of the 'distance that remains to be covered'. At the central level, 31,584 vacancies were filled in 2009-10 and 14,506 recruitments have so far been done in 2010-11.

The ministry had sanctioned 11,985 posts to the NSG for its four regional hubs, two regional centres and the operational headquarter at Manesar, Gurgaon. The procurements done by the central paramilitary forces include assault rifles, carbines, pistols, bullet-proof jackets, mine-protected and bullet-proof vehicles, armoured troop carriers, rescue boats, grenade launchers and night vision equipment.

The decline in militancy in Jammu & Kashmir was discernible, and the three-member team of interlocutors to explore peace in the state had been making steady progress.

---

13. The MHA had faced lot of flak for late despatch of NSG commandos to counter terrorists during 26/11.

14. For instance, he despatched a helicopter to keep surveillance during violence in Kandhmal (Orissa) soon after the demand was made by Chief Minister Naveen Patnaik.

Border Security

The responsibility for border intelligence had been extended to Directorate of Revenue Intelligence (DRI) and NIA apart from MI, BSF (Border Security Force), IB and RAW. He also put border fencing, floodlighting and construction of border roads on fast-track. Two schemes were launched for computerisation and networking of the Central Reserve Police Force (scheme called SELO) and BSF (a scheme called Prahari), the two largest paramilitary bodies. The interlinking could usher better man-management, resource management, information management and good decision support system for the forces.

The Mumbai terror attack had thoroughly exposed the gaps in coastal security. In fact, it was beyond belief that the terrorists could reach the city through the sea route undetected. Though a Coastal Security Scheme was formulated in 2006, its actual execution began in 2009 after the Mumbai terror attack when Chidambaram announced a project entailing issuance of identity cards to villages located on the 7,517 km-long coastline and setting up of coastal police stations, check posts, outposts and operational barracks. By November 2011, National Population Register (NPR) data work had been completed in all coastal states and Union Territories—Gujarat, Tamil Nadu, Puducherry, Kerala, Goa, Lakshadweep, Daman & Diu, Karnataka, Andhra Pradesh, Orissa, Andaman & Nicobar Islands, West Bengal and Maharashtra.

Anti-Maoist Insurgency Plan

Believe it or not, the most violent movement in India was not terrorism or insurgency but Left-wing Extremism (LWE). Addressing a gathering of collectors of most LWE-affected districts of the country in September 2011, Chidambaram observed that the Maoist insurgency has killed 10-times more people that year than those killed by terrorists in the country. "While 26 persons were killed in terrorist violence and 46 killed in insurgency (27 in Jammu and Kashmir), 297 persons were killed in Naxal violence. That is 10 times of those killed in terror incidents," he had said. He observed that three issues—trust deficit, governance deficit and development deficit—must be settled before the government wins the hearts and minds of villagers in naxal-affected states.[15]

In 2005, the home ministry had established a high-level panel to probe ways to stem the rising tide of LWE. In its report, the committee noted:

> While the mechanism constituted for countering naxalism envisaged a multi-pronged approach, over the years the State response has tended to remain largely police centric, with the main effort being to counter the movement with superior force. The approach has often swung from one extreme—that of using overwhelming force—to the other, structured around "ceasefires" and "peace talks." While it is recognised that the naxal problem goes well beyond mere law and order dimensions, the broader socio-economic issues have not attracted serious attention....[16]

When Chidambaram took office, the Maoist insurgency was gaining strength in Chhattisgarh, Jharkhand, Bihar, Orissa, West Bengal, Maharashtra, Andhra Pradesh, Madhya Pradesh and Uttar Pradesh. In fact, violence in the so-called red corridor peaked during 2012 recording death of 713 civilians (*vis-à-vis* 591 in 2009) and 285 (317 in 2009) policemen. The security forces, on the other hand, were able to neutralise 171 Maoists in 2010 (against 219 in 2009). Chhattisgarh in particular had a bloodiest 2010 with Maoists killing 142 civilians and 164 security personnel.

To combat LWE, the MHA under Chidambaram adopted a two-pronged holistic approach that supplements the efforts of state governments through security-related and development-related interventions. In security intervention, apart from directly deploying central armed police forces, the government actively participated in capacity-building efforts of the states through schemes like the security-related expenditure, special infrastructure and construction or strengthening of fortified police stations.

The MHA decided to open 20 Counter-insurgency and Anti-Terrorist (CIAT) schools, which will impart specialised training to state police undertaking counter-insurgency operations, jungle warfare, and counter-terrorism in affected states such as Bihar, Chhattisgarh, Orissa, and Jharkhand. Of these, seven CIAT schools distributed across Bihar, Chhattisgarh, Jharkhand, and Orissa have been sanctioned. Furthermore, the MHA decided in 2008 to carve out 10 battalions from the CRPF in

15. *The Tribune*, Chandigarh, September 14, 2011.
16. Ramana (2011).

order to create a specialised force exclusively to fight the Maoists.[17] These should realistically be completely operational by 2013. These battalions would be established at a total cost of about ₹ 1400 crore (roughly ₹ 900 crore for infrastructure, and about ₹ 500 crore for training).[18]

Chidambaram stressed on filling vacancies in the state police and central paramilitary forces, generously allocated funds for schemes for their modernisation including upgradation of their weaponry, initiated work on linking them up through technology, constantly argued for air support to them and fast-tracked their training in jungle warfare.

The second approach involved economic development packages. In November 2010, Chidambaram announced a two-year Integrated Action Plan (IAP) in 60 naxal-hit tribal and backward districts. The districts were spread over these nine states[19] where the IAP was aimed at improving basic infrastructure like road, power and health. The IAP focused on effective implementation of the Provisions of the Panchayats (Extension to the Scheduled Areas) Act, 1996 and the Scheduled Tribes and Other Traditional Forest Dwellers (Recognition of Forest Rights) Act, 2006 (Forest Rights Act). While the district component was administered by the Ministry of Panchayati Raj, the state component was supervised by the Planning Commission.

In 2010-11 alone, each of the 60 districts was given a block grant of ₹ 12.5 crore. In 2011-12, the grant was increased to ₹ 30.0 crore and 18 more districts were added to the beneficiary list.

It is interesting to note that connectivity, employment, market access and education have direct socioeconomic impact on geography. More so, a secure environment allows the benefits of growth and development to percolate down to the intended beneficiaries. Detailed Project Reports

17. The sanctioning of India Reserve (IR) battalions and raising of Commando Battalions for Resolute Action (CoBRA), the specialised force trained for counter-insurgency and jungle-warfare operations, added to the states' firepower. Thirty-seven IR battalions were sanctioned to nine LWE-affected states. Provision was made for raising two companies per battalion as commando units/specialised forces for which additional financial assistance of ₹ 6 crore was provided by Central Government for each IR battalion. Ten battalions of CoBRA were raised as part of CRPF.

18. Ramana (2011).

19. Andhra Pradesh, Bihar, Chhattisgarh, Jharkhand, Madhya Pradesh, Maharashtra, Orissa, Uttar Pradesh and West Bengal.

(DPRs) for over 25,671 km road length to connect 10,129 habitations for 33 LWE-affected districts in eight states were cleared by October 2009.[20] An amount of ₹ 5,659.39 crore was released for these roads. Not only this, a number of households were provided employment under the National Rural Employment Guarantee Scheme (NREGS)—now rechristened as Mahatma Gandhi National Rural Employment Guarantee Scheme (MGNREGS). Further, ₹ 2,228.95 crore were released for electrifying all the villages and habitations under Rajiv Gandhi Grameen Vidhytikaran Yojana (RGGVY), in addition to Sarva Shikha Abhiyan (SSA) which spent ₹ 737.65 crore and Indira Avas Yojana, under which 150,369 houses were sanctioned and 76,729 were allotted.[21]

According to the MHA, the number of casualties in Maoist violence has shown a decline in 2012 compared to 2010 and 2011. According to official statistics, violence claimed the lives of 287 civilians and 113 security force personnel till 30 November 2012. In 2011 and 2010, the casualty figures were 611 and 1,005 respectively.[22]

"We have to do better... It is a long haul," Chidambaram told the Rajya Sabha in May 2012, hoping that the government would get an upper hand on the situation "eventually."

Technology to Secure India

Technology wizard Tim Berners-Lee often says that "Data is a precious thing and will last longer than the systems themselves."

Data is as important to a comprehensive intelligence-sharing mechanism as it is to any other field of applied mathematics. To integrate databases and place them before intelligence agencies, the MHA under Chidambaram launched implementation of National Intelligence Grid (NATGRID), a programme that will integrate 21 databases like land records, internet logs, phone records, gun records, driving licence, property records, insurance and income tax records and make them available in real time to 11 intelligence agencies to sniff a terrorist plot. Personnel from RAW, IB,

20. Ministry of Home Affairs (2010).

21. Ibid: 24.

22. *MHA Report Card*, November 2012.

MI, Revenue Intelligence, National Security Council etc., in liaison with the NATGRID will sift through the data for actionable intelligence.

Interlinking of databases—from driving licence and bank account details to immigration records—will drastically curtail the time taken for security agencies to retrieve information about individuals. This system will also lubricate the flow of real-time, actionable intelligence sharing among various intelligence agencies.

A major component of the NATGRID, in fact, is expected to come from the private sector. "The government realises the major technological expertise in the private sector and therefore, it is seeking to increase the role that it plays in this area in such projects," G.K. Pillai, Union Home Secretary, had declared.[23]

Crime and Criminal Tracking Network and Systems (CCTNS), another ambitious mission mode project under the National e-Governance Plan, was conceived by Chidambaram. CCTNS plans to interlink about 20,000 police stations, finger print bureaus and forensic laboratories, etc., on a national databank of crime and criminals and would help people lodge and track complaints online. It will have a linkage with databases of other agencies of criminal justice system like jails, immigration, courts and passport authorities. It is about creation of a nationwide networking infrastructure for evolution of IT-enabled state-of-the-art tracking system around 'investigation of crime and detection of criminals.' "Training is a big component of CCTNS project and steps have been initiated to ensure that suitable training is imparted to everyone on the ground, right from the police stations upwards," Pillai had said. Being implemented by National Crime Record Bureau (NCRB), the pilot was launched in January 2013.

Another revolutionary decision Chidambaram took was about the implementation of Mission Mode Project on Immigration, Visa and Foreigners Registration and Tracking (IVFRT). The project, aimed at developing a secure and integrated service delivery framework to enhance security and facilitate immigration, issue of visas and registration, will help the country keep an eye for criminals against whom Look Out Notices (LoCs) are out and check entry of unwanted or blacklisted persons. The

23. Inclusion (2011).

project planned to interlink 169 missions in foreign countries, 77 Indian check posts, 7 FRROs and 640 foreign registration offices.

Since the data including the photo biometric document would come to central processing system of Central Foreigners' Bureau (CFB) too, it would keep security agencies in the loop on every single person who will check into the country. The project was operationalised in Indian High Commission at Islamabad in June and in the Indian mission in London in November 2011. It has also been implemented in Bangladesh. Designed by National Informatics Centre (NIC), the project is scheduled to be completed by September 2014.

The Way Ahead

Addressing IB officers on 23 December 2009, Chidambaram described the proposed National Counter Terrorism Centre (NCTC) as an outfit capable of "preventing a terrorist attack, containing a terrorist attack should one take place, and responding to a terrorist attack by inflicting pain upon the perpetrators."

In 2008, the Second Administrative Reforms Commission recommended that MAC should be converted into NCTC with personnel drawn from different intelligence and security agencies. A review of the current architecture of counter-terrorism uncovered several gaps and deficiencies and the need was felt for a single of control and coordination of all counter terrorism measures.

The Cabinet Committee on Security (CCS) cleared the institution of the NCTC in January 2012. The NCTC will be an integrated platform that will collect, evaluate and analyse intelligence, maintain a databank and coordinate counter-terrorist operations. Headed by a full time director, the NCTC will make sharing of intelligence and follow up operations efficient, faster and better coordinated. The operations division of the counter-terrorism body has been given powers to arrest and carry out searches under Section 43 (A) of the Unlawful Activities (Prevention) Act, 1967.

Although the NCTC was to be set up from 1 March 2012, that could not be done as a few chief ministers have expressed their misgivings over police powers being given to the NCTC. The controversy that followed has stalled the movement on this front until now. Progress on NCTC would definitely forge greater coherence in intelligence sharing and operational response. It is indeed sad that facile arguments about federalism and privacy have been advanced to derail some anti-terror and anti-insurgency capacity-building. Each terrorist attack makes it abundantly clear that India lacks a central coordinating body to process raw intelligence and share actionable intelligence with states.

Much work also need to be done to shore up India's cyber security. It calls for a three-tier system. One, creation of requisite technical talent to strengthen our IT system; two, an effective legal framework; and three, an efficient security infrastructure that could use technology with ease and the law towards achieving the objective of securing information assets of the nation.[24] As changes in the economy are leading to increased use of IT and data processing, the need for a comprehensive data protection and security law can't be postponed any longer. While such legislation should ensure personal data protection, it should balance the need for data sharing for legitimate needs, including that of national security.

These are some of the areas where India must break a new ground.

All in all, most of the tasks Chidambaram initiated within the first six months of his taking over as Home Minister have either been achieved or on track to their accomplishment by the time he left office on 31 July 2012, to become the Finance Minister yet again. The facts speak for themselves: what he achieved in his first one-and-half months surpassed what his immediate predecessor could not achieve in four-and-half years in office.

Having seized the moment and crafted a brand-new philosophical, technological and operational framework for internal security, the legacy that Chidambaram left behind at the MHA was impressive. It's for his successors to build on it.

References

Business Standard (2010). "Our Police will be Effective in 7-8 years", Q&A with G.K. Pillai, Home Secretary, *Business Standard* (New Delhi), 14 February.

Dhanjal, Gursharan (2011). "Trojans in India's Cyber Security", *Inclusion* 2 (Special Issue): 4-5. New Delhi.

24. Dhanjal (2011).

Inclusion (2011). "The Canvas for Change is Huge: An Interview with G.K. Pillai," *Inclusion* 2 (Special Issue): 22-25. New Delhi.

———. (2012). "Chidambaram on Chidambaram", *Inclusion* 3(2): 56-63. April-June. New Delhi.

Ministry of Home Affairs (2010). *Annual Report 2009-10*. Government of India. p.23

Ramana, P.V. (2011). "India's Maoist Insurgency: Evolution, Current Trends and Responses", in Michael Kugelman (ed.), *India's Contemporary Security Challenges*. Washington, D.C.: Woodrow Wilson International Center for Scholars. p.41.

10 India: From Value Added Tax (VAT) to Goods and Services Tax (GST)

Parthasarathi Shome[1]

Introduction: Early Application of the Credit Principle

India has been on the reform path in its indirect tax structure since 1986 when the VAT-related credit principle of allowing credit against tax paid on inputs against tax collected on sales was initiated. It reflected the government's White Paper, *Long Term Fiscal Strategy*, of December 1985. This principle was introduced on selected commodities, at the Centre, up to the manufacturing stage of the production-distribution chain. It reflected the Indian Constitution's allocation of taxing powers to the Centre up to the manufacturing stage while the power to tax sales (or the distribution stage) had been given to the states. Subsequently, the number and dispersion of tax rates were reduced; the credit principle was extended to an increasing number of commodities. Thus, the Centre's excise structure went through a modified VAT phase (or MODVAT) and subsequently was called Central VAT (or CENVAT) when the credit principle became universal and the rates collapsed into a single rate together with a few exceptional rates. In 1995, a positive list of five services was introduced to be taxed at a lower rate; the rate and number of services were brought up over the years, and input tax credit between goods and services was featured. Though services have not been mentioned in the taxing powers under the Constitution, the Centre took the step of taxing them through the residual category that has been assigned to it by the Constitution. Currently, all major services are taxed with a negative list of exempted services. The CENVAT rate and the service tax rate are the same though they are not yet equivalent.

1. All opinions are exclusively those of the author.

At the state level, after a decade of preparation from 1998, a VAT on goods was introduced in 2005, from manufacturing stage forward. Since the CENVAT rate is included in the base of the state level VAT (SVAT), there is cascading or a built-in tax-on-tax effect. Further, a tax on interstate trade whose rate is determined by the Centre (hence Central Sales Tax or CST) but is collected and retained by states continues, though it is planned to be phased out. Since the CST paid in the exporting state is not given credit in the importing state, the tax gets embedded in the downstream distribution chain. Thus it cascades. Thus, the present combined Centre-states indirect tax structure exhibits considerable progress that has already been made, though several lacunae remain.

An improved structure in the form of GST is, therefore, being proposed. It will run in parallel at the Centre and state levels, and will comprise seamless taxation through the entire chain of production and distribution and also include both goods and services under both the Centre and states. However, there are important goods that are proposed to be excluded from the GST base, rendering it not comparable with GST structures across the world. The global practice of equalising GST rates has also not been guaranteed. The GST was planned to be introduced on April 1, 2010. However, progress towards a robust, meaningful structure has been in fits and starts. GST's introduction is, therefore, awaited.

In what follows, Section II will traverse the ground recalling the emergence of the VAT, pointing towards the fits and starts that it suffered in the process of introduction. It then clarifies the current CENVAT/service tax structure at the Centre and the VAT/CST structure of the states to illustrate where cascading occurs in the system. It also comments on the potential revenue productivity of the VAT. Section III focusses on the ideal structure for an Indian GST, the particular challenges reflecting the fact that the GST, being also at the level of states, would have to address the issue of interstate trade while ensuring the GST's nature as a consumption tax,[2] and other concerns that have arisen between the Centre and states since the GST will cover both levels of government. Section IV concludes

2. This implies that, when GST is paid by an importing dealer from state B to an exporting dealer in state A, the revenue collected has to be transferred from A to B where the consumption of the traded commodity takes place.

by citing some international experiences and whether there is scope for India to draw any salient conclusions from them.

II

Value Added Tax

Emergence of VAT

In December 1995 (when a Congress-led government was at the Centre), in a conference called by the Union Finance Minister, he asked state finance ministers to study the ramifications of the prevailing distortive state taxes (comprising the sales tax) on domestic goods and services as well as the tax on interstate trade (CST). Prior to this period, states outcompeted each other by lowering sales tax rates to attract investment until four floor rates—by category of goods—were agreed upon among themselves. However, several negative features remained in the overall structure including multiplicity of rates and exemptions.

In December 1996, a task force comprising experts in taxation and state level finance secretaries submitted its first report on phasing out the CST that recommended a reduction of the CST rate from 4 per cent to 2 per cent, and further reduction based on certain conditions. Subsequently, state chief ministers formed an Empowered Committee of state finance ministers (EC-VAT) to consider introduction of a VAT that would alleviate the remaining lacunae in the improved sales tax.

In 2002, the Central government led by the Bharatiya Janata Party (BJP), in a conference of EC-VAT, announced plans for the introduction of VAT in all states from April 2003. They agreed on a minimum set of common features in every state's VAT legislation. A model VAT structure was circulated to all states. It was agreed that CST would be phased out. Except Haryana which was a special case, all other states postponed the implementation of VAT, however, in the last minute, with impending general elections.

Reasons for Not Introducing the VAT in the First Round

To begin with, all states were not adequately prepared. Some states were hurrying through their VAT legislation in state assemblies even in the last week of March. Second, it was apprehended by the traders that a VAT would increase their paper work and was more complicated. Third, the VAT was proposed to replace sales tax and some minor taxes such as the work contract tax, lease tax, turnover tax and luxury tax but octroi, a distortionary tax on entry to municipalities, was to remain as well as taxes on selected services so that the VAT would be an incomplete reform. Fourth, state-level excise duties would continue in their present form instead of being included in the VAT base so that the information chain would be truncated and affect administration adversely.

There were other reasons. Fifth, traders apprehended that prices of certain products would rise, e.g., medicines and drugs, due to an inevitable increase in their effective tax rates. Sixth, from the states' point of view, the fact that revenue gains would be uneven among states was a big obstacle unless the Centre came in to compensate the revenue-losing states. Thus, the anticipated benefits did not match up to the lingering adverse political economy of VAT introduction at that point in time.

The Second Round in the VAT's Introduction

A Congress-led government was elected in April 2004. In January 2005, EC-VAT completed a White Paper on VAT. It proposed rates of 4 per cent and 12.5 per cent, with a common base and exemption list and a pool of about 40 exemptions that could be of local importance, from which each state could pick 10 exemptions. Though there was a peculiarity that the lower rate of 4 per cent covered capital goods and raw materials that, under the credit principle, would be credited out anyway and that, therefore, it would have been better to reserve the lower rate for goods of consumption by lower income deciles as is common global practice; nevertheless, on the whole the VAT structure was superior to the sales tax that it replaced. The distortionary CST continued, however.

On April 1, 2005, the state-level VAT was introduced. States ruled by the BJP or other parties such as the Samajwadi Party (SP) and the Dravida

Munnetra Kazhagam (DMK) desisted. The experience from the VAT was salutary. Revenue growth from the VAT was 25 per cent p.a. in contrast to an average of 12.5 per cent from sales tax for five years prior to VAT's introduction.

VAT remains a shining example of fiscal federal cooperation as the Centre assured a formula-based compensation for revenue loss incurred by states based on their previous best three years' revenue which turned out to feature a growth rate of 17.5 per cent p.a. The compensation would be given for three years, on a declining scale from 100 per cent to nil. ₹ 5000 crore were allocated. While most states experienced revenue gain, some large manufacturing states lost but were compensated from the compensation fund, resulting in the Centre's exhausting the budgeted amount for compensation. In view of the revenue gain, eventually all states introduced VAT reflecting its revenue productivity.

An important cause of revenue expansion was, first, the extension of the tax base to traders/retailers i.e., the taxpayer base. Earlier, under the sales tax, the practice in many states was merely to add a premium to the manufacturing value to derive the effective tax base. Second, many states that earlier applied rudimentary tax administration methods began to tax goods in a comprehensive manner for the first time, thus expanding the effective tax base.

VAT's high revenue productivity has been observed internationally. If the general VAT rate is x per cent, its yield should approach $1/2x$ per cent of GDP as per the Shome Index of VAT Productivity. For this to be achieved, the VAT base needs to be broad in its scope and its administration should be modern and supported by appropriate information and communication technology (ICT) back-up so that it can minimise leakage. Countries such as Chile and New Zealand have been successful. With a VAT rate of 18 per cent, both countries had achieved VAT revenue collection of almost 9 per cent of GDP. Other developed countries, such as, the United Kingdom (UK), have not been successful. With a standard VAT rate of 17.5 per cent, the UK collects slightly less than 6 per cent of GDP, i.e., around $1/3x$ per cent of GDP. While leakage from VAT collection is not too high, European Union (EU) members are subject to the Sixth Directive on VAT. A member can enter the EU with an existing exemption regime but if they remove an exemption, they cannot reinstate it. Thus, there is a tendency to maintain exemptions as they are. Many developing economies collect around 1/3*x* of GDP in VAT revenue.[3]

Returning to the Indian case, the next phase was a Centre-state agreement to phase out the CST. Under this principle, the CST rate of 4 per cent would decline by 1 per cent p.a., reaching 0 per cent by April 1, 2010, when a GST would be introduced. While the process was initiated, the process of reduction stalled at 2 per cent, reflecting several factors. First, states became increasingly vocal regarding the amount of compensation that they should receive for revenue loss from the lowering and eventual abolition loss of the CST. First, they clarified that they were not being compensated for the revenue loss that they were suffering from CST reduction from 4 to 2 per cent. Further, they have taken the position that the revenue loss from CST abolition is a permanent one so that they expect the Centre to work out a perennial compensation mechanism for this loss. The Centre appears to have been unable to alleviate the states' concerns or work out a midway solution, and the Centre-state fiscal federal relations appear to be at a crossroads with the Chairman of EC-VAT recently declaring publicly that there is a sense of distrust in this relationship.

Second, if the CST is to be abolished, the current mechanism based on filling out forms to administer and check the interstate trade flow would be lost. Interstate trade would then have to be tracked through a clearing house mechanism that is explained later. Without a robust, ICT-based clearing house mechanism, the CST cannot, or perhaps, should not, be abolished. Thus, much work remains to be done in completely phasing out the CST.

Thus, considerable cascading remains in the present indirect tax structure. It may, therefore, be useful to demonstrate at which points cascading occurs. This is attempted in self-explanatory Figure 10.1. While formal estimates are not available, if one uses the current tax rates that are not credited out in the process of production and distribution, then a quick calculation of the embedded tax in manufacturing climbs beyond 20 per

3. In India, if the state level VAT is considered where the rates are 12.5 percent and 4 percent, and the fact that services fall outside the VAT net, then VAT collection is above 1/3*x* of the relevant GDP base.

cent, which escalates the final effective tax rate on the commodity. It is not too surprising that Indian manufacturing has suffered a significant decline in its share of GDP and has also become less competitive in international trade.

Figure 10.1

Cascading in Indirect Tax Structure

Goods	*Cascading*	*Services*
Manufacturing • CENVAT (Centre) • ITC—allowed within CENVAT[1]	• CENVAT – cascades within regionally dispersed firms – ITC for capital goods given over two years	• Service Tax (Centre) • ITC allowed between CENVAT and Service Tax.
WHOLESALE (Dealers) • Base includes (CENVAT ⇓ cascading VAT (States).	• State level VAT – cascades at three points (as shown)	• ITC not allowed between State level VAT and Service Tax.
RETAIL • ITC allowed within state level VAT but not for ⇓ services cascading. • Interstate trade is taxed by CST for which there ⇓ is no ITC cascading.		

Note: [1] However, ITC is allowed only within a unit, not within a firm across its various units situated in various jurisdictions.

III

Goods and Services Tax

The concept of GST was mooted to remove the remaining lacunae in the present indirect tax structure, originally planned to be introduced on April 1, 2010. This final phase of reform progressed up to a point but has been held back for various reasons. Recalling the developments, in December 2007, a GST committee convened by the Union Finance Minister and EC-VAT submitted a report recommending a two-chain GST for the Centre and states covering both goods and services and with the input tax credit (ITC) principle applicable through both chains. There would be no credit across the Centre and state chains since that would imply anomalous revenue ramifications between them where revenue sharing is determined by the Finance Commission every five years as per the Indian Constitution. That ideal GST structure is illustrated in Figure 10.2.

Figure 10.2

Ideal Structure of GST

Centre CGST		**States** SGST
1 general rate (1 lower rate could be accommodated)		1 general rate (1 lower rate could be accommodated)
	Selected Features	
• Broad base including petroleum, alcohol and tobacco	• Parallel chains → No ICT between CGST and SGST	• Broad base including petroleum, alcohol and tobacco
• Goods and services to be taxed at general rate	• Cascading removed from overall GST system	• Subsume smaller taxes • Goods and services taxed at general rate
• A few low-income consumption items at lower rate	• No CST on interstate trade → Inter-state Goods and Services Tax (IGST) to operate	• A few low-income consumption items at lower rate
• Full ITC across multiple units of a firm		• Abolish CST • Full ITC across states • Monitor interstate trade with computerised infrastructure • Install clearing house (at central government level or at selected banks) for accounting and payments for trade (IGST)

The currently prevailing proposal for the GST structure has much to be desired. First, the rate structures for Central GST (CGST) and state GST (SGST) have not been agreed upon. A significant flaw here would be to have different rates for goods and services. The whole point of a GST is not to have to differentiate between goods and services and, instead, to have a seamless relationship that would negate all judicial cases over disagreements in classification. Having different rates for goods and services will be quite inconsistent with global practice on VAT or GST. India must follow global practice in order for its GST to be internationally meaningful.

GST Base

The crux of a GST is to have a broad base that would, in turn, enable a low tax rate. Therefore, the GST base should be as broad as possible. The list of exemptions from both states and the Centre, presently numbering in the hundreds, should be further reduced under the GST. If India has to have a GST, these numbers for exemptions are too high.

There are other significant exclusions from the base. Almost half the revenue coverage—petroleum, alcoholic beverages and tobacco products—are planned to be kept out of the GST base. The advantage of keeping them within the GST base is that the tax administrations at central and state levels will have the necessary information on the complete upstream to downstream process of production and distribution. Therefore, it is important to bring in petroleum and alcoholic products into the GST base. What countries do in order to get more revenue from these products, since tobacco and alcohol are considered to be demerit goods and petroleum is a non-renewable resource, is to levy excises on them and then impose the GST rate. This should be done in India also and a revenue neutral configuration could be worked out. Government departments should also ideally be within the GST base, as is the case in many countries, again to structure the GST in a seamless manner. However, if political economy considerations make it impossible to cover defence, for example, then it has to be accepted (defence has essentially remained outside central excises also).

Implications of Consumption Tax on Interstate Trade Mechanism

The GST should be a consumption-based tax. Therefore, for SGST, a method has to be found such that the revenue from interstate trade goes to the state that imports and consumes rather than to the state that produces and exports a good or service. The appropriate method is for the producer/exporter state to collect the revenue from the purchaser/dealer (from an importing state) and to pass on that revenue to the importer state's exchequer. This can be facilitated by transmitting the collected money in a clearing house and, from there, to transfer the money to the importing/consuming state.

Theoretically, the clearing house can be the central government itself i.e., the states send in the collected revenue to the central government which, in turn, sends the revenue stored with it to the various importing states. The practical question is, first, who would finance the creation of this clearing house and, second, how long would an importing state wait for its due revenue to arrive. A list of designated banks could also act as a clearing house but for this arrangement also, banks would have to be compensated as a service provider. Whether it is the banking system or the central government that acts as a clearing house, a computerised system needs to be developed for it. It has to be capable of distributing revenue collected in one exporter state to all states where the goods have gone to be consumed (and it has to repeat this exercise for every exporting state, and continuously over time). Such a comprehensive computer system is not yet in place.

What is continuing now is a two per cent CST and the revenue is being retained by the exporting states. These states want compensation from the Centre if they remove CST (which is necessary to make the GST into a consumption-based tax). Reflecting its overall fiscal position, it would be a mammoth task for the central government to feasibly compensate states perennially for the abolition of CST, which is what is being effectively asked by the states. Recalling that, when the state-level VAT was introduced, the compensation for revenue loss by the Centre for the states was kept at only ₹ 5000 crore and that too, it was for a finite period of three years based on a formula for diminishing compensation. A new compensation formula needs to be threshed out for CST abolition based on diminishing revenue compensation from the Centre to states. Thus, Sarma and Bhaskar's (2012: 74) recent suggestions that:

- The Centre should settle the CST compensation dispute with the states immediately.

- The Centre should provide a firm assurance upfront to states that they will provide compensation to states for possible losses in implementation of GST for a period of at least five years as suggested by the Thirteenth Finance Commission.

are likely to turn out to be more challenging than at first glance.

The CST has been brought down from the original four per cent rate to two per cent in anticipation of a consumption-based GST. But given the lack of computerisation to monitor interstate trade, reports indicate that VAT evasion has grown by attributing more to interstate trade which has only a two per cent CST rate than declaring it as within-state sale (which faces a higher VAT rate). Information based on a pilot project in a manufacturing state that is examining if a taxpayer reports the same turnover in tax returns for different taxes—income tax, excise and customs, service tax, VAT—reveals that reported turnover can be very different for different taxes by the same taxpayer. Thus, measures to minimise tax evasion must be installed before GST is introduced or CST is abolished.

There are other unresolved issues between the Centre and states. The state-level VAT and the Centre's CENVAT have thresholds over which these taxes apply. These are ₹ 10 lakh for states and ₹ 1.5 crore for the Centre. The Centre prefers to bring down its threshold but the states basically think of it as encroachment into their small taxpayers that they prefer to keep as exclusively theirs. Ideally, they should not impose any restriction in the Centre's decision regarding its own threshold just as they should be able to maintain their own threshold without the Centre's interference and based solely on their administrative capacities.

Service Tax Concern of States

One issue is, in what manner the current service tax will be subsumed, and what its effects will be under the GST. The states will also tax services under the GST (within their chain of SGST). But they remain unconvinced about the revenue potential from this base expansion. This is because, under the current state-level VAT, while there is no revenue coming from service tax (since this tax remains outside state VAT), under a future GST, SGST will obtain revenue from service tax but also give input tax credit for service tax paid by taxpayers. Thus, the states are not confident about how much net revenue they will gain by being able to tax services under the SGST.

Structuring the GST Council

Finally, the mechanism of decision-making in the GST Council has to be carefully calibrated. The original proposal that was flawed was based on a simple majority of states present at meetings that could amend rules. That would allow a handful of states to be able to change fundamental operations at the Centre's behest. Now, as is being interpreted, the new proposal requires a consensus that could result in too strict a requirement for changing rules. It could imply that the Centre could never make changes to its liking. Instead, states that are not present should also be allowed to vote within a specified time period. If say, the Centre reserves $1/3^{rd}$ of the voting power and the states $2/3^{rd}$, and any change also requires $2/3^{rd}$ majority, then changes can occur only if all states are opposed to the Centre, or the Centre carries half the states with itself. This kind of voting requirement could be complemented with other combinations for different type of changes. Given the enormity of the implications for Centre-state economic—and political economy—relations of GST reform, the voting aspect of the GST Council over and above its administrative structure, requires fine toothcomb consideration and analysis before a final decision is made.

The GST Bill proposes a dispute resolution authority to ameliorate any action by a state or the Centre that adversely affects the harmonised GST structure. The states have, however, expressed their opposition to the formation of a supra body that would have the power to dictate them on matters of dispute resolution. The EC prefers the GST Council to devise an appropriate mechanism to resolve disputes rather than another body, according to its Chairman, with 'legislative supremacy'. It has asked for the Bill to be amended accordingly and feels that, if a dispute cannot be resolved at the GST Council, then the matter should pass to the level of the judiciary. These matters—of the GST Council and of dispute resolution—remain to be resolved to the satisfaction of both the Centre and the states.

IV

Concluding Remarks

India has come a long way in its indirect tax reform. Final reform poses a challenge, in particular because both the Centre and states play significant roles in this area of taxation and the reform encompasses both levels of government considered together. Other fiscal federal countries have not fared as well as India. Argentina has a central VAT and its provinces have uncoordinated provincial tax structures, many of which cascade. Brazil's states have often made unilateral changes in their respective VAT structures even though they meet regularly under Conselho National de Politica Faezendária (CONFAZ), a council similar to India's EC-VAT. Even though CONFAZ is convened by their Central government's Deputy Finance Minister, it has little sway over the fiscal or policy behaviour of states, possibly reflecting the narrow VAT at the Centre that applies only to a short list of industrial products.

Canada has a complex GST buttressed by an advanced ICT infrastructure. The central government has its own harmonised GST. It administers its own harmonised GST but also the provincial GSTs of smaller provinces such as New Brunswick, Nova Scotia and New Foundland. The province of Ontario administers its own GST while the centre administers the harmonised GST there. The province of Quebec, on the other hand, administers both the harmonised and the provincial GST. Some mineral-rich provinces such as Alberta, Saskatchewan and Winnipeg apparently have not introduced a provincial GST. Overall, Canada's is no doubt a complex GST structure.

Thus, examining global experience among fiscal federal countries, India has accomplished more in terms of VAT uniformity and in ameliorating possible deleterious distortions for economic decision-making. Nevertheless, despite its complex centre-provinces arrangements, the Canadian GST may have some salient characteristics that may be useful for India, reflecting several expectations that Indian states have placed on the table before the Indian GST can become viable. First, states want flexibility in their GST rate structure. They are eschewing the single rate concept and prefer a floor rate and a narrow band on top, while allowing only two—standard and lower—rates within the band. Second, they want flexibility on rates during emergencies such as floods or droughts when they should be allowed to put rates of ordinary times in abeyance. These preoccupations are comparable to those prevalent in the Canadian model and should not be impossible to alleviate, even though they would imply higher taxpayer compliance costs and would require deeper levels of ICT support than currently envisaged.

In conclusion, India needs to reformulate its GST Bill with patience and perspicacity. The objective should be to achieve a low rate structure and ample base with few, if any, rational exemptions, effective and transparent administrative organisation and rules, supported by a fully installed, world-class computer system at the central, state, and interstate levels, while being cognisant of modern taxpayer (or customer) concerns. The last, increasingly crucial aspect of customer facilitation across tax administrations globally, is a matter worthy of special attention and may be addressed on another occasion.

References

Agurrie, C. and Parthasarathi Shome (1988). "The Mexican Value Added Tax: Methodology for Calculating the Base", *National Tax Journal* 41: 543-54. December.

Bagchi, A. (1995). "Inter-Governmental Fiscal Relations: The Cases of India and Indonesia", in J. Roy (ed.), *Macroeconomic Management and Fiscal Decentralisation: EDI Seminar Series*. Washington D.C.: Economic Development Institute of The World Bank.December.

———. (1997). "A State Level VAT? Harmonising Sales Taxes: A Comparison of India and Canada", in Parthasarathi Shome (ed.), *Value Added Tax in India: A Progress Report*. New Delhi: Centax Publications Pvt Ltd. pp.273-97.

Bird, Richard M. (2000). "Subnational VATs: Experience and Prospects", Symposium in Honour of John F. Due, *93 Annual Conference of National Tax Association*. Santa Fe, New Mexico. November (draft).

Cnossen, S. (2012). "Introducing a Modern GST in India: Need for Further Debate", *Tax Notes International*. 66 (13): 1267-83, June.

Karnataka Tax Reforms Commission (2001). *First Report and Final Report*. Bangalore, India.

McMorran, Ronald T. (1995). "Mechanisms to Alleviate Cascading", in Parthasarathi Shome (ed.), *Tax Policy Handbook*. Washington D.C.: International Monetary Fund.

Mukhopadhyay, S. (2005). *The Economics of Value-Added Tax: Theory & Practice*. New Delhi: Centax Publications Pvt Ltd.

National Institute of Public Finance and Policy (1995). *Taxation of Services: Scope for Extension*. New Delhi.

Sarma, J.V.M. and V. Bhaskar (2012). "A Road Map for Implementing the Goods and Services Tax", *Economic & Political Weekly* XLVII(31), August 4.

Shome, P. (1992). "Trends and Future Directions in Tax Policy Reform: A Latin American Perspective", Inaugural Speech, *Annual Conference of the Center for Inter-American Tax Administration (CIAT)*. Jamaica; reprinted in *Bulletin for International Fiscal Documentation* 46: 452-66, September.

———. (1994). "Fiscal Federal Relations and Macro Economic Management: Selected Latin American Experiences", Inaugural Address, *Sixth Regional Conference*. Santiago de Chile: UN Commission for Latin America and The Caribbean (ECLAC).

———. (ed.) (1995). *Tax Policy Handbook, International Monetary Fund*. Washington D.C.

———. (1996). *Fiscal Policy in the 1990s—Needed Reforms and Ramifications for the Financial Sector.* Sir Purshotamdas Thakurdas Memorial Lecture. Mumbai: Indian Institute of Bankers. December.

———. (ed.) (1997). *Value Added Tax in India: A Progress Report.* New Delhi: Centax Publications Pvt Ltd.

———. (2002). *India's Fiscal Matters.* New Delhi: Oxford University Press.

———. (2002). "Value Added Tax: Structure and Administration", in *India's Fiscal Matters*. Chapter 4. Oxford University Press. pp.154-78.

———. (2012). *Tax Shastra: Administrative Reforms in India, United Kingdom and Brazil.* New Delhi: Business Standard Book.

Varsano, R. (1999). "Subnational Taxation and the Treatment of Interstate Trade in Brazil: Problems and a Proposed Solution", *Decentralisation and Accountability of the Public Sector. Annual World Bank Conference on Development in Latin America and the Caribbean.* Valdivia, Chile. July.

Zee, Howell H. (1995). "General Sales/Turnover Tax—Tax Cascading: Concept and Measurement", in Parthasarathi Shome (ed.), *Tax Policy Handbook.* Washington D.C.: International Monetary Fund.

11 Second Decade of Securities Market Reforms

An Evaluation

U.K. Sinha

It is a privilege to be invited to contribute to this volume in honour of P. Chidambaram, a formidable intellectual, a liberal reformer and a leader ready to face challenges and take difficult decisions. His sense of anticipation is legendary and it has served the nation immensely on multiple occasions. One incident I remember takes me back to early October 2008. In various parts of the world—including India—economists, financial sector specialists, government officials and politicians were trying to cope with the implications of the collapse of Lehman Brothers. In India, there were feeble early indications of investments in money market mutual funds (MF) coming down to a trickle and redemption requests gathering momentum as Indian corporates having global operations were finding it difficult to raise short-term money abroad. Even Indian banks having branches outside India were unable to raise a small amount of short-term money in the global markets. Chidambaram immediately understood that the small waves of fear about liquidity could turn into massive tides unless contained immediately. One late evening, he insisted that the Reserve Bank of India (RBI), Securities and Exchange Board of India (SEBI) and representatives of MF industry—which happened to be me—gather early in the office of the Reserve Bank and take measures to arrest the worsening sentiments affecting financial markets. A decision was taken as an exceptional measure to enable banks to provide lines of credit to the asset management companies (AMC) up to half per cent of their net demand and time liabilities. A press release was issued before the trading hours began that day. The market operated normally, all redemptions were honoured and there was no panic. The actual money borrowed turned out to be less than 50 per cent of the limit prescribed. A major crisis had been averted.

The very fact that SEBI, the RBI and Government of India (GoI) could work through overnight to resolve a potential crisis helped India tide over the situation without any hiccup. Chidambaram's contribution to financial sector reforms in India, however, travels much beyond this episode.

Looking back, foundations for economic reforms including industrial, fiscal and trade components of 1990s were laid through financial sector reforms. A system—where bank deposits or savings of workers could primarily be appropriated by the government for its fiscal management; where rates charged by banks were not free and categorisation of bank assets was not uniform; capital raised from market required approval from government for timing, quantity and price; households had limited avenues to invest in the market; and foreigners had the door shut for portfolio investments and very limited opportunities for direct investment—was obviously not going to serve the larger agenda of economic reforms. In the first decade of reforms, substantial progress was made towards deregulating administered rates of interest, capital adequacy of banks received focus, prudential norms were made uniform and transparent, need for development of financial institutions to face competition and migrate into banks and efforts towards global integration of financial services were recognised and action initiated. In the securities market, measures were taken to insulate capital raising from government control, create an independent market regulator and open the market for foreigners. By the end of the first decade of reforms, a nationwide trading system which was anonymous, screen-based and order-driven was available across the country. Dematerialisation of securities was enforced, MF and foreign institutional investor (FII) regulations were put in place, and disclosure-based regime for capital raising, central counter party for novation and rolling settlement of trades and derivatives trading in single stocks and in indices were introduced. In some of the measures and also in setting up some new institutions, India became comparable to the best markets in the world.

However, in spite of these developments the market remained narrow and shallow and market supervision came under severe challenge with multiple examples of market misconduct and manipulations in which investors lost money—the most famous being the Ketan Parekh scam of 2000-01. These episodes exposed limitations of the measures adopted and highlighted the need for next level of reforms; many of which required legislative as well as market development and supervision steps. The next level of challenges which emerged at the end of the first decade can broadly be classified into three areas:

(i) making the domestic market more attractive for capital raising by the corporates;

(ii) drawing domestic household savings and foreign investors into the market; and

(iii) managing risk, making the market safe and protecting interests of investors.

Serious attempts were made to address many of these challenges in the second decade of reforms. Amendment of SEBI Act in 2002 giving it wide-ranging powers, the Securitisation and Reconstruction of Financial Assets and Enforcement of Security Interest (SARFAESI) Act, 2002 for securitisation, and amending Securities Contract Regulation Act (SCRA) to provide for demutualisation of stock exchanges in 2004 laid the legal foundation for future reforms. Annexure A-11.1 aims to capture major reforms in the securities market. This paper will attempt to evaluate the measures within the three broad categories listed above.

Making Capital Raising Attractive

Primary Market Reforms

Improving the timelines for rights/public issues, enhancing price discovery and encouraging larger retail participation in primary issuance process were the major focus areas of primary market reforms during the last decade. Accordingly, timeline for rights issues was reduced from 16 weeks to just about 6 weeks; and timeline between public issue closure and listing reduced from 22 days to 12 working days. For enhancing price discovery, book building mechanism was further strengthened and concepts like 'Anchor Investors' and Application Supported by Blocked Accounts (ASBA) in public offering were introduced. Monetary limit on retail individual investor application was increased from ₹ 1 lakh to ₹ 2 lakh and SEBI (Issue of Capital and Disclosure Requirements) Regulations, 2009 was notified. Recently, steps have been taken for electronic IPO through nationwide broker terminals, and enhanced accountability of merchant bankers has been introduced. The volumes have increased rapidly in this decade as evidenced in Table 11.1.

Table 11.1

Market Capitalisation to GDP

(%)

	1992	*2000*	*2007*	*2010*
Hong Kong	165.4	368.6	561.4	481.0
Malaysia	158.9	124.7	174.4	172.6
Singapore	99.5	159.3	210.2	177.3
UK	84.9	174.5	137.2	137.4
South Africa	79.7	154.2	291.3	278.2
USA	71.7	152.6	142.5	117.5
Japan	63.2	67.6	101.7	75.1
Australia	44.1	89.4	151.5	128.5
Canada	41.9	114.1	153.5	137.0
South Korea	32.4	32.2	107.1	107.4
India	26.5	32.2	146.4	93.6
Brazil	11.6	35.1	100.3	74.0
Indonesia	8.6	16.3	49.0	51.0
Turkey	6.2	26.1	44.3	41.8
China	4.3	48.5	178.2	80.4
Russia	0.0	15.0	115.6	17.9

Source: World Bank (*http://data.worldbank.org/indicator/CM.MKT.LCAP.GD.ZS*).

Corporate Governance and Divestment of PSUs

Corporate governance drew more focus. Institutional investors were encouraged to develop voting policies, shareholders advisory firms came up and e-voting was mandated. Rules were framed for minimum public share holding in listed companies and timelines drawn up for non-compliant companies. However, in spite of repeated extension of timelines, close to 200 companies—PSU and private—are still having overwhelming promoter stakes. Takeover regulations of 1997, which were amended in 2002, were further changed in September 2011 providing for higher threshold and size for open offer and removal of differential pricing for promoters and other shareholders. Measures for buybacks, rights, bonus issues and delisting were taken in order to deal with corporate needs as well as to provide fairness and quality. Apart from corporate dependence on securities market to raise capital, another facilitator for increased vibrancy in the capital markets since 2003 is the government's disinvestment policy, which is directed towards reducing the financial burden on government, securing wider ownership and encouraging competition and market discipline. Disinvestment of public sector undertakings (PSUs) also provides the much-needed investment avenues to investors in securities market. In fact, the offloading of public sector shares as part of the disinvestment programme gave significant boost to the revival of equity market during 2003-04. A number of PSUs like MUL, IBP, IPCL, CMC, SAIL, ONGC, etc., successfully divested their targeted stakes.

New Products and Processes

Any discussion on the efforts towards making capital raising attractive in the Indian markets, would be incomplete without touching upon some of the new and innovative products and processes introduced recently. This includes Indian Depository Receipts (IDRs), ASBA, small and medium enterprises (SME) Platform, and Alternate Investment Funds (AIFs), to name a few. ASBA was introduced as a new mode of payment in public issues through book building wherein the application money remains blocked in the bank account of the applicant till allotment is finalised. The intent was to speed up the issue process and to deal with complaints relating to refund of investors money in public issues. Further, in recognition of the need for making finance available to needy SMEs, recognised stock exchange having nation-wide trading terminals have been permitted to set up stock exchanges trading platform for SMEs. Bombay Stock Exchange (BSE) and National Stock Exchange (NSE) launched their respective SME platforms in March 2012. More recently, with a view to extending the perimeter of regulation to unregulated funds and ensuring systemic stability, increasing market efficiency and encouraging formation of new capital, SEBI has notified the Alternate Investment Funds (AIF) Regulations.

Savings and Investments

Mutual Funds

In mutual funds, the number of players increased, asset under management (AUM) grew and the regulatory regime became more transparent and robust. The AUM of MFs in India grew nearly nine times since 1998-99 from about ₹ 68,200 crore at March end 1999 to ₹ 6,11,400 crore at March end 2012. MF industry also witnessed the entry of more foreign players. During this period, the maximum annual net inflow of ₹ 1,53,800 crore was observed during 2007-08 and the maximum annual net outflow of ₹ 49,400 crore was noted in 2010-11. Of the 14 years from 1998-99, there have been net outflow in four years, of which three have been after the crisis in 2008. Apart from market sluggishness, distribution incentives, regulatory and tax arbitrages enjoyed by similar financial products *vis-á-vis* mutual fund units, also had their share of impact on crowding out flow of savings into MF industry. As a result, the pace of growth in AUM has slowed down to only 16 per cent over the four years since 2007-08.

The abolition of entry load in 2009 was an event which substantially impacted the entire business model of the industry. Recently, measures such as transaction charge on MF subscription for distributors, fungibility of total expense ratio, incentive to MF for penetration beyond top 15 cities, incentive for direct investment in MF, cash transaction in MF up to ₹ 20,000, encouragement for long-term holding in MF, and dealing with mis-selling through innovations like product labelling and proactively penalising mis-selling have been taken. It has also been decided to chalk out a long-term policy for MF growth in order to boost the process of institutionalisation of retail investments in securities markets.

Foreign Portfolio Investment

Since the time when FIIs were permitted to invest in the Indian stock market (1992-93), their net cumulative investments in India has increased to $ 14,048.2 crore as on March 31, 2012. Except for the financial years 1998-99 and 2008-09, net FII inflows have always been positive. After reaching peak yearly inflow of $ 1,644.2 crore in 2007-08, the yearly net inflow post the crisis has surpassed the pre-crisis level with net inflows of $ 3,025.2 crore, in 2009-10, $ 3,222.6 crore in 2010-11 and $ 1,892.3 crore in 2011-12, thus reflecting that India has emerged as an even better investment destination after the global financial crisis.

FIIs were permitted to trade in exchange derivative contracts and invest in sponsored American Depository Receipt (ADR)/Global Depository

Receipt (GDR) programmes, government bonds, corporate bonds and divestment by the government in listed companies. Aggregate FII investment limits were progressively increased from $ 175 crore in 2004-2005 to $ 2,000 crore in government bonds and from $ 50 crore to $ 4,500 crore in corporate bonds. Occasional concerns regarding participatory notes (PNs) led to qualified foreign investors (QFIs) being allowed to directly participate in the securities market through equity, mutual funds (MFs) and corporate bonds.

Pension Funds

Pension sector has seen first stage progress in the last decade. Participation in pension investment in India has traditionally been through employers in the organised sector, limiting the access to pension of majority of workers in the unorganised sector. Efforts of pension reforms culminated in setting up of the Pension Fund Regulatory and Development Authority (PFRDA) (October 2003), introduction of New Pension System (NPS) (December 2003), and introduction of the PFRDA Bill in Parliament (March 2005). Central government made the NPS mandatory for its new recruits (except defence forces) from 1 January, 2004. The NPS architecture, consisting of the NPS Trust, Central Recordkeeping Agency, Pension Fund Managers, Trustee Bank and Custodian, was made operational for Central government employees from 1 April, 2008. The NPS architecture has also been offered to the state governments. Starting 1 May 2009, any citizen of India desiring to open an NPS is allowed to do so. Government introduced a co-contributory pension scheme 'Swavalamban' in the Budget 2010-2011. However, Employees' Providend Fund Organisation (EPFO) and other statutory pension funds still maintain pooled investment approach with no choice to the workers and have desisted from investing even a small portion in equity. The size of the Indian pension fund market is approx over ₹ 7,50,000 crore. NPS had ₹ 1,51,63 crore of AUM on 31 March 2012. So far there are more than 0.36 crore NPS subscribers of which about 28 per cent are central government employees, 37 per cent state government employees, 3 per cent organised private sector employees and rest 32 per cent from unorganised sector. Retirement benefits in India, in one form or the other are available to only about 12-13 per cent of the working population. There is a tremendous untapped potential in this sector.

Market Integrity and Investor Protection

The 2000s witnessed the advent of newer and innovative trading systems, practices and procedures, previously unheard of. Technology had started gaining ground in the form of concepts such as internet trading, mobile trading, etc. This was followed more recently by the dawn of complex trading practices like Algo and high frequency trades, co-location, etc. In such a scenario, upholding and maintaining market integrity was of paramount importance. Important measures taken for maintaining market integrity included strengthening the enforcement power of SEBI, robust risk management norms, market monitoring mechanism and equitable governance norms in market infrastructure institutions like stock exchanges and clearing corporations.

Enforcement

The SEBI (Amendment) Act, 2002 provided comprehensive provisions relating to investigation by SEBI including power to pass interim orders pending investigation or inquiry, enhanced penalties for major violations upto ₹ 25 crore or imprisonment of 10 years and power to pass cease and desist orders. Procedural steps were taken to expeditiously resolve cases of violations by passing quasi-judicial orders, instituting legal proceedings or through consent process. Some landmark decisions have come out of SEBI and a multi-member appellate body, Securities Appellate Tribunal (SAT) has helped enhance trust in the enforcement mechanism.

Risk Management

The establishment of central counterparties, T+2 rolling settlement, straight through processing, derivatives trading (including currency futures), short selling, margining for institutional investors in the equity cash segment, know your customer (KYC) norms and minimum public float, etc., are some of the major steps in the direction of strengthening risk management framework in Indian securities market. Strengthening of robust risk management systems in secondary market (Table 11.2) has ensured that there were no defaults in the system even when there were unprecedented movements in the markets.

Table 11.2

Developments in Securities Settlement System

Development	*Year*
Margin based on VaR	Jul 2001
Compulsory T+5 rolling settlement for all scrips listed and traded in any stock exchange in India.	Jul 2001
Index-based market-wide circuit breaker	Jul 2001
T+3 rolling settlement	Apr 2002
Straight Through Processing (STP) for securities transaction	Dec 2002
T+2 rolling settlement	Apr 2003
Real Time Gross Settlement (RTGS) of Funds	Mar 2004
Mandatory processing of all institutional trades executed on the stock exchanges through STP	Jul 2004
Separate trading window for block deals	Nov 2005
Launch of Securities Lending & Borrowing Scheme	Apr 2008
Commenced clearing & settlement of currency derivatives transactions through clearing banks.	Aug 2008
Commencement of settlement of corporate bonds	Dec 2009
Commenced settlement of corporate bond transactions	Dec 2010
Commenced settlement of Commercial Paper (CP) and Certificate of Deposit (CD) transactions	Apr 2012
Securities Contracts (Regulation) (Stock Exchanges and Clearing Corporations) Regulations, 2012	Jun 2012

Source: SEBI publications.

The Task Ahead

The first decade after 1991 saw substantial progress in the regulatory architecture, trading mechanism, growth and volume of the market, introduction of new class of investors like foreign portfolio investors, and shifting from merit-based to disclosure-based capital raising. In comparison, the second decade was more challenging and the gains have been modest. Introduction of new products or new trading mechanism ran into serious differences of opinions and led only to incremental progress. Corporate bond market is one such example. The regulatory preference for bank loans *vis-á-vis* corporate bonds has also contributed towards the same. The interesting thing is that the legislative intent has been very clearly articulated through enactment of SARFAESI Act and through trading of securitised instruments but the traditional thinking that bank loans are preferable and once sanctioned have to remain on the books of the bank forever run rather deep. Government bond market is also largely illiquid.

Interest rate derivatives are another example in which two successive efforts, one made in 2003 and another in 2009, failed to enthuse the market. In the currency derivates market, there is an over the counter (OTC) forward market as well as a screen-based currency market. But it is the third market outside India in Singapore and Dubai, i.e., the non-delivery forward market, which is growing. Corporates end up going outside the country for raising resources as well as for hedging the exchange risk. Issues of policy and regulatory differences need to be resolved so as to serve the needs of economic growth.

The international experience in deepening and broadening the market has been that retail money comes to the market not through individuals but mainly through institutions like pension funds, insurance companies or MFs. While the effort to mobilise foreign portfolio money in the country has been successful, the same cannot be said about the domestic money. Many of the FIIs investing in India are pension funds, trusts, endowment funds, etc. They are investing in India to take benefit of growing Indian economy even though they have the choice to invest in other countries also. In spite of enabling provisions from the Ministry of Finance, the largest pension funds in the country do not invest in the equity market and run defined benefit pension schemes and administered rate of return having no individual retirement accounts or portability. Rectifying fragmented regulatory arrangement and having uniform fiscal incentives for pension products should be a subject of high priority.

Lack of convenience, high costs and lack of awareness are other deterrents in mobilising domestic savings into the market. The cost of trading in the country is today quite high mainly because of steep statutory cost. While some measures have been taken to remove irritants in areas like KYC, a single KYC across financial markets is still quite some distance away. Given the high penetration of mobile telephones in India and increasing transition towards smarter handheld devices, technology needs to be leveraged for enhanced participation.

Trust is a very important element in an individual's decision to park his savings into the market. Events of market misconduct—the last big one being the Ketan Parekh scam in 2001—have also jolted the confidence in the market. A stronger investor protection mechanism along with a clear-cut policy on insuring/compensating investors needs to be put in place to protect investors from losses due to fraud or events outside of market risks. The task for the next decade will continue to be how to further empower regulatory institutions and provide accountability on them so that they remain alert.

A related task for the next decade would be to deal with the question of multiple regulators. There are instances where unscrupulous people have been able to raise large sums of money by navigating through paths in-between the jurisdiction of various regulators. In one such case the Supreme Court of India has recently passed a judgment asking the concerned entity to refund over ₹ 20,000 crore to investors. Similar instances of raising money through plantation or housing finance schemes, chit funds and other innovative products are reported to be flourishing as these fall in-between various regulators, ministries and between the Union and the state governments. There is a serious need to look at the consolidation of various regulators in the market. Hopefully, Financial Sector Legislative Reforms Commission (FSLRC) is looking into this area and government would be able to rectify the situation quickly.

Post global financial crisis, systemic stability of financial markets is getting increasing attention of regulators and policymakers globally. It is now well recognised that securities regulators also have to contribute to the monitoring and prevention of systemic risks. While steps have been taken for monitoring systemic risks in the Indian securities market, the regulatory mandate of preserving systemic stability in securities market needs to be reflected in the regulatory mandate.

Financial markets are rapidly changing world over. Technology is playing a crucial role. Regulators are increasingly required to deal with new products, processes and market misconducts. Traditionally, securities market regulators have relied a lot on legal expertise. Given their diverse and dynamic mandate, there seems to be a need for multidisciplinary approach in capacity-building. Securities market regulators need to supplement legal expertise far beyond strong technological infrastructure to also include expertise in the area of financial technology, forensic, behavioural science, financial economics, financial education, human resource development, etc.

Annexure A-11.1

Major Reforms and Movement in Sensex

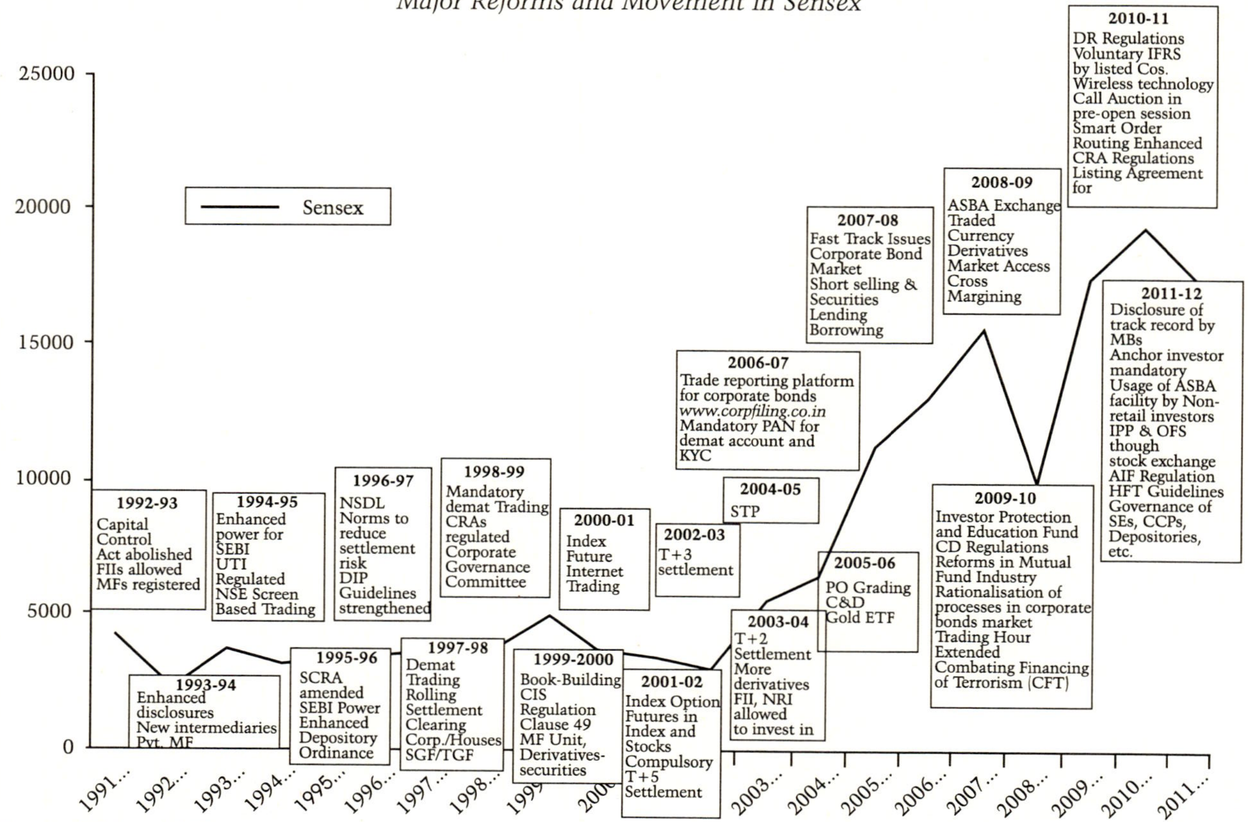

Source: SEBI and BSE

12 Indian Exchanges at Crossroads

Vijay L. Kelkar

Introduction

During the 1990s when I was the Secretary, Ministry of Petroleum and Natural Gas, I had the privilege of working with P. Chidambaram who was at that time the Finance Minister of India. As the Finance Minister, he was very supportive of the hydrocarbon sector reforms. In fact, he has been a source of inspiration and support to all those who were attempting to take the Indian economy on a more rapid growth path. During his tenure as Finance Minister (2004-2008), the Indian economy saw the highest-ever growth rates in history. Major reforms such as introduction of value added tax (VAT), rewriting the Direct Taxes Code, notification of the Fiscal Responsibility and Budget Management (FRBM) Act were undertaken under his leadership. In the area of capital markets, his attempts to pioneer the much needed second round of reforms were significant, which included liberalisation of the regulatory regime for foreign institutional investors (FIIs); initiating the idea of setting up alternate trading platforms for small and medium enterprises (SMEs) to raise equity and debt from capital market; steps to galvanise the corporate bond market, raising limits for overseas investment by mutual funds and so on. He also focussed on instilling confidence in retail investors by setting up an investor protection fund under the aegis of Securities and Exchange Board of India (SEBI). In his budget speech of 2007-08, Chidambaram proposed the idea of self-regulating organisations (SRO) for different market participants under regulations that would be made by SEBI. He has always been ahead of his time and it would be no exaggeration to say that he has been the torchbearer of the second wave of securities market reforms. In this paper, I shall deal with an important component of this wave, which relates to stock exchange reforms.

Acting as a lynchpin, stock exchanges have assisted capital markets in India to play an increasingly important role in determining the pace and pattern of economic growth. This critical institution is currently at a crossroads, as some policy decisions regarding its governance and ownership have become imperative because of two major reasons. First, in the recent global financial crisis, it has been seen that 'conflict of interest' in systemically important financial institutions (FIs) can be potentially very disruptive. Since exchanges play both commercial and regulatory role, there is an inherent 'conflict of interest' in the exchange business (for more detailed discussion, please see Section II). Second, it is being increasingly argued that not allowing exchanges to get listed would hurt their natural evolution as for-profit organisations and the full benefits of demutualisation may not be realised. It is also suggested that listing would not only mean easier financing for exchanges but also more nimble decision-making.

The last time the Indian exchanges were at a crossroads was some 20 years ago, when the question was whether the exchanges would be demutualised or not. Until then, exchanges were not-for-profit organisations and were run like 'clubs', which had a membership of brokers. The brokers operated the exchanges primarily for their own benefits. This, unsurprisingly, gave rise to a number of governance problems, which are quite well known and need not be discussed here. The idea behind the policy decision to demutualise, which meant a transformation of the exchanges from non-profit mutual organisations to for-profit shareholder-owned enterprises, was that these for-profit exchanges would be disciplined by profit-seeking investors and this would mean higher accountability to the shareholders.

Demutualisation of exchanges roughly coincided with the establishment of India's capital market regulator, the SEBI, which took a number of initiatives to modernise the capital markets. Following these measures, the Indian capital markets have grown tremendously with exchanges and SEBI playing a central role: price discovery has become more efficient resulting in better resource allocation; transactions have become faster, safer and cheaper; the number of investors has risen; and markets have become globalised. Overall, the Indian markets have become larger, deeper, diversified and more sophisticated. The impressive achievements of Indian exchanges in their macroeconomic roles (such as improving allocative efficiency, reducing cost of capital, fostering democratic capitalism, enhancing financial stability, acting as an instrument for global integration and so on) have been widely acknowledged. Clearly, the recent pressures to reform the exchanges are emerging in the context of the exchanges' role as a firm and not because of underachievement in their macroeconomic role.

Reforms have become necessary to essentially address three critical and inter-related questions. First, with exchanges turning into for-profit entities, there arose a conflict of interest since exchanges also perform regulatory functions.[1] How should the conflict be managed? In the past two decades, this 'conflict of interest' was not a matter of major concern, as the exchanges viewed market integrity in their own enlightened long-term self-interest and generally refused to compromise their regulatory roles to advance their commercial objectives. In the light of the recent financial crisis, systemic risk resulting from 'conflict of interest' is being viewed as too serious a matter to be left to the discretion of any market player or set of players. It merits regulatory attention. In the context of exchanges, the case for this is even stronger when listing is contemplated (see below). Second, as a natural next step to demutualisation, should an exchange be allowed to list itself and if so, under what conditions? Third, to protect the public interest, is there a need to take further safeguards to the special ownership regime for exchanges that already exist? Are the existing restrictions on ownership enough to manage the 'conflict of interest', when an exchange gets listed?

To address these issues, the SEBI has recently notified new regulations known as the Securities Contracts (Regulation) (Stock Exchanges and Clearing Corporations) Regulations 2012 or SECC Regulations 2012. This paper seeks to put the regulatory challenges in perspective and examine to what extent the SECC regulations can meet these challenges.

---

1. The regulatory functions of the exchange are three-fold: member regulations, listing regulations and market surveillance regulations. Member regulations comprise regulations relating to registration of members, dispute resolution, compliance with capital adequacy, books and accounts, and so on. Listing regulations comprise framing new listing standards including rules for corporate governance and shareholding reporting and monitoring the corporates' compliance with the same. Market surveillance regulation consists of market conduct rules, trading rules and market investigation.

Managing the Conflict between Commercial and Regulatory Roles

Of the three issues mentioned above, the conflict between commercial and regulatory roles of the exchange is the most critical. It is the drive for profit that determines the scope and intensity of this conflict. For example, a for-profit regulatory organisation may be unwilling to commit adequate resources to enforcing regulation vigorously. Similarly, under pressure to generate high returns on investment, an exchange may be less willing to take action against customers or users who are a large and direct source of income for the exchange. The real problem is that while both the costs and benefits of the commercial function are evident, only the cash outlays part of the regulatory function is clear. The benefits of regulation are more difficult to quantify and hence, may not be given adequate importance. The 'spill-over benefits' from better regulation cannot be fully captured by the 'firm', i.e., the exchange. Hence, it is more than likely that there will be under-investment in improving regulation.

To address the conflict of interest that can arise between the market and regulatory function of stock exchanges, the regulators across the world have adopted different models. One model is to create a 'Chinese wall' within the exchange between the regulatory departments and the rest of the exchange. This however is not the only option. There are other ways to insulate the regulatory functions from commercial pressures. For example, all exchanges could be divested of their regulatory roles, and these could be entrusted to a newly created industry-wide SRO. Yet another alternative is that the government regulator assumes all the regulatory functions and there is no frontline regulator.

Recently, SEBI has chosen the first of the above option: that is, creation of a 'Chinese wall'. The modalities of this arrangement have been notified in the SECC regulations. To enhance the autonomy of the regulatory departments of the stock exchanges, SEBI has prescribed a policy of 'Chinese wall', which would separate the regulatory departments of stock exchanges from other departments. Implicit in this regulation is a requirement that no individual in the regulatory departments would have any role to play on the business side. Further, the employees in the regulatory departments would be physically segregated from those in other departments including those with respect to access controls and would not be allowed to communicate any information concerning regulatory activity to anyone in other departments. In exceptional circumstances, the employees from other departments may be given confidential information on 'need to know' basis with the intimation to the compliance officer.

As part of the 'Chinese wall' policy, SEBI has decided that the governance structures of exchanges would be such that the heads of each of the regulatory departments (membership, listing and the surveillance), report directly to a separate independent oversight committee, each chaired by a public interest director.[2] These heads of departments are also required to report simultaneously to the exchange's MD/CEO. These committees have been entrusted with the responsibility of addressing the conflicts of interest in respect of: (a) member regulation, (b) listing functions, and (c) trading and surveillance functions. Clearly, the aim is to subject the regulatory functions of the exchange to direct monitoring by an independent oversight committee of the governing board with the ultimate aim of addressing 'conflicts of interest'.

An important question is whether the 'Chinese walls' are effective in practice. Their effectiveness as a regulatory instrument is yet to be proven worldwide. Indeed, there has been enough empirical evidence against the efficacy of the 'Chinese walls' from the investment banking and mutual fund industry and other financial conglomerates which provide a range of financial activities.

Massa and Zahid (2005) show that there exists a flow of information between the banking and mutual fund divisions of the financial conglomerates despite the 'Chinese walls'. They found that mutual funds reap an unfair advantage by acquiring 'inside' information from their banking divisions and invest more heavily in the stock of firms to which the commercial banking arm of the group has lent. Studies by Acharya and Johnson (2007) found that, "In the absence of perfect 'Chinese walls' within banks, the credit derivatives market provides the trading desks of relationship banks a trading mechanism through which the information possessed by loan officers about a firm can be exploited, and, in turn,

2. Public interest director means an independent director representing the interest of investors in securities market and who is not having any association directly or indirectly which, in the opinion of the board, is in conflict with his role.

transmitted to public markets." Bodnaruket *et al.* (2008) showed that on the basis of their inside information, financial conglomerates acquire stakes in the companies to which they have provided advisory services. According to the authors, "the results are consistent with much anecdotal evidence about the potential insider trading behavior of financial intermediaries and the breach of Chinese walls."

In the specific context of the exchange, it is difficult to see how and why the conflicts would disappear or be effectively addressed with the erection of 'Chinese walls'. After all, the two functions remain in the same entity and that entity as a whole has an interest in promoting its own business. Further, would the head of the regulatory department consider it worthwhile to report a wrongdoing to the independent board without the knowledge of the CEO? Consider the following evidence, which although is in the context of whistleblower policy, is directly relevant here.

> According to the Lehman Bros. Bankruptcy Examiner Report, Matthew Lee, a senior vice president of Lehman Bros. finance division, was aware of accounting improprieties at Lehman Bros. In May 2008, he sent a letter to Martin Kelly, his superior and the Lehman Bros. controller, about the Repo 105 transactions used by Lehman Bros. to move assets off the balance sheet at quarter-end. There was no response to the letter.
>
> Why didn't Lee use the employee hotline to report the issue directly to the audit committee? Perhaps Lee decided that sending a letter to a superior was risky enough without further jeopardising his career by going to the audit committee. There is no evidence that Lehman Bros. created any reward for providing legitimate information on the employee hotline. In any event, Lee was laid-off less than a month after sending the letter (Lipman, 2012).

Clearly, there are pitfalls in the proposed model, as there are inadequate incentives for the regulatory departments to report honestly to the board and in case they do, there is no protection guaranteed to the staff. Although the SEBI regulations provide that the heads of regulatory departments can appeal to the respective committee in case a stock exchange takes action against them, it is not clear how much can they rely on their 'right to appeal' to protect their interests. Further, there are practical difficulties for a board committee to exercise oversight on a daily basis. Perhaps in view of these considerations, SEBI has envisaged that the model proposed by them is only an interim one and its long-term goal is to set up an independent

SRO specifically for the member regulation (SEBI Press Release of April 2, 2012). Thus, out of the three types of regulatory functions carried out by the exchanges—member regulation, listing functions and surveillance functions—SEBI has a vision of divesting exchanges of only their member regulation, albeit in the long run, while there is no plan for the other two regulations as of now. The problems of these two regulations, particularly the surveillance function, remaining with the exchange must, however, be recognised. In case of surveillance, an exchange has access to only partial information about a member's trading: namely, the trade information *vis-à-vis* that particular exchange. To take a simple example, it is entirely possible that a member does all 'purchases' on one exchange and all 'sales' on another. If the exchange—from which the member purchases—does surveillance on the basis of only the information that it has access to, it may reach an erroneous conclusion.[3]

This implies that for surveillance to be effective, all trading members need to be collectively supervised by a centralised agency (say an SRO), instead of having different exchanges to monitor and supervise the behaviour of the members. Thus, it is important to recognise that the grounds for requiring the exchanges to give up their surveillance function goes beyond the need to address 'conflict of interest'. In fact, cues can be taken from the US regulatory model where surveillance functions of the main exchanges, New York Stock Exchange (NYSE) and Nasdaq, are outsourced to Financial Industry Regulatory Authority (FINRA), an independent SRO, though exchanges are still accountable to the Securities and Exchange Commission (SEC) for the standard of regulation and for any regulatory failing. In the context of India, it would be relatively easy to implement a similar model, as SEBI already has in place an Integrated Market Surveillance System (IMSS) which integrates data from stock exchanges, depositories and clearing corporations.

The alternative of the industry-wide SRO raises a question relating to its funding, which needs to be addressed, but that may not be a very difficult task. What may prove to be a bit challenging though is to find institutional mechanisms to keep the 'industry lobbying' functions of the SRO distinct and separate from its 'regulatory' tasks, as has been borne out by the Indian experience.

---

3. Further, regulatory duplication for members is of no less significance.

Finally, although a discussion on the option of SEBI taking over all the regulatory responsibilities that the exchanges are currently holding may appear inopportune in the light of the SEBI's recent regulations, it is perhaps prudent to keep this option open and explore its possible use. While examining this option, we have to ensure that SEBI, the state regulator, has adequate capacity in terms of skilled human resources. Experts feel that advanced technologies would help the state regulators to have electronic trails and using them, they can catch any instance of market abuse. The fact, however, is that technology is not just the preserve of regulators; deviant market players can and do use technology to stay ahead of the regulators. So, the case for high quality and well-paid staff in adequate number at SEBI, who are capable of efficiently exercising the regulatory responsibilities, becomes that much stronger.

Should Exchanges be Listed?

The question as to whether exchanges should be listed has been widely debated. Those in favour hold that like in some of the Organisation for Economic Co-operation and Development (OECD) countries, listing is a natural event to follow demutualisation and hence, disallowing listing could defeat the purpose of demutualisation. They emphasise the advantages of listing, such as increasing the scope of raising capital at a lower cost, providing exit route to shareholders and promoting transparency and better governance of exchanges. But, there are downside risks too.

The problem is that the conflict between the commercial and regulatory roles of the exchange, if unresolved, will get exacerbated if an exchange gets listed, because listing would create incentives for the management to get more closely aligned with their share price performance, which would effectively be the barometer of management efficiency. Listing would also induce a more short-term orientation for the management. Falling share prices (of an exchange), for example, which may be due to reasons outside the control of the exchange, may induce the exchange management to be lax on its regulatory role at a time when enforcement of regulation may actually need strengthening. Clearly, in such a situation, the exchanges' incentives to play their macroeconomic role more effectively would be weakened.

An important point to note is that while several exchanges around the world have already listed themselves, most of them are in mature markets where the regulatory roles of exchanges have been hived off.

In India, the SECC Regulations has for the first time permitted a stock exchange to get listed, provided, the exchange has:

- complied with the provisions of SECC Regulations, particularly those relating to ownership (See Section IV of this paper) and governance;
- completed three years of continuous trading before applying for listing; and
- obtained prior approval of SEBI.

While listing has been permitted so that an exchange, as a firm, gets an opportunity to realise the benefits of listing, pre-conditions for listing have been set with the aim of ensuring that the exchanges' macroeconomic role is not hampered with and the possibility of the listed exchanges raising systemic risk in the economy is preempted. Of particular importance in this respect are the governance reforms outlined in the SECC regulations aimed at resolving the conflict between the regulatory obligation and commercial operations of the exchange, because as stated earlier, listing aggravates conflict. Recognising this, SEBI has directed that the stock exchanges be permitted to list when they put in place the appropriate mechanism (the 'Chinese wall' policy) for tackling conflicts of interest.[4] Our discussions in Section II, however, shows that the 'Chinese wall' policy suggested by SEBI may not truly be the most effective mechanism, although the long-term goal of independent industry-wide SRO may potentially be. So,the key question is one of sequencing of listing: would it not be better if exchanges were to list after the independent SRO comes into being? Further, SEBI envisages that the independent SRO to be established in the long term would assume responsibilities relating only to member regulations. What about the problems resulting from the exchanges retaining the listing regulations and the market surveillance? Could the new SRO not take on these two types of regulations as well?

4. SEBI has also directed that a stock exchange will not be allowed to list on itself.

There are some who argue that listing will not complicate matters even if the exchanges continue to have their regulatory functions. This argument is based on the premise that exchanges are too concerned about their 'reputational capital' to neglect their regulatory obligations and if they do, they would collapse the next day! In real life, this rarely happens. It may take considerable amount of time before these exchanges are exposed and it may take much longer, possibly years, for their reputational capital to erode to a point that they actually collapse. Meanwhile, the damage to the economy would have been significant.

It may be noted here that one key benefit of exchange listing from the economy's viewpoint—namely, improved governance of exchanges—can be attained by exchanges acting as if they were listed—that is complying with the provisions of 'Clause 49' of the exchanges' listing agreements, even though they are not listed. Indeed, the SECC Regulation 2012 mandates that the disclosure requirements and corporate governance norms of (unlisted) stock exchanges match those of listed companies.[5]

Another indirect benefit of listing lies in the fact that it facilitates mergers, which can potentially raise the efficiency of the merging enterprises. Demutualisation, *per se*, enables mergers, but listing makes mergers much easier. Globally, mergers—in the first wave—have been between large exchanges in matured markets, the motivation being primarily a reduction in technology costs—an issue of lesser importance in the emerging markets. More recently, a new trend has begun, where exchanges in matured markets have started acquiring small stakes in fast-growing regions such as Asia and the Middle East, essentially to hedge the risk of slower growth in their own markets. The trend is likely to pick up momentum in the coming years. This kind of acquisition can potentially undermine the market development efforts of exchanges in the emerging markets. For example, an exchange of a developed country that takes over an emerging market exchange may care little about the market development in the hinterland, with a resultant loss to the developing economy.

Furthermore, cross-country exchange mergers have often failed reportedly on grounds of preserving national interest. The recent example

5. Clause 35 of SECC Regulations 2012 states that, "The disclosure requirements and corporate governance norms as specified for listed companies shall *mutatis mutandis* apply to a recognised stock exchange and a recognised clearing corporation."

of two proposed exchange mergers which failed to materialise due to vested national interests are between (a) the Australia Securities Exchange (ASX) and the Singapore Exchange (SGX) and (b) London Stock Exchange (LSE) and Canada's TMX.

The SGX-ASX merger proposal was opposed on the grounds that it was "contrary to the national interest."[6] The Australian authorities apprehended that "not having full regulatory sovereignty over the ASX-SGX holding company would present material risks and supervisory issues impacting on the effective regulation of the ASX's operations, particularly its clearing and settlement functions." They were also concerned that the proposed acquisition would undermine Australia's efforts to "build Australia's standing as a global financial centre in Asia."[7] Similarly, the LSE-TMX deal was opposed reportedly on the grounds of nationalist pride. The deal was largely viewed in Canada as a British takeover which led to concerns that "smaller Canadian companies would find it difficult to list on the combined exchange and that a variety of financial and legal services now conducted in Canada would cross the ocean to Britain" (Austen, 2011). These two instances are clear evidence that even today exchanges are viewed as some kind of 'national assets' and cannot simply be driven by their interest as firms and further, one of the major benefits of listing, namely facilitating mergers to generate efficiency, may not materialise in the case of exchanges.

The upshot of the discussions in this section is that exchanges are generally viewed as a 'special class of firms', because they are systemically important and have often been a source of 'national pride'. At the same time, like any other firm, exchanges have needs and aspirations. So, the policies related to exchanges need to be re-evaluated from the perspective of both 'exchange as an institution of systemic significance' and 'exchange as a firm'. From the viewpoint of exchange as a firm, the case for listing is relatively strong and clear-cut, given their growing aspirations, capital requirements and need for greater visibility on one hand and the minimal costs (to the exchange) resulting from listing on the other. From the systemic viewpoint, however, the case for exchange listing may not be as

6. Australian Deputy Prime Minister and Treasurer, Media Release No.030 on Foreign Investment Decision dated April 8, 2011.

7. Ibid.

strong as made out by some. As our earlier discussions indicated, listing may facilitate mergers of other firms but not necessarily of exchanges. Further, the benefits such as improved disclosure and transparency can be generated even without listing through a simple regulatory fiat. Clearly, from a systemic viewpoint, the benefits of exchange listing are at best limited. In such a situation, the 'systemic' costs of listing must be minimised for the economy to gain from exchange listing which would entail some safeguards.

Thus, while an exchange's needs 'as a firm' cannot and should not be underestimated, it is only an appropriate sequencing of reforms that would ensure that listing does not raise systemic risk or reduce the effectiveness of the exchange's macroeconomic role. In other words, safeguards need to be in place before listing occurs. SEBI's regulations reflect this line of argument. But the key question is whether the safeguard—in the form of 'Chinese wall'—is truly effective and if not, are we showing enough urgency to accelerate the timetable for the creation of the industry-wide SRO which could potentially be a superior alternative.

Reforms in the Ownership Structure

The final issue relates to the ownership structure of exchanges which also has a bearing on exchange governance. Given that the exchange is entrusted with vital economic functions, dispersed ownership structures have been adopted by stock exchanges the world over, so that there is no undue influence of any single individual on decision-making. In line with this thinking, most regulatory regimes in the world (including in India) have imposed ceilings on individual shareholding in the range of 5-15 per cent of the total; only in exceptional cases, and after seeking specific approval from the concerned regulator or government, individual shareholding has been allowed to exceed 15 per cent. There is, however, a contrary view that limiting the maximum permissible holding to a very small percentage of the exchange's share capital would reduce the incentives for the shareholders to take adequate interest in the progress of the stock exchanges. There is little doubt that, on balance, the large benefits obtained from limiting individual ownership would far outweigh the possible costs.

The SECC Regulations 2012 have directed that at least 51 per cent of the paid-up equity share capital of a stock exchange be held by public and no person resident in India (individually or together with persons acting in concert) is allowed to hold more than 5 per cent except a stock exchange, depository, insurance company, banking company or public financial institution, which may acquire or hold (either directly or indirectly, either individually or together with person acting in concert) upto 15 per cent of the paid-up equity share capital of stock exchange. Further, no person—not even a stock exchange or a depository—resident outside India can acquire or hold more than 5 per cent of the paid-up equity capital of a recognised stock exchange. The combined holding of all persons outside India should not exceed 49 per cent of the exchange's total paid-up equity capital. These regulations also call for application of 'fit and proper' criteria for the shareholders of the stock exchanges.

These prescriptions relating to exchange ownership structure are in line with best global practices. Also, their implementation has no bearing on the questions discussed in Section II and III, respectively. Therefore, regardless of how these questions are addressed, the SECC regulation on exchange ownership structure can be undertaken.

Concluding Remarks

Timing and sequencing are important factors that determine the success of any institutional reform programme. This is, especially, so in the case of financial markets. The world has yet to emerge completely from the financial crisis. Any error in judgement in introducing exchange reforms in a country such as India can wipe off decades of progress in a very short time. So, we have to pay adequate attention to timing and sequencing of exchange reforms that are currently being discussed.

While designing exchange reforms, policymakers need to ensure that no incentives are created at the micro level that are not aligned with the macroeconomic role that exchanges are expected to play. After all, exchanges serve the capital market which is a very delicate market having economy-wide implications. We have very limited knowledge of what can go wrong in the exchange industry with policy changes, but we do know that wrong incentives for exchanges can lead to a breakdown of trust and subsequently to the failure of exchanges, no matter how big they are and have disastrous effects, much worse than bank failures. So, let us make policy changes with due care to make sure that attempts to address the needs of exchanges as firms do not undermine their macroeconomic role. The last time the Indian exchanges were at a crossroads, the SEBI nudged them in the right direction and the results speak for themselves. Now, with the global economy more close-knit and the financial sector more complex, the need to choose the right path and sequencing appears even stronger.

References

Acharya, V. and T.C. Johnson (2007). "Insider Trading in Credit Derivatives", *Journal of Financial Economics* 84: 110-141.

Alexander, D. (2011). "London Stock Exchange Drops $3.4 Billion Bid for TMX Group", Business Week, June 29. Accessed on July 30, 2012 *(http://www.businessweek.com/news/2011-06-29/london-stock-exchange-drops-3-4-billion-bid-for-tmx-group.html)*

Armitstead, L. (2011). "Canadian Group Maple Launches Hostile Bid to Scupper LSE Deal with Toronto Exchange". Accessed on July 30, 2012 *(http://www.telegraph.co.uk/finance/newsbysector/banksandfinance/8573404/Canadian-group-Maple-launches-hostile-bid-to-scupper-LSE-deal-with-Toronto-exchange.html)*

Austen, I. (2011). "London and Toronto Exchanges Call Off Merger". Accessed on July 30, 2012 *(http://dealbook.nytimes.com/2011/06/29/london-and-toronto-exchanges-call-off-merger/)*

Australian Treasurer (2011). "Foreign Investment Decision". Media Release, 8 April. Accessed on July 30, 2012 *(http://www.treasurer.gov.au/DisplayDocs.aspx?doc=pressreleases/2011/030.htm&pageID=003&min=wms&Year=&DocType=0.)*

Bekaert, G., M. Gomes, P. Garcia and C.R. Harvey (1995). *The Role of Capital Markets in Economic Growth*. Catalyst Institute.

Bodnaruk, A., M. Massa and A. Simonov (2008). *Investment Banks as Insiders and the Market for Corporate Control*. Available on *http://ssrn.com/abstract=966202*

Carson, J. (2011). "Self Regulation in Securities Market", *Policy Research Working Paper*. The World Bank.

Christiansen H. and A. Kolderstova (2009). "The Role of Stock Exchanges in Corporate Governance", *OECD Paper*.

Credit Suisse (2011). *Global Exchange M&A: An Asian Perspective*. Asia-Pacific Exchanges.

CWA (2011). "Council of Financial Regulators: Review of Financial Market Infrastructure Regulation", Consultation paper by Common Wealth of Australia.

Jalan, B. (2011). *Review of Ownership and Governance of Market Structure*. Securities and Exchange Board of India

Kelkar, V. (2011). "On the Economics of Stock Exchange", *Annual (second) Shri R. Venkataraman Endowment Lecture*. Madras School of Economics. March 29.

Lee, R. (2010). *The Governance of Financial Market Infrastructure*. Oxford Finance Group.

———. (2011). *Running the World's Market*. Princeton University Press.

Lipman, F.D. (2012). "From Enron to Lehman Brothers: Lessons for Boards from Recent Corporate Governance Failures", *Directors Notes*. The Conference Board.

Massa, M. and Rehman Zahid (2005). "Information Flows within Financial Conglomerates: Evidence from theBanks–Mutual Funds Relationship". Working Paper available on *http://faculty.insead.edu/massa/Research/bankfunds.pdf (accessed on July 26, 2012)*

Michael, S. and A. Saeed (2011). "A Tale of Two Exchanges: How Singapore Lost Down under in ASX Bid". *Thomson Reuters*. Accessed on July 30, 2012 *(http://graphics.thomsonreuters.com/AS/pdf/ASX_2104mv.pdf)*

Osler, Hoskin and L.L.P. Harcourt (2011). "Global Stock Exchange Consolidation and the Battle for TMX", *Capital Market Review*.

SEBI (2011). *Review of Ownership and Governance of Market Structure. http://www.sebi.gov.in/commreport/ownershipreport.pdf* (Accessed on July 11, 2012)

———. (2012). *Securities Contracts (Regulation) (Stock Exchanges and Clearing Corporations) Regulations*.

———. (2012a). *Securities Contracts (Regulation) (Stock Exchanges and Clearing Corporation) Regulation, 2012*. Accessed on July 12, 2012 *(http://www.sebi.gov.in/cms/sebi_data/attachdocs/1340272091708.pdf)*

SEBI Press Release (2012). *SEBI Policy on Market Infrastructure Institutions (MIIs) and Exit Process for Non-operational or Derecognized Stock Exchanges*. SEBI PR No.40/2012 (2 April). Accessed on July 12, 2012 *(http://www.sebi.gov.in/sebiweb/home/list/4/23/0/0/Press-Releases)*

———. (2012a). Ownership and Governance Norms for Market Infrastructure Institutions. SEBI PR No. 66/2012 (21 June). Accessed on July 12, 2012 *(http://www.sebi.gov.in/sebiweb/home/detail/23988/yes/PR-Ownership-and-Governance-norms-for-Market-Infrastructure-Institutions)*

13 An Agenda for Nine Per cent Growth

Tarun Das

The happy days of nine per cent plus GDP growth in the Indian economy are not long past. Those were the days when P. Chidambaram was Finance Minister. Only a couple of years. And yet, the decline in growth over the past 18 months has led to pessimism, doom and gloom analysis and forecasts as well as fall in confidence levels.

This, of course, is typical of Indian psychology. A little bit like the euphoria-excessive—when India wins the World Cup in cricket and the doomsday statements when India subsequently loses to England and Australia. Quite a bit is due to the low level of self-esteem and self-confidence Indians suffer from. A hangover of the two centuries of colonial rule and the fact that it took the information technology sector, at the turn of the century, to enable Indians, especially Indian industry, to look the world in the eye and stand shoulder to shoulder with the best. That was a huge turning point for India's self-esteem but only a beginning.

The last 10 years have seen a transformation of India, its economy and industry, which has been unprecedented. Competitiveness and confidence came. Comfort with globalisation came. Investment and acquisitions came. And all of it, together, took India to earlier unimaginable heights of nine per cent plus GDP growth.

But, the global economy and its deep crisis had more challenges in store for the Indian economy. Plus, the fact that since 2009 the focus shifted from high economic growth to social reforms, social development and social inclusivity, to help build a more equitable society. In effect, a different developmental and growth model from many other countries. Unfortunately, whilst the idea was great, the prerequisite for all of this has to be high economic growth to generate the resources which are essential for social reforms.

It's now a turnaround job to get back to nine per cent. Not impossible. Certainly possible. But, the constant refrain by many seeking 'bold reforms' seems unnecessary and unwise. Likewise, the song of passing fresh legislation since bipartisan support in Parliament is the exception and certainly not anywhere near the rule. And, even new policies, such as opening multi-brand retail to FDI, are fraught with challenges because of divergent political views.

So, what is the way forward? Or rather, back to nine per cent growth levels? Is it a pipedream? Is it impossible? Is it feasible? Here are some suggestions to make it happen. None of these are earth-shaking but just focussing on specifics, the micro rather than the macro. On execution and implementation. On moving ahead where there is space and opportunity.

First, the public sector industries in the country are still a very significant part of the economy, especially in manufacturing, steel, capital goods, defence production, etc. Their weightage in India's industrial production is significant but they seem to be the orphans of the Indian economy. Many of the public sector undertakings (PSUs) have the ability to enhance their investment, capacity, production and export, given support by way of quick approvals and facilitated implementation.

This just does not happen. These orphans are subjected to political and bureaucratic interference, many demands, huge delays in approvals and the country loses out. The economy suffers. Some of the finest corporates in the country are NTPC, BHEL, BEL, HAL, etc, to name just a few. If the owner and parent could give positive attention to the public sector and free them, equip them with truly independent strong boards and autonomy, this group could help add nearly one per cent to India's GDP growth.

There is urgent need to review the handling of PSUs by government. Right now, there are several ministries and departments 'administering' PSUs. The need now is for an independent 'Public Sector Authority' (PSA) to deal with all of the PSUs in a coordinated manner. Ministries are supposed to be for policymaking, not to manage or oversee management. Let the PSA be formed to deal with this aspect, mandated to build a strong, competitive public sector.

This may sound like heresy but, around the world, there is increasing acceptance that the mixed economy model is the way to go—a strong private sector and a strong public sector. France is an excellent example of this model. India was. India needs to get back to its roots.

The public sector is in heavy investment industries and sectors. Not easy for private sector to generate the huge resources required for very long-term returns to accrue. Therefore, to safeguard India's national security, the public sector has to continue to play a significant role in the national economy. There is no choice. This is a 'given'.

Another aspect of public sector rebuilding is the disinvestment process. This needs to be restarted so that the people of India have shares in PSUs, are actually and directly shareholders, seeking strong corporate governance and accountability. This is just not about generating funds for the deficit to be reduced though this, too, is very critical. It is also for the long-term sustainable viability of the PSUs. In the short term it also aids the deficit reduction challenge which the finance minister faces currently.

A study of PSU boards does show that many respected persons are members of such boards. In spite of this, the perception is strong that PSUs are not independent, are subject to political and bureaucratic direction and intervention. Creating a separate, independent PSA will go a long way towards freeing PSU chiefs from the day-to-day harassment from different quarters. The PSA will not eliminate this challenge but, at least, the variations in demands and pressures would be greatly minimised.

The public sector, therefore, is a big part of the answer to bring back nine per cent GDP growth and the sooner PSUs get this recognition and support, the sooner the target will be achieved.

A second major area for action is infrastructure—roads and highways, railways, ports, airports, waterways, housing, urban development, etc. These are huge areas of economic activity often managed by single authority, e.g., NHAI/roads and highways; Railways; Airport Authority of India (AAI)/airports except where private sector has taken over, such as Hyderabad, Bangalore, Mumbai and Delhi; Port Trusts/ports; Inland Water Transport Authority/water; National Housing Bank and HUDCO/housing; JNUURM/urban development. There are others such as DMIC/Delhi Mumbai Industrial Corridor.

What is their implementation record? How are these functioning? From all accounts, not too well. Hence, 'construction' of infrastructure which is a huge lever for economic activity and employment, is at a level far below potential.

Across the country, these agencies, and others in similar areas, need to increase construction activity through implementation of projects and programmes. The finance minister, who is, the most efficient and competent minister-level 'manager' needs to review the situation agency by agency and get them moving faster forward.

Infrastructure, especially construction of any kind anywhere in the country, can add one per cent to GDP growth. No question about that. And, it can be done. Its all about management of implementation. Its all about the 'how' (to do), going beyond the 'what' (to do). This is actually the strength of the private sector—getting projects done on time and within budgets. But, there is no reason why the various agencies mentioned earlier cannot do likewise. If there is need, and there may well be, external expertise can be associated or inducted to strengthen and deepen the implementation and execution capability.

A third area of attention is the private sector.

Before the deregulation of the early 1990s, the private sector was a 'bit' player in the economy. A general perception was that the private sector was either out of or in the corner of the economy 'room'. But, over the last 20 years, the private sector has evolved and is located in the centre of the room. It, therefore, can make a huge difference to the economic growth of India.

Today, the private sector is not investing or indicates that the problems are such that investment is not possible. How is this to be tackled? Macro-statements, speeches and talk have no value. No conviction. Confidence and investment will happen only if there is action and problems, perceived or real, are addressed and resolved. This, again, calls for 'micro' action. The top 100 companies/groups (Tata Group alone has, reportedly around 100 companies) and the top echelons of the finance ministry, supported by other relevant ministries, need to engage each major corporate group in an urgent dialogue.

The dialogue is not to be 'academic'. It is to be very practical and focussed. What project is planned? Where is the bottleneck? How is it to be resolved? And, resolve it fast.

This is only the top 100 but their tentacles connect with thousands of ancillaries, vendors, suppliers, and partners. So, in the process of clearing the implementation of the top 100, the small and medium enterprise (SME) sector in the country will benefit.

And, if this exercise is extended beyond the top 100 to the next 100 and so on to touch 500 companies of the private sector, India will gain another one per cent or more in GDP growth.

The final suggestion in the area of manufacturing and infrastructure relates to defence production. It is slightly more long-term in impact but hugely important.

India's defence budget is massive. India's requirements of defence equipment are enormous. For the Army, Air Force and Navy. Not to mention the paramilitary and other security forces.

Currently, India's needs are met largely through imports, essentially from the private sector MNCs overseas. It is commonly said that over 70 per cent of defence equipment needs are imported. Less than 30 per cent made in India. This ratio can be reversed: 70 per cent made in India, 30 per cent imported. The result, huge additionality of production, skills, technology and employment within the country.

One key issue is technology. India needs and wants up-to-date, advanced technology. Not outdated. Not obsolete. Not inefficient. Good enough to deal with possible conflict situations.

Technology is the most precious asset to any company which has developed it, owns it. It takes years of R&D to develop state of the art technology and no company is going to part with it under any circumstances. Sales—Yes. Transfer or sharing? No. And yet, India needs local manufacture. For this, the companies must be allowed to manufacture in India with management and ownership control. Twenty-six (26) per cent FDI is no good. Forty-nine (49) per cent FDI will not work. Fifty-one (51) per cent to 100 per cent has to happen. Plus, long-term stability assured. No retrospective changes ever!

And, this can change the defence production scenario in India. Plus, one per cent additional GDP growth just from the defence sector because the numbers are so big as to be almost frightening. Massive industrial assets would be created in India. Costs would fall. People would get jobs and training—from the blue-collar to the top manager. This is a huge win-win for India. And, enhance national security.

The impact of rapid growth of the public and private sectors in manufacturing, as well as defence production, would lead to an explosion of new enterprises in the small and medium industry sector, so vital to entrepreneurship building and employment. At a conservative estimate, the whole range of manufacturing and infrastructure industries can add at least two percentage points to India's economic growth and several points to its industrial growth.

The Indian economy currently has a structure very different to 25-30 years ago. The new player, and a significant one at that, is the services sector. Not just information technology. Engineering, consulting, legal, accounting, maintenance, retail, etc. This segment of the economy has truly exploded with growth and entrepreneurship over the last 10-15 years, representing over 50 per cent of the country's economy.

Though the services sector growth has slowed over the last 18 months, any pick-up of the economy, signs of which are emerging, will automatically bring an upswing in the services sector. Representing, as it now does, well over 50 per cent of the economy, its growth rate reverting to double-digit figures will add significantly to the GDP growth of India.

And, this growth is not necessarily dependent on government action, except to provide an enabling environment for enterprise and growth. After a lapse of three years, since 2009, there are clear signs of government initiatives to do just that.

Finally, for agriculture, which was 40 per cent of GDP 30 years ago but is now only 15 per cent, an annual growth of 3 per cent per annum is a reasonable expectation, given the actions being taken for modernisation, storage, prevention of waste, expansion of food processing industries, etc. Whilst agriculture will not add big numbers to the GDP growth rate, its steady growth itself is an important benchmark for higher growth. There are two issues here: first, efficient management of food stocks so as to contain inflation; second, looking at agriculture growth beyond food grains.

So, a brief review of industry, infrastructure, services and agriculture shows the way to get back to the much higher rates of growth, nine per cent and above, which India experienced in the 2004-2008 period. The structure of the economy has changed enormously in recent decades which provides the framework for higher growth. In this, the private sector plays a much larger role but the public sector too has a major part to play.

In addition, the savings and investment rates, currently are way higher at more than 30 per cent of GDP, compared to just over 20 per cent in the 1980s. The current level reflects a decline over the high 30s a few years ago but it is still much higher. Also, the private sector's share in savings and investment is much more than before. Its efficiency of use of capital is higher which, again, adds strength to the economy, giving cause for confidence in achieving the high growth rates which India has achieved.

What is it that Government Needs to Do? Or, Not to Do?

A number of things—more space and freedom to all of industry and entrepreneurship making business easier to do. This applies to both the public and private sectors. And, this would include a de-freeze on issues such as environment and land, both of which have held back growth and investment.

A critical way forward for government, which has started with the increase in diesel prices, is to control the deficit: in fact, reduce it and bring back balance in the economy's financial and fiscal health. This is what the government needs to do, allowing the rest to happen in a free flow.

The economy is again poised for a confident return to nine per cent growth with the leadership team in place in North block, managing the finance ministry, a proactive Prime Minister and his team and expert advice coming in from the fiscal consolidation and tax sides. Already, confidence levels are rising and sentiments are on an upswing.

The agenda for nine per cent growth is neither unreal nor unachievable. Practical, steady policies, management and implementation, which are already in evidence, under the leadership of Chidambaram are showing the way to a renewal of the nine per cent legacy. First, get back to seven per cent growth in 2013. And, then, the higher, tougher jump to nine per cent. The dream team is in place. India is on the way back.

14 Agriculture Growth in India

The Hope and Despair Syndrome

Y.S.P. Thorat

My association with P. Chidambaram dates back to Reserve Bank of India (RBI) days, but particularly during my stint with National Bank for Agricultural and Rural Development (NABARD) which required working closely with him as the head of the finance ministry. One of the first initiatives we worked on jointly, for instance, was the initiative taken by him in 2004 to double credit to the farm sector. The original slogan gave us some trouble because it implied a quantitative doubling of credit while the best which could be done under the circumstance was doubling the rate of growth in credit. Yet, the idea was taken up by Chidambaram. He worked out the implementation strategy with great attention to detail, piloted it with zeal and monitored it with a diligence which ensured that in the next three years, despite significant odds, the desired outcome was achieved. In fact, at his quarterly meeting with the chiefs of public sector banks (PSBs), the progress of the flow of credit to the farm sector used to be the first item on the agenda.

Another memory of Chidambaram is the way he used to handle meetings with PSBs and financial institutions (FIs). His understanding of the subject and grasp of the agenda was firm, based on facts and backed by meticulous reading of everything put up to him. Coupled with his prodigious memory, this was often lethal as many of us realised at our expense. One often thought at the time that he micro-managed and went into unnecessary details. But in hindsight it appears that in an environment characterised by convenient generalisations and glib explanations, his approach was a breath of fresh, if cold, air. He neither generalised nor minced his words and would inevitably pin the participants to specific answers, specific action points and specific timeframes.

He saw far. For instance, at that time regional rural banks (RRBs) had been reduced to a footnote in the banking agenda. Since nearly everything in regard to them was required to be routed through their sponsor banks, most of them were suffering from serious identity-related issues. Chidambaram, however, recognised their potential for last-mile connectivity and for the first time, convened a meeting at his level to discuss their problems with a view to find constructive solutions. When the first meeting was convened, we thought it would be a one-off affair. No one, least of all RRB chairmen, believed that they would be treated on an equal footing with their commercial bank counterparts and given the same consideration as them. Yet it was so. We were wrong. It was not a one-off meeting. He regularly met with RRB chairmen and addressed their issues—both operational and HR—thus injecting a new feeling of hope, confidence and self-worth into them. The RRBs have much to be grateful to him.

I saw Chidambaram at his best during the days following the submission of the report of the Vaidyanathan Committee (2004) which examined whether there was a case for recapitalising cooperative credit institutions. To begin with, he was agnostic, if not a sceptic. He accepted that cooperatives in select areas were indeed doing a credible job but was disinclined to buy the argument that systemically, they were the best institutions for moving rural credit and should, therefore, be capitalised. Before formally submitting the report, the Chairman and I, as Member Secretary, made a presentation to him. We had done our homework and thought we would sail through. We were wrong. Chidambaram questioned the assumptions, arguments and data put forward and challenged our enthusiasm regarding the recapitalisation proposal. He came around only when it was made clear that we were not proposing a unilateral transfer of funds but recapitalisation contingent on measurable reforms in law, policy and operations. The Prime Minister commended the report to state governments at the meeting of the National Advisory Council the following year. However, cooperation being a state subject, Chidambaram was given the task of building a consensus across the board. Among his many fine hours, this was one. He worked tirelessly and ceaselessly with us—Prof Vaidyanathan, Vinod Rai, myself, a few others—and met state governments individually and jointly on a number of occasions to work out the lowest common denominator of acceptance. There were occasions when we felt that the Centre was conceding more than what was warranted to the states, but little did we realise that what we were witnessing was the fine art of real politics being practiced in a democratic framework led by a coalition government. It is to his credit that he succeeded. Credit cooperatives like regional rural banks have much to thank him for.

Contrary to belief in certain quarters, he had a pragmatic and sound 'ground level' grasp of agriculture and related issues, particularly on the credit side and was concerned in a serious and constructive way with the welfare of farmers. He was, of course, right in this because what happens in the agriculture sector touches the lives of most Indians—whether it is the decreasing share of agriculture in the total GDP or the increasing divergence between growth trends in the total economy and those in agriculture.

In this paper, I will be focussing on the agriculture sector as Chidambaram often spoke about it in context of the need for serious reform. He felt that the significance of the agriculture sector in India was not restricted to its contribution to GDP but to the complementarities which it shared with other sectors of the economy. He often emphasised that agriculture growth alone had the potential to accelerate rural development and also reduce poverty. In his view the real task was not merely to boost credit to the farm sector but to bring in a series of reforms relating to subsidy and infrastructure which would change the paradigm itself. Agriculture employs roughly half the workforce. An average Indian still spends almost half his total expenditure on food. Consequently, accelerating agriculture growth and sharing it inclusively among people and across regions is, and must be, the prime agenda and touchstone of our policy.

Let us look at a few facts. The growth performance in agriculture has over the long haul been low and fluctuating. From the Ninth Five Year Plan (FYP) onwards, agricultural growth has 'lingered' at around 2.5 per cent. Although the growth rate improved to around 3.5 per cent during the Eleventh FYP, the differential in the performance of agriculture and the overall economy continues to be worrisome. This is reflected in the steady fall in the share of agriculture in GDP from around 30 per cent in 1990-91 to about 14 per cent in 2010-11. Secondly, not only has agricultural growth been low but its volatility has been six times that of overall growth. Thirdly, there have been significant changes in the composition of agriculture GDP over time. Today, food grains constitute around 20 per cent of the total value of output from the sector which is less than the contribution from the livestock sector (25%) and almost equal to that of the horticulture sector (20%). Fourthly, although gross capital formation (GCF) in agriculture has increased from 8.6 per cent in 1996-97 to 20.1 per cent in 2010-11, it is still far lower than the overall GCF in overall GDP. It is significant that within investment, public investment in agriculture forms no more than about 20 per cent of the total investment in the sector.

On the structural side, Indian agriculture is characterised by small farmers. Fragmentation and subdivision has been steadily increasing and, as a result, the number of operational holdings increased from 7.1 crore in 1970-71 to 13.77 crore in 2010-11. It is worth noting that during this 40-year period, small farmers more than doubled their share in total 'operated' area to about 44 per cent implying that now, a significantly large area is characterised by 'small farming'. The estimates also suggest that small holders contribute about 51 per cent of the value of agriculture output.

On the irrigation front, the country has an overall irrigation potential of around 140 million hectares (ha). Of this, only about 109 million ha have been created and around 80 million ha utilised. Although gross irrigated area as a percentage of gross cropped area (GCA) increased from 34 per cent in 1990-91 to 45.3 per cent in 2008-09, wide variations continue to persist in the irrigation coverage across states and across crops with 65 per cent of agriculture continuing to be undertaken in dryland and resource poor regions

Since mid-1970s, the net sown area (NSA) in the country has stagnated at around 135-40 million ha while the GCA has fluctuated between 185 to 195 million ha from 2000 onwards thereby putting a significant constraint on cropping intensity. Coupled with this there has been a stagnancy/decline in yield growth for most of the crops compared to the 1990s. Among food grains, yield indices of rice and wheat have declined to 1.68 and 1.14 respectively during 2000-01 to 2011-12 relative to 3.19 and 3.10 during 1980-81 to 1990-91. The yield indices of pulses have shown only a marginal increase from 1.61 (during 1980-81 to 1990-1991) to 1.91 (during 2000-01 to 2011-12). While, no doubt, there are a few exceptions as in case of Bt Cotton, maize and groundnut, these constitute the exception rather than the rule. All of the above facts have implications which point to the need for formulating a cogent agricultural policy that will lead to a sustained growth in agriculture and ensure that the requirements of both farmers and food security are fully met.

Greater integration of the agricultural sector with the overall economy and the dovetailing of the Indian economy with the global economy has brought in its wake specific challenges and concerns. Globalisation, an expanding middle class and diversification of the food basket have been fuelling corporate interest in agriculture as a source for raw material for agri value chains and the focus is now increasingly on marketing of produce. National, regional and local marketing systems are also gearing up to adopt best practices in procurement, storage, transport, packing and processing of food products. Though their present market share is relatively small, food supermarkets are a reality and expected to play a significant role in the years to come as caterers to the growing urban demand for quality farm produce delivered in modern formats. This in turn will hopefully create a pressure for higher food quality standards leading to new and innovative procurement systems. Indian corporates may also seek to capture larger market shares in the expanding international trade in primary commodities and processed foods and, therefore, demand increasing volumes of quality produce from domestic producers. However, the major constraint in this regard is the highly fragmented nature of production and low per capita surplus of small and marginal farmers which will tend to limit their ability to access the market and leverage better returns for their produce. Aggregation in all forms, whether of land or provision of agri and farm management services, appears to be the appropriate way to enable small landholders to participate and take advantage of the emerging opportunities in the sector. This highlights the need to put in position policies that can absorb the 'not so advantageous' impact of the globalisation process.

Other changes are also taking place. At the ground level, for example, the hitherto identifiable distinction between the rural and urban sectors has gradually given way to a sort of 'rural–urban continuum' characterised by the imprint of the services sector. This transformation is, in part, captured in the compositional shift in the consumption pattern in the rural areas. Rural India is now an important part in the domestic consumption story, not only because 70 per cent of its population lives in rural areas but also because it has 56 per cent share in national income, 64 per cent share in expenditure and 33 per cent share in savings.

Interestingly, farm income which used to contribute about three-fourths of the rural income has dropped to 30 per cent (2010). Non-farm growth which includes the services sector has been substantial and an estimated 42 per cent of rural households are reported to be drawing their income from non-farm sources, particularly traditional services (27 per cent). Overall, the WTO regime, while being beneficial in certain respects, has raised concerns in regard to food security and the subsidy regime. The crux of the matter is that while globalisation works through macro parameters, its impact is felt at the micro level and, therefore, the channels of its transmission need to be understood and responded to appropriately.

The volatility in agricultural output points to the need for putting risk coping mechanisms in position. The skewedness in the distribution of landholding coupled with the predominant share of small farmers, implies the need for promoting institutional arrangements designed to ensure that growth (along with its diversification) benefits the small and marginal farmers. Given the fact that it is the private sector investment which is mainly holding agriculture growth together, sustained investment can be best ensured by giving the private sector a better 'reformed' incentive structure. Further, there is a need to align agricultural production with the consumption basket, especially from the food inflation perspective. Urgent institutional reforms, better management and maintenance are also called for to stem the deteriorating performance of public surface irrigation schemes. This may involve engaging water user associations and even unbundling large surface schemes into storage (dams), transmission (main canals) and distribution water channels at the farmer's level.

Groundwater irrigation, which is presently the biggest source of irrigation, suffers from over-exploitation in most states. Excessive dependence on groundwater for irrigation has several implications, including an ever-increasing decline in the groundwater table, drying up of a large number of wells, low well productivity, rise in well and pumping depths, deteriorating groundwater quality and salinity ingress. There is also little doubt that free or low pricing of power for irrigation has contributed to the problem in a significant way. Consequently, major reforms in the power sector including improvement in the quality and availability of power are absolute preconditions for improving the overall groundwater situation in the country.

In regard to research, the major responses so far have been in regard to irrigated agriculture and our understanding of the solutions for sustainable development of dry land areas (and farmers depending on such land) continues to leave much to be desired. These regions which are home to the majority of small and resource poor farmers must be enabled to move from the periphery of policy attention to its centre.

Agricultural growth strategy has for a long time focussed mainly on the production phase. In the context of food grains policy, concerns have been raised regarding the simultaneous presence of high food inflation and large food grains stocks in our granaries. It has been argued that, in creating a better food grains policy, it is imperative to look at the entire system of food grains production, procurement, release and distribution.

Besides improving storage facilities, there is a need to redesign the mechanics of procurement and release of food grains to the market to ensure that the impact on prices is in the desired direction. Coupled with this there needs to be a strong initiative for improving marketing conditions and encouraging private sector participation by reforming the Agricultural Produce Marketing Committee (APMC) Acts. Appropriate changes in these legislations can boost private sector involvement and investment in the development of regulated markets, backup logistics, efficient warehouse receipt systems, futures markets and the infrastructure for imports and exports. This is particularly relevant for the high value agriculture segment which is currently hostage to high post-harvest losses and weak farm-firm linkages. The introduction of the Model Act in 2003 was directed towards permitting private market yards to undertake direct buying and selling and promote and regulate contract farming in high value agriculture. Although many states have adopted the new Model Act, albeit with modifications, its impact on farmers in terms of better prices for their produce and a reduction in the high differences between farm harvest prices and consumer prices continues to be weak.

Storage infrastructure in the country needs to be increased and upgraded. Around 30 per cent of fruits and vegetables grown in India (40 million tonnes) get wasted annually on account of gaps in the cold chain, poor infrastructure, insufficient cold storage capacity, non-availability of cold storages in close proximity to farms, poor transportation framework, etc. India wastes more fruits and vegetables than it consumes. Operating costs for Indian cold storage units are over \$60 per cubic metre, per year compared to less than \$30 in the West. Energy expenses make up about 28 per cent of the total expenses for Indian cold storages compared to 10 per cent in the west. The data speak for themselves and bring out the need to give focused attention to post-harvest issues. Efforts at creating storage infrastructure should also consciously ensure that the benefit of this infrastructure does not accrue to large farmers only. Recent technical studies have pointed out that unless facilitative arrangements like pledge financing facilities and warehouse receipts are put in place, the benefits of the storage infrastructure may not accrue to small and marginal farmers.

Making small farmers participate in the growth process is critical. The shift toward consumer-driven markets, an integral element of market liberalisation and globalisation, implies that the small farmer is increasingly being asked to compete in markets that demand much more in terms of quality and food safety. As small farms diversify into higher-value products, they will be increasingly required to meet stringent demands of sophisticated markets. There is, therefore, an urgent need to support institutions such as producers organisations and other arrangements which can aid and dovetail the output of small farmers with the demands of markets at home and abroad.

Lastly, there is the vexatious question of 'subsidy'. Research studies show that the marginal returns evident in terms of poverty alleviation or accelerating agricultural growth are much lower from input subsidies than from investments in rural roads or agri-R&D or irrigation. There is always a trade-off between allocating money through subsidies or by increasing investments. The investment option is much better than subsidies for sustaining long-term growth in agricultural production and also to reduce poverty faster.

There are several other areas of importance for the growth of the agriculture sector including enhancing public sector investment in research, effective transfer of technology, institutional reforms in the research set up so as to make it more accountable and geared towards delivery. These include conservation of land, water and biological resources, the development of rainfed agriculture, development of minor irrigation, timely and adequate availability of inputs, support for marketing infrastructure and an increase in flow of credit, particularly to the small and marginal farmers.

15 Reformer by Instinct and Choice

N.K. Singh

No contemporary economic history of India can be written without recognising and commending the far-reaching contribution of P. Chidambaram. He is both a reformer by instinct and choice. His first impulse is to begin from the drawing board and, given an incisive analytical mind, never allow myriad complexities to detract his focus. He has invariably exercised options to improve consumer choice, enhance productivity and unleash competition. His critics sometimes suggest that he is obstinate and unrelenting, if not downright arrogant. There is no doubt that he does not easily suffer fools. Sometimes the clarity of his logic and compelling persuasive analysis can be mistaken for inflexibility. He remains unruffled by transient resistance.

This piece examines his contribution in four segments—in the areas of trade policy, expenditure reforms and tax reforms, and briefly touches on the multiplier synergy between development and peace. I was fortunate to be a part of some of these initiatives.

My association with Chidambaram dates back to 1991 when he was the Commerce Minister and India was in a full-blown balance of payments (BoP) crisis. Being actively engaged in negotiating satisfactory arrangements with IMF and the World Bank, I quickly realised that liberalising the trade regime was critical. India at that time, notwithstanding incremental and halting of liberalisation, had stringent import-export controls. In fact the office of Chief Controller of Imports and Exports was a venerable and feared institution even though its only function was to permit private importers to effect imports at their own cost and risk. Trade and industry waited with bated breath each year for the annual import policy popularly known as the 'Red Book'. Similarly, there were crippling export restrictions and a substantial part of the trade was canalised which meant that trade could only be undertaken by state trading entities like the State Trading Corporation (STC) or the Metals and Minerals Trading Corporation (MMTC). As part of the foreign trade control regime, average tariffs were at stratospheric levels touching almost an average of 130 per cent in 1990-91. When Chidambaram became the commerce minister he took no time to thoroughly overhaul the antiquated trade regime. Imports were liberalised and canalisation near ended. The supplementary trade policy announced in August 1991 decanalised 16 export items and 20 import items and the role of the state monopolies like trading corporations substantially reduced. The 'Red Book' on import policy was renamed as the 'Green Book' marking not only a substantial change in the import regime itself but more importantly representing a mindset change. All this was accomplished at a time when the foreign exchange reserves were meagre, permitting limited flexibility. In July 1991, he liquidated the office of the Chief Controller of Imports and Exports. This move would have been considered as anti-national even a few years ago. The liberalisation of India's trade regime under Chidambaram was hailed both nationally and internationally as a major departure in India's overall economic strategy. By the time Chidambaram left the commerce ministry in April 1996, most of the trade and external sector reforms envisaged by him had been accomplished. The Indian economy was on a firmer footing than ever before.

The importance of trade reforms addresses several questions. Theoretical literature supports the view that open economies grow faster than closed ones. Trade openness has growth enhancing effect in the host country through efficiency gains, competition and technology transfer. Empirical evidence suggests a high co-relationship between trade openness, investment and economic growth. Trade expansion raises productivity and offers greater economies of scale. Rising exports alleviate foreign exchange constraints and provide access to international markets. According to the *World Development Report*, published by the World Bank, the main advantage of the outward-oriented strategy over the inward-oriented strategy is that it promotes a more efficient use of resources and encourages capital inflows.

Foreign trade in India had suffered from discretionary controls and restrictive policies for over four decades after independence. The persistent current account deficits (CADs) left the Reserve Bank of India (RBI) little option than impose exchange control restrictions on all foreign exchange transactions. Trade remained an insignificant contributor to national income owing to limited exportable surplus, fostering policies of protectionism and inward-oriented policies characterised by import substitution, self-reliance and self-sufficiency. As a consequence India's share in world trade which stood at around 1.8 per cent in 1950 gradually declined to 0.5 per cent by 1991. Liberalisation of the import control regime in India in the 1980s, particularly in the category of open general licences (OGL) no doubt did open imports somewhat. The growth in exports was however sluggish in the initial years due to slowdown in world trade. As a result the trade deficit went up from $ 590 crore in 1984-85 to $ 910 crore in 1988-89 and the CADs rose from $ 240 crore to $ 890 crore during the same period. Although exports maintained healthy growth it was overshadowed by growth in imports. By 1990-91, there was a marked deterioration in India's BoP. In addition to this, the volatile external situation, high fiscal deficits and growing external debt culminated in perhaps the worst-ever economic crisis in India in 1991.

The broad-based trade liberalisation programme initiated in response to the BoP crisis of 1991 marked a significant turnaround in India's highly protected trade regime. In fact, reforms in trade and external sector formed a major ingredient of the reforms programme to restore the macroeconomic balance. Apart from the exchange rate devaluation and a move to a unified market determined exchange rate system, the new trade policy sought to end the quantitative restrictions (QRs) on imports besides phasing out import licensing, removal of QRs, rationalisation of tariff structure, decanalisation and reduction in the tariff rates.

While some liberalisation measures were the result of a growing conviction that they were necessary to make exports competitive in the international market, some believed that they were undertaken as a consequence of the stabilisation and structural adjustment programme. Be that as it may, the overall performance over the next three years, measured in terms of the usual parameters of growth and stability, clearly exceeded expectations. The CAD, which had touched 3.2 per cent of GDP in 1990-1991, came down to a far more comfortable level of 0.4 per cent by 1993-1994. Foreign exchange reserves increased to a respectable level of 8.6

months of imports by the end of 1993-94 from its precarious level of less than a month in 1991. Exports grew at an average of 20 per cent for the period and the CAD situation improved significantly varying between 1 per cent and 1.8 per cent of GDP. The rate of growth of GDP improved from 0.8 per cent in 1991-92 to a decent 5.3 per cent in 1992-93 which further accelerated to 6.2 per cent in 1993-94.

Reaping the benefits of greater integration with the world economy was an important objective of opening the economy to trade and foreign investment. In the first few years of reforms significant progress was made towards this objective by removing QRs and lowering tariff barriers. However, building a consensus on external liberalisation was far from easy. Indian industry which supported the external liberalisation and removal of import restrictions on capital goods later demanded a 'level playing field' to adjust to external liberalisation as tariff levels came down and the pressure of competition from imports increased. India's import duties were among the highest in the world in the pre-reforms period. It also used QRs through import licensing measures as an instrument of policy. Significant progress was made in reducing tariff rates and in dismantling QRs in the initial years of reforms. Import licensing was virtually abolished in the first two years of reforms while the customs duties were also brought down significantly. The removal of import licensing and tariff reductions led to a more open economy in tune with the policy of economic liberalisation. As Commerce Minister, Chidambaram was instrumental in pushing through reforms in trade and external sectors through deregulation of trade, removal of trade barriers, rationalisation of tariffs and putting an end to the licence permit *raj*. All these resulted in a more meaningful integration of the Indian economy with the global economic order.

Chidambaram moved as Finance Minister on 1st June 1996, when I was the Expenditure Secretary. It was a coalition government which had a limited mandate and it was generally believed that it may not last too long. As Expenditure Secretary, I perceived his restlessness in a policy of incrementally expenditure driven portfolios. He encouraged me to move towards zero-based budgeting, realising though that as long as there are myriad ways in which expenditures were being sanctioned a uniform expenditure policy was difficult. Tentative steps towards portfolios rationalisation was beginning to take shape. Expenditure reforms had long been delayed in India for several reasons.

1) The classification of expenditure itself between Plan and non-Plan expenditure is a bit fallacious, both in terms of organisation and methodology. Organisation because the non-Plan expenditure is under the purview of the Expenditure Department while Plan expenditure is in the domain of the Planning Commission. No doubt, even for Plan expenditure, the approval of new projects are subject to standard financial scrutiny procedures. Methodologically all expenditure constitute an outgo from the consolidated fund of India and giving preference to new projects or schemes as against maintenance was a misplaced priority. What was the use if assets created earlier are flogged, depleted or badly maintained due to lack of resources while new projects were being constantly sanctioned.

2) Every public expenditure generates vested interests within the bureaucracy and between the Centre and the states. Since staff is sanctioned which are project related, even after the basic purpose of the project has been either fulfilled or subsumed in a larger project, it continues to remain in public portfolio because staff attrition is scarcely practiced. Central ministries or organisations assigned for public outlay soon develop institutions in states, and the combined effect of lobbies both at the Centre and the states reinvent reasons for the perpetuation of the scheme.

3) Expenditures which have a populist character in terms of entitlements or connected with anti-poverty schemes are rarely abolished since they are perceived to be electorally unacceptable. The purpose of many of these measures are rarely tested by accepted outcome methodologies. Expenditure portfolios, instead of folding, only tend to grow in size and complexity. Zero-based budget as a concept has yet to be fully applied and a basic review of government's expenditure policy is overdue. Subsequently, no doubt, accountability through better monitoring procedures, creation of an independent evaluation office and the outlay-outcome statements placed in Parliament are credible initiatives

for better expenditure management. It is never easy when it comes to expenditure to shed the baggage of the past and to restructure policies which are relevant in a more contemporary context.

I moved as Revenue Secretary in August 1996 when Chidambaram was still the Finance Minister. He had already commenced significant tax reforms in my predecessor's time. The rationale of these tax reforms were:

1) To simplify and reduce the number of rates, both for direct and indirect taxes. It was well known that income tax rates varied widely from 20 to 40 percentage points and was liable for periodic changes. Corporate tax rates were high at 40 per cent for domestic companies with an additional penalty of 10 per cent for foreign companies. Multiplicity of rates, both for excise and customs created uncertainty with enormous discretion to change them to suit either individual interest or respond to some other collateral circumstances. The first important thing was to compress and rationalise multiplicity of taxes, both direct and indirect.

2) The proportionality of revenue realisation from direct and indirect taxes was skewed in the Indian context. Indirect taxes constituted the major source of revenue realisation representing 76 per cent as against direct taxes which constituted only 24 per cent. Part of the problem was historical because realisation from customs duties and corporate taxes was not part of the common divisible pool of the states. Central government in order to keep their fiscal deficit at acceptable levels and generate larger revenues had a strong temptation to continue with high rates of customs and corporate taxes. Thus the rationalisation of *inter se* proportionality between indirect and direct taxes was a major challenge. The best international practice, of course, was a much higher portion of revenue emanating from direct instead of indirect taxes. The tax reform had to move in that direction. Within the indirect tax, the proportionality of dependence from revenues from petroleum and oil products was excessive and needed significant moderation.

3) Garnering higher revenues does not necessarily imply higher rates of taxes. The alternative hypothesis that moderate tax create virtuous circles of compliance in fostering higher rates

of economic growth by leaving larger disposable incomes in the hands of private individuals and investors is a widely accepted feature of tax reform all over the world. Indian tax rates were not only too many but far too high which penalised growth and discouraged honest tax payers.

Chidambaram introduced in the budget of 1997-98 far-reaching tax reforms. This popularly came to be known as the 'dream budget'. This was an exercise with which I was closely associated. This budget addressed all the three tax reform initiatives which have been outlined above. The budget lowered income on income tax rates, it removed surcharge on corporate taxes, reduced corporate tax rates and abolished the gift tax. It slashed the maximum marginal income tax rate for individuals from 40 per cent to 30 per cent and cut the income tax rate for domestic companies to 35 per cent from the earlier 40 per cent. Peak customs duty was reduced from 50 per cent to 40 per cent, and the excise duty structure was simplified. Individual investors were no longer required to pay dividend tax (Annexure A-15.1).

The Union Budget of 1997 extended the scope of service tax to cover a larger number of services which has over the years become an additional and important source of resource mobilisation. The rationalisation of the excise rates and their progressive convergence was an important initiative which laid the foundation of a goods and services tax (GST) which is currently under discussion.

Literature on whether Laffer curve exists is somewhat mixed, namely the principle that lower rates of taxes improve compliance and augment gross tax collections. Significant improvement in tax realisation was however witnessed subsequent to the tax reforms in 1997. It helped in raising both the tax-to-GDP ratio in over all terms and broadening the tax base. Empirical evidence elsewhere suggests that a 10 per cent decline in tax rates enhances government revenues by 14 per cent. In the Union Budget 1997-98, tax rates were reduced for all tax payers from 22 to 16.3 per cent. But revenues remained constant due to improved compliance, and the tax payers base increased from 0.55 crore to 0.68 crore in the very next year. Over the next six years overall compliance increased by 50 per cent—from a mere 11.9 per cent of tax payer population to 18.20 per cent. Besides, while direct taxes have built-in progressivity given variations in rates to income slabs, indirect taxes are generally perceived to be regressive. The incidence of excise duty is across the board and spares no category of consumers. Increased dependence on direct taxes is socially more equitable and better designed in an economic strategy which emphasises growth inclusiveness.

Chidambaram's far-reaching reforms introduced in the 1997 Budget was coupled with introduction of a voluntary disclosure income scheme (VDIS). This was based on the premise that unrealistic and discretionary tax rates of the past may have inhibited many tax payers in voluntarily complying with tax rates. By reducing income tax rates to just 10, 20 and 30, it sought to enlarge the tax base with a modest entry tax of just 10 per cent. At the same time, the 30 per cent highest tax rate was designed to discourage tax evasion endemic in our system. It is a tribute to this policy that successive governments and finance ministers have not tampered with the basic structure of income tax of just three rates. The VDIS brought immediate tax collection of nearly ₹ 10,000 crore, while ₹ 33,000 crore declared by over 3.5 lakh individuals permanently entered the tax stream. The VDIS scheme was imaginatively marketed. The scheme was also upheld by Supreme Court. Similarly, retrospectively speaking, the policies of that time have resulted in the tax-to-GDP ratio improving to 11 per cent and the proportion of direct taxes to indirect taxes improving from 24:76 in 1997 to 54:46 in 2010. The dependence on indirect taxes progressively came down over this period. Within the indirect taxes, the duty structure for excessive dependence on the petroleum sector also have been significantly moderated. Peak customs duty which Chidambaram had announced to be aligned with average developing country rates have also come down and are now 10 per cent which is not very different than rates prevalent in the region. Similarly, excise rates have also come down while service tax introduced by Chidambaram in the same budget has become a significant revenue earner for the states. Chidambaram had announced the formation of an Expert Group in that Budget for new Direct Taxes Code (DTC). It has taken long but both the GST and DTC are in the public domain and, hopefully, sooner than later will become part of our overall policy.

Any piece on Chidambaram cannot be completed without mentioning the importance of his last innings as Home Minister in which he thoroughly modernised our intelligence and enforcement apparatus. The relationship between development and peace is well accepted and multiple peace dividends were reaped as a result of his characteristic zeal for systems modernisation.

The Indian economic story has and will go through many ups and downs. The current stagnant phase of both policy and outcomes should not blind us to accept that not only has India seen better days but also experienced a period of 'high noon' of economic growth, unprecendented in recent times. Chidambaram has been a key architect in catapulting the India growth story—a story widely acclaimed as India's long-awaited arrival on the global scene.

ANNEXURE A-15.1

Table 1

Income Tax Rates in India for the Highest Slab

(%)

1956-57	87.5
1962-63	72.5
1971-72	85.0
1974-75	70.0
1977-78	60.0
1984-85	55.0
1992-93	40.0
1997-98	30.0
2011-12	30.0

Source: Reserve Bank of India, *Empirical Fiscal Research in India: A Survey* and *Economic Survey* (various year).

Table 2

Corporation Tax Rates for Select Years

Year	*Domestic Company*		*Foreign Company*	
	Closely held	*Widely held*	*Closely held*	*Widely held*
1980-81	45	65	50	70
1984-85	55	65	50	70
1987-88	50	60	50	65
1991-92	40	50	50	65
1997-98	35	35	48	48
2001-02	35	35	48	48
2009-10	30	30	40	40

Source: Same as Table 1.

Table 3

Customs Duty Rate in India for Select Years

Year	*Peak Rate*
1991-92	150
1992-93	110
1993-94	85
1994-95	65
1996-97	50
1997-98	40
1998-99	45
2004-05	20
2009-10	10

Source: Same as Table 1.

Bio-Sketch of P. Chidambaram

Date of Birth:

September 16, 1945.

Education:

Bachelor of Science in Statistics from the Presidency College, Madras.

Bachelor degree in Law from Madras Law College.

Master of Business Administration from Harvard Business School, US.

Positions in Public Life:

1969: Started off career as a lawyer in Chennai.

1972: Member, All India Congress Committee (AICC).

1973-76: President, Youth Congress, Tamil Nadu.

1976-77: General-Secretary, Tamil Nadu Pradesh Congress Committee.

1984: Elected to 8th Lok Sabha from Sivaganga constituency, Tamil Nadu.

1985: Made Joint Secretary, All India Congress Committee.

1986-89: Appointed Union Minister of State, Personnel, Public Grievances and Pensions in the Rajiv Gandhi government. Also served as Union Minister of State, Home Affairs (Internal Security).

1989: Re-elected to 9th Lok Sabha from Sivaganga, Tamil Nadu.

1990-91: Served as member of the committee to review Lok Sabha Secretariat Rules, 1955; the consultative committee under the Punjab State Legislature (Delegation of Powers) Act, 1987; Public Accounts Committee; and the consultative committee, Ministry of Finance.

1991: Re-elected to 10th Lok Sabha from Sivaganga, Tamil Nadu.

1991-92 and 1995-96: Union Minister of State, Commerce (Independent Charge).

1996: Quits the Congress party and joined a breakaway faction of the Tamil Nadu state unit of the Congress party called the Tamil Maanila Congress (TMC). Re-elected to 11th Lok Sabha on TMC ticket from the same constituency in Tamil Nadu.

1996-98: After the general elections produced a hung parliament, the TMC joined forces with a few national and regional level parties and formed the coalition United Front government at the Centre, with the Congress party supporting it from the outside. Chidambaram was appointed the Union Minister of Finance for the first time (with additional charge of Law, Justice and Company Affairs till April 1997).

1998: Re-elected to 12th Lok Sabha from Sivaganga, Tamil Nadu.

1998-99: Served as member of the Committee of Privileges; Committee on Finance; and the Consultative Committee, Ministry of External Affairs.

1999: Lost election to the 13th Lok Sabha from Sivaganga, contested on behalf of the TMC.

2001: Left the TMC and formed his own party, Congress Jananayaka Peravai, centred on the Tamil Nadu politics.

2004: Reunited with the Congress, after merging his party with it. Re-elected to 14th Lok Sabha as Congress party candidate from Sivaganga.

2004 (May)–2008 (Nov.): Union Cabinet Minister, Finance.

2008 (Nov.)–2012 (July): Appointed Union Home Affairs Minister.

2009: Re-elected to 15th Lok Sabha from Sivaganga.

2012: Appointed as the Union Finance Minister for the third time in his career.

Achievements as Union Minister

As Union Minister of State, Personnel, Public Grievances and Pensions in Rajiv Gandhi government (1985-1989)

- The entire rules regarding disciplinary action were rewritten.
- Maternity leave rules were relaxed and privilege was extended to unmarried pregnant women.
- Rules governing procedure of Union Public Service Commission examinations were streamlined and Curriculum in the Lal Bahadur Shastri National Academy, Mussoorie, was reformed.

As Union Minister of State, Home Affairs (Internal Security) in Rajiv Gandhi government (1986-1989)

- For the first time, a status paper was brought out that envisaged a clear roadmap for capacity-building and expansion of central paramilitary forces.

As Union Minister of State (Independent Charge) for Commerce in P.V. Narasimha Rao government (1991-92 and 1995-96)

- India's erstwhile heavily restricted foreign trade policy was radically changed in tune with the wider economic reform process initiated by the Union finance minister in 1991.
- Import licensing controls were dismantled in a big way.
- Movement towards market-determined foreign exchange rate regime was set in motion.
- India's export policy liberalised industrial licensing procedures were rationalised to make room for private sector-led export boom.

As Union Finance Minister in H.D. Deve Gowda government (1996-97) and I.K. Gujral government (1997-98)

- Economists acclaim the Budget 1997-98, widely known as the Dream Budget, brought discipline in government spending and launched an ambitious tax reform programme for the first time in India.
- The Dream Budget gave a huge fillip to economic reforms in India and included lowering income tax rates, removal of the surcharge on corporate taxes, and reduced corporate tax rates.
- The daring scheme to halt tax evasion, or Voluntary Income Disclosure Scheme, boosted tax compliance to unprecedented levels.

As Union Finance Minister in Manmohan Singh government (2004-2008)

- India posted GDP growth rates of 7.0, 9.5, 9.6, and 9.3 per cent in these years, effectively raising India's economic profile around the globe. Inflation was tamed to an average 5.5-6.0 per cent.
- In the Budget of 2008, the move to waive farmers' debt played a role in boosting aggregate demand in the Indian economy, helping India insulate itself from the impact of recession.
- Tax-GDP ratio moved up sharply up to 2008.

- Higher GDP growth rates and increased government revenues aided the government to roll out welfare programmes like National Rural Employment Guarantee Act intended to achieve financial inclusion.
- Financial Inclusion Fund (FIF) and Financial Inclusion Technology Fund (FITF) set up.
- Value Added Tax introduced. Moreover, foundation laid for the introduction of Direct Taxes Code and Goods and Services Tax, two key steps in broader taxation reform in the country.

As Union Home Affairs Minister in Manmohan Singh government (2008-2012)

- To curb extreme left-wing militancy in various parts of the country and to bring development to those areas, an Integrated Action Plan for the Left Wing Extremist Areas was launched.
- Overall reform of the country's police force accelerated in order to facilitate merit-based, transparent recruitment and modern training. Emphasis was also laid on equipping them with latest high-tech weaponry.
- To strengthen coordinated response on internal security and to beef up the government's counter-terrorism abilities, a slew of measures were taken, like the setting up a National Intelligence Grid (Natgrid), the Crime & Criminal Tracking Network & Systems (CCTNS), the Multi Agency Centre (MAC) and the Mission Mode Project on Immigration, Visa and Foreigners Registration & Tracking (IVFRT).

As Union Finance Minister in Manmohan Singh government (2012-)

- Economic reforms given a fresh lease of life, as sectoral caps in foreign direct investment were eased significantly on multi-brand retail, aviation and broadcast industries. In single-brand retail, caps were removed altogether.
- Unveiled a five-year action plan to cut fiscal deficit to 5.3 per cent of GDP for 2012-13 and further down to 3 per cent by 2017-18.

Published Work:

View from the Outside: Why Good Economics Works for Everyone (2007): A collection of his columns published in the Indian Express between 2002 and 2004.

Index

M

N

P

R

S